A Handbook of
International
Peacebuilding

· ·

John Paul Lederach
Janice Moomaw Jenner
Editors

. . . .

A Handbook of International Peacebuilding

Into the Eye of the Storm

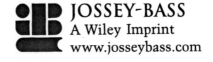

JOSSEY-BASS
A Wiley Imprint
www.josseybass.com

Published by Jossey-Bass
A Wiley Imprint
989 Market Street, San Francisco, CA 94103-1741   www.josseybass.com

Jossey-Bass books and products are available through most bookstores. To contact Jossey-Bass directly call our Customer Care Department within the U.S. at 800-956-7739, outside the U.S. at 317-572-3986 or fax 317-572-4002.

Jossey-Bass also publishes its books in a variety of electronic formats. Some content that appears in print may not be available in electronic books.

Library of Congress Cataloging-in-Publication Data
A handbook of international peacebuilding: into the eye of the storm /
[edited by] John Paul Lederach.—1st ed.
    p. cm.
Includes bibliographical references and index.
ISBN 978-0-7879-5879-4
    1. Peacekeeping forces. 2. United Nations—Armed Forces. I.
Lederach, John Paul.
JZ6374 .H36 2002
341.5'84—dc21   2002007064

FIRST EDITION

Contents

· ·

Part III: So Are You Coming to Help Us? Advice from the Ground

Part IV: Intervention Matters: From Money to Ethics

Acknowledgments

The first conversation we had with Alan Rinzler, executive editor at Jossey-Bass, about the possibility of an edited handbook for international peacebuilding seems like a long way back. He appeared to be convinced that this would all flow smoothly toward publication. He may not have said exactly, "Get the right people, and the pieces will fall in place," but that was the feeling we got from the conversation. He was right. Doing an edited volume may be a little like quiltmaking. If it is done well, you end up with something warm that is a piece of art. If you don't get it right, you have a blanket nobody wants.

We got the right people to write the chapters. As the chapters arrived in our offices, it turned out there was very little editing needed. These folks can talk straight, and they can talk straight from their experiences. Our greatest acknowledgment is to our community of authors, a wonderful experience of cooperation, ideas, and mutual encouragement. We cannot thank them enough.

We are deeply appreciative of the editing staff at Jossey-Bass, particularly Amy Scott and Lasell Whipple, who have helped to shape and mold this project from the beginning to its publication. We also thank our respective institutions, which provided us with support, encouragement, and time to accomplish this work. Thanks to Scott Appleby at the Joan B. Kroc Institute for International

Peace Studies at the University of Notre Dame and to our colleagues at the Conflict Transformation Program at Eastern Mennonite University, particularly Ron Kraybill, Lisa Schirch, and Howard Zehr, who helped with the initial conceptualization of this project.

We are grateful to a number of students at the Conflict Transformation Program who were our first readers. Their advice and reactions were invaluable as we made decisions about adding some new chapters and editing others. And we are deeply grateful to the many peacebuilders around the world who have blessed our lives professionally and personally.

Finally, we are appreciative for the opportunity to work together as coeditors. This was a project that flowed along, and we hope will make a contribution to this field.

July 2002   John Paul Lederach
                                                       Janice Moomaw Jenner

Introduction

· ·

I Just Got a Call

John Paul Lederach

As I hang up, the sudden silence in the room draws my attention to the sharp buzzing in my ear. It may be due to the sound of the telephone that just rang. Or maybe it is the strain of listening twenty minutes over a long-distance international call, the crackling of a bad connection adding to the difficulty of communicating across languages that are not our native tongues. Or maybe this buzz is my head swimming with questions about the request, or what actually felt like a desperate plea, to help with some conflict resolution workshops in a country I have never visited, with people I do not know well, in a situation of violent conflict. The request seemed very genuine. I can feel my heart pounding with anticipation and anxiety. The situation described sounded like an unbelievable opportunity but rife with danger. How do I know this is the right thing to be doing at this time in this context? And are these people whom they say they are? How are they seen by others in the situation, particularly those directly involved in the fighting? Is there anyone already doing this work? Is this the best use of their and my time and resources? Will this be like parachuting into a place with quick answers and then leaving, or is this the start of something that could be truly important and make a difference over the long haul? It is no wonder my head is spinning.

Over the past twenty years of active practice in international conflict transformation and peacebuilding, I have received hundreds of these inquiries, and the demand seems to be growing. Some are easier to field because they come from existing relationships in places where I have worked. Others, like the call I just had, come out of the blue. In all of them, the questions remain much the same and just as perplexing. The exponential growth of this field I broadly refer to as peacebuilding creates excitement and ambivalence. For me, the excitement is clearly the incredible rise of interest and pursuit of alternative nonviolent and creative ways to address human conflict across our globe. Three decades back in the 1970s, those of us in the field of conflict resolution did not have such well-defined and sought-after practices like those of alternative dispute resolution, mediation, conciliation, violence prevention, early warning systems, community reconciliation, nonviolent peacekeeping, trauma healing, second-track diplomacy, or problem-solving workshops, to mention only a few of the many arenas of today's range of peacebuilding activities. There were far fewer voices, almost no existing university degree programs, and barely a handful of training initiatives. Today, these creative alternatives are no longer seen as peripheral but are making direct headway into mainstream thinking and practice at local and high political levels. There are now far more practitioners and rising practitioners who work full time or would like full-time engagement and are sought as resources for responding to conflict zone all over the world.

The ambivalence I noted is also rooted in the very growth of the practice. Peacebuilding has too often moved rapidly and seamlessly from local domestic applications to deeply complex international settings with little time for assessing the appropriateness of intervention or the full development of capacities as practitioners respond to opportunities and requests for help. This is perhaps most apparent in the rise of requests coming from the significant number of destructive conflict situations across our globe. A 2001–2002 survey of world conflicts lists twenty-three high-intensity, seventy-nine low-intensity, and thirty-eight violent political conflicts (Jongman,

2001–2002). I venture an educated guess that some form of conflict transformation and peacebuilding initiatives was being conducted by some sector of the society or international organizations in every one of those settings. In many of them, a multiplicity of organizations and people, often operating without knowledge of each other, are proposing responses to conflict based on experiences primarily gained through short-term training and practice in settings other than one in which they are working. The ambivalence is rooted precisely in the fact that we have moved too quickly without sufficient guidance into the complexity of many international violent settings of conflict. The ambivalence is also deeply connected to how we practitioners of one approach or another within peacebuilding make decisions about responding to the kind of telephone calls and request I just received and our capacity to develop responsible action in very difficult settings.

My experience is that international peacebuilding is genuinely well intended by people who are deeply concerned and want to make a difference. But good intentions are not sufficient for ensuring appropriate action, process, and outcome. It is also my experience that high-quality training programs and even direct application learned in one setting are important keys to personal and programmatic development as that practice and work expand to new settings. However, particularly for people who are moving for the first time into complex international applications of their practice, the experience they have gained and models they have developed in home settings through practice or training do not automatically guarantee a smooth transfer—if transfer is even appropriate—in other situations, and it may not be sufficient to ensure good coordination of the approach with a broader set of peacebuilding activities and efforts in those new arenas of application.

This handbook outlines a response aimed at building on the opportunity and addressing the ambivalence of international peacebuilding. We propose that a set of basic and very practical guidelines, articulated from the direct experiential base of the best and most seasoned international peacebuilders, is useful to have before all of us as we assess the opportunity and challenges of specific decisions and the development of process design. A number of important assumptions, ideas, and criteria have guided the development of this handbook and were used as the various chapter authors were contacted and shared their advice.

First, we chose the word *handbook* with an image in mind that places the emphasis on the "hand" portion of the word. We wanted a guide with such a practical focus, a quality of advice, sufficiently light and to the point, that it would be tucked away in carry-on luggage as people traveled. Sometimes *handbook* refers to large-scale, encyclopedic volumes—something like the software reference books that accompany the latest version of a program. Generally, these sit on library and personal reference bookshelves and receive an occasional visit. Accompanying these larger volumes is often a smaller one, written with a direct-to-the-idea quality, easy to follow and easy to comprehend. These guides often sit beside the computer and are thumbed through often. It is this idea of "thumbed through" that we sought to provide. If we are successful, copies of this handbook around the world will be used so much that they will have tattered corners. We have asked the authors to write with this image in mind: to the point, concrete, and identifying the most important elements of advice they can contribute.

Second, we are using the broad terminology of conflict transformation and peacebuilding to cover an extensive and growing array of practices, approaches, and models aimed at finding more constructive and nonviolent ways to respond to conflict. We chose not to narrow to one professional set of lenses or approaches, but rather to keep this open to a more sweeping population of persons working across national boundaries. Our intention is not to provide the specifics of a design for a particular profession or application within this broad field, but rather to raise a set of questions and provide advice useful across the board for those moving internationally into settings of complex, protracted, and often violent conflict.

Third, we assume that there will be no shortage of people, practitioners, and trainers who are available and interested in doing conflict transformation and peacebuilding work internationally. And we also believe there will be no shortage of requests, opportunities, and initiatives that will keep a regular flow of them crossing borders. Furthermore, given historical patterns and economic realities, we assume that a significant number of these peacebuilders will be coming from North American settings into conflict zones across the globe. Although we believe that the ideas, proposals, and advice put forward by the authors in this book are valid and useful to people from any setting, we have oriented the advice primarily to North American peacebuilders traveling abroad to practice for the first time in an international setting. However, we seek advice from people located in the Northern and Southern Hemispheres where many of the conflicts are taking place.

Fourth, we have asked the authors to speak directly from their experience and to identify the most important lessons learned from the hard school of on-the-ground practice. This advice includes concrete counsel, cautions, and questions and in some cases a frame of reference and guidelines for improving the practice and relationships with partners in the receiving communities. We have also asked some people from areas of protracted conflict, who over the years have gained a great deal of experience of what it feels like to receive outside offers of help, to provide cautions and advice to the arriving peacebuilder.

Finally, the flow and conceptual framework of the handbook follows a logical sequence of questions often asked by any of us working in international conflict zones, from first contact through the initial phases of process design and assessment. The range of questions has been shaped and reshaped with the participation and proposals of many the authors in the book. Clearly, no book is exhaustive. Our intention was to reflect on the most significant questions and challenges facing peacebuilders who are, in a context of great need and with authentic commitment to be constructive, initiating and supporting a peaceful change process and strategy.

A Handbook of
International
Peacebuilding

. . . .

Part I

· ·

The Invitation

Get a Sense of the Big Picture

Y ou have just received an invitation to carry out what appears to be an important, urgent, and useful set of peacebuilding activities in a place you have never even visited. You know you have developed and have confidence in the set of skills the caller was asking for, but is this the right thing for you do? Where do you even start to answer that question?

We suggest you begin by looking at three basic sets inquiries: Who is asking you to come, and where do they fit in? What are they asking you to do, and how do you fit in? Why are you going? In the end, these inquiries should help you visualize a bigger picture and a broad frame of reference. They do not answer all the specifics you will need to have clear before you make a final decision, but they should help you assess at a first stage whether you have a place in the picture. Just because you received an invitation and felt the heart tug of the urgency is not enough reason to intervene. Good intentions and the availability of professional capacities are not sufficient justification to move into a setting of protracted conflict. Entry requires thought, assessment, and discernment. It starts by getting a sense of the big picture.

1

. . . .

Who Is Calling?

Sue K. Williams

Let's begin with the first point of inquiry: how to assess who is requesting your participation. At a superficial level, this would seem to refer to the person who is calling you. But when you are dealing with settings of protracted conflict, it is important to think beyond the initial point of contact. Remember that in settings deeply divided by conflict, those you are connected with or perceived to be influenced by will carry more weight than who you are, what you do, or what you believe.

We asked Sue Williams to reflect on her experience in responding to requests and first points of contact. Sue has lived in Northern Ireland for the past fifteen years. (She is American by birth and now has dual citizenship.) She has lived and worked for most of her professional life as a mediator and a trainer in conflict transformation and in development in places like Northern Ireland and various countries in Africa and Asia. With her husband, Steve Williams, she coauthored a book on mediation strategies, Being in the Middle by Being at the Edge *(1994). She comes from a Quaker background and has worked as director of policy and process skills with the training program Responding to Conflict, located in Birmingham, United Kingdom, and she is now an independent consultant based in Derry, Northern Ireland.*

Carefully read what she writes in response to the inquiry, "Who is calling?" She suggests that it is important not only to gain a sense of the person (and his or her organizational affiliation) calling you, but to understand the person's location within the setting of conflict. You need a picture of your point of contact in reference to a web of relationships on the ground locally, nationally, and internationally. Assessment of who is calling requires you to think about networks, levels of networks, perceptions, and who has defined the need behind the request.

. . . .

When the telephone rings (or the e-mail, fax, or letter arrives), the journalist's time-honored questions present themselves: Who? What? When? Where? Why? and How? This chapter deals primarily with the first question, which in many ways seems the most fundamental. If the "who" is right, the rest may be negotiable.

When the telephone rings at my house, there's no knowing who may be calling, from where, or about what. Sometimes a caller opens up a whole new world to me by involving me in a distant conflict. As I find out more about the situation, and perhaps end up working with the people there, I learn to care deeply about what happens. In this sense, the who of a request is especially important, because peacebuilding involves us at deep levels. What could appear to be a simple request of providing technical assistance for a limited period of time is the beginning of a commitment to people dealing with a specific, violent conflict. For this reason, I look quickly beyond what is being asked, where, and focus on who is doing the asking.

Who Is Actually Making the Request?

There is someone asking, and my decision will depend in large measure on that person. This is partly because peacebuilding is, by its nature, collaborative, which means that the different parties need to be able to work creatively together. It is not a package, as though they were ordering a computer and I intended to deliver and install it. In our case, the product may be a mediation initiative, a consultation, a training, or a strategic review, but no matter what it is, it will require that I work closely with the sponsoring organization, local partners, individual parties and their organizations, local communities, and perhaps local authorities.

The Who Assessment

Getting a good sense of the individuals and organizations asking for your assistance is vital. The following questions can help clarify whether you want to consider accepting this particular request.

Step 1: Assessing the Person and the Organization

I start with a series of questions that make reference to what I do and do not know about the person calling, the organizations involved, the situation, and the kind of work proposed—for example:

- Is it someone I know or from an organization I know? If not, how did they get my name? What do I know about them? Whom do I know who is likely to know them?

- Are they insiders to the situation in question or outsiders? How are they perceived by others in the situation?

- Do they have a profile locally, nationally, or internationally? Are they known for certain kinds of initiatives and for independence or with strings attached? Do they have a political or economic bias that might be important to the work proposed?

- Are their values and approach compatible with mine?

- Do they have a track record of doing good work in a responsible and interactive way? What have they actually done? Do they have the capacity to do this kind of work in this place? Do they understand it conceptually? Can they support it financially and organizationally?

- What will happen to the results of this work? Will the partners compete for ownership of the result? Will one organization claim credit for more than it has done and risk exposing or discrediting important local initiatives? Will decisions about what happens next be made by those most involved, by those with power or money, or by those in key positions?

Some of these questions are likely to be relevant for any request, and each leads to others. At the same time, of course, the others who are involved will be asking these same questions about me.

Step 2: Assessing How the Organization Is Placed in the Specific Context

I begin with questions about where this initiative comes from. This is important because it tends to determine whose understanding of the problem serves as the basis for the work. It is also important to know as much as possible about all the organizations that may be involved, how they relate to each other, and particularly how they relate to the key parties. If this work is aimed at political parties, armed groups, governments, refugees, community groups, women, or youth, then how does the organization that is calling me and the network of organizations relate to them, and how do they perceive the potential work?

We can approach this question by addressing purpose and entry: Are the groups contacting me an appropriate point of entry to achieve the aims of this initiative? Included in this question is an assessment of the aims themselves. Are they appropriate aims (realistically, politically, ethically), and can this group, with my assistance, select the right people, get them there, and follow up with them?

One call I got came from a familiar partner, a U.S.-based nongovernmental organization (NGO), to document and advise a local initiative in a violent conflict in South America. The first step was to make contact with two international NGOs (INGOs) based in

Europe. However, the initiative itself was at the community level
within the country, with some liaison and campaigning work at the
national level. At the national level, one INGO was active on this
issue, along with two national NGOs (NNGOs). At the regional
level, there was also a local NGO (LNGO), as well as the previous
actors, with various relationships among themselves. And at the
level of the real work, there were three distinct communities (each
of which actually consisted of several smaller communities) to
which each of the other organizations related in various ways (see
Figure 1.1).

Such a complex structure, with both myself and the inviting
agency so far removed from the action, raises several immediate

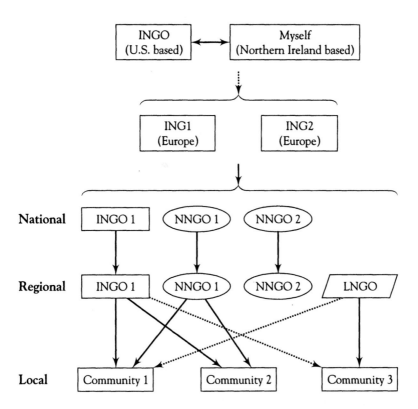

Figure 1.1. The Organization of a Local Initiative in South America.

questions and warning flags, highlighted by questions that go beyond intentions to the framing of needs and problems:

- What is the presenting problem or issue? Who has defined it? To whom was it seen as a problem or need? These are the key questions.

- What kind of consultation process was used to define the need in designing this initiative? Who was involved, and who was not?

- What did those most actively involved (the community and those working with them) think of the proposed initiative and my involvement?

- How do all the organizations and levels relate to each other? It is important to know the history between the organizations and to understand who can help with or obstruct the work in progress.

- Is there political conflict not just between governments and armies but between and within organizations? The more organizations and levels there are, the greater the likelihood is of rivalry and conflict between them. (In some cases, this was managed very well, but in others, I've been caught in significant internal organizational disputes.)

- Within the organization, who wields power over this initiative, and how do they deal with others? This can be a real stumbling block. I've found myself trapped in the role of fronting an activity for an organization that talks about participation and collaboration but actually engages in hierarchical tyranny.

Step 3: Assessing the Political Significance

Peace is, and will be seen as, political. We are, after all, working in situations of potential violent conflict.

Because there is a history of deep conflict, there is a history of mistrust. Any activity will be viewed initially through the lenses of caution and suspicion. In some situations, the political overtones of conflicts may arise from ethnic, religious, linguistic, or cultural overtones. It is vital to understand as much as possible about the nuances of both the situation and the relationships involved, particularly those with whom you will be working closely.

Because much of my work is political, I will use an example where the issue itself was political. I received a request to provide mediation training to a selected group of eminent persons who were potentially in a position to mediate between the various political parties (and their associated militias) during an upcoming election in a central African country. I was not familiar with the national NGO requesting my involvement; an acquaintance had referred me. As they described their situation and their plan, several things struck me as significant in deciding whether to proceed:

- The situation was urgent. Elections were soon to be held, each party had an armed militia, and the pattern was that thousands of people were killed at each election.

- Although I knew the region, the kind of work, the language, and some of the cultures, I told the caller I thought I had insufficient experience in this situation. The caller replied that with my experience of political mediation and command of French, I was as close to ideal as they were able to find. In the following days, I did more research on the political situation, but I was very cautious about my suitability.

- The national NGO requesting assistance seemed to have a realistic understanding of what could be done to build on the skills of the team and to provide on-call support for problems emerging later.

- Those selected for the mediation team seemed to
  represent a significant level of credibility and generally
  might be perceived as either individually independent
  or collectively balanced (bishops, university professors,
  and retired diplomats). There was one former prime
  minister, who might offer too high a profile and insufficient independence of the political conflict.

After doing extensive research with books, articles, on-line, and
with a network of colleagues, I decided to accept the offer. As things
turned out, the person with the high political profile was a useful
entrée in the short term but an obstacle in the long term, which
confirmed my experience that high status can be an asset and a dis-
advantage, either or both, at particular moments in the process.

Civil war broke out one hour after I arrived in the country for the
training. Although I was trapped in the shelling, telephones in
the capital continued to function. We ended up doing a mini-
workshop by telephone, and the mediation team negotiated two
cease-fires, during the second of which the French Foreign Legion
managed to evacuate my location.

This example also illustrates another lesson: one rarely ends up
doing what one envisaged, but the flexibility and willingness to do
what seems possible often may produce useful results.

Step 4: Striving for Creative Synergy

The total effect of an initiative may not be the sum of the inputs
and component parts. Among the other factors that can be extremely important are timeliness, excitement, the right people, flexible funding, a shared strategy, and embedding the initiative in a
larger process. This leads to another set of questions related to the
who assessment:

- Is this timely? This is the most important factor of all
  because it encompasses the activity, the people, and

the situation. Timeliness is hard to assess in objective terms; I rely primarily on the evaluation of experienced, well-informed local peacebuilders.

• Is the strategy underlying this initiative shared by many actors? If yes, what you are doing can fit into a body of work. If no, then it will have only itself to depend on. It is important to know what other peace initiatives are being undertaken and how this one fits with them.

• Is there flexibility in strategy and funding? This issue is particularly important if the work goes well and prompts ideas for other action. In this case, flexible funding and organizational strategy can take advantage of developments and support creativity.

I raise these questions with the people or organizations making the request. The answers are not always clear immediately. Examples that spring to mind include some that far exceeded any reasonable expectation of their impact and some that involved so many competing forces that they accomplished far less than was invested in them by all concerned. Again, the judgment seems to be intuitive, based on juggling many different factors and imponderables, such as what people did not say.

Ask questions about funding in the early stages. I would never advise refusing a request purely on the basis of lack of funding, both because this is philosophically unacceptable and because my experience is of having agreed to a few initiatives without any funding that turned out very well. But most effective projects do find supporters, so there would have to be good reasons to explain why a good piece of work lacked funding.

Conclusion

It is useful to be clear about which situations and requests to avoid. My own list includes the following:

- Strings attached to funding (especially governmental funding) in which funders insist that one of their people participate in the event. The biggest risk to avoid is being seen as an espionage operative.

- Organizations you do not trust or with which you have fundamental philosophical differences. It is better to be explicit about differences than to assume they will be sorted out later.

- International organizations you cannot find out anything about. A lack of information is more understandable in the case of local organizations but still needs to be pursued.

- Acting on ignorance. Ignorance is not neutrality and will catch up with you sooner or later.

- Initiatives in which everything is coming from outside, with little or no connection to people and organizations on the ground.

If you don't know enough about an international organization, ask people who seem likely to know. This is still a small domain, and there are probably fewer than six degrees of separation (that is, a chain of not more than six people will connect you to anyone else).

If you don't know a local or national organization, ask local people or long-time expatriate workers.

Don't forget to reflect systematically on your own experience, documenting it and trying to see clearly what it is trying to teach you. Important resources for this kind of reflection have been the books (and personal advice) of British peace activist Adam Curle and the late H. W. van der Merwe, long-time executive director of the Centre for Conflict Resolution in South Africa, and the processes and products of the Local Capacities for Peace Project

(LCPP), a project of the Collaborative for Development Action in Cambridge, Massachusetts. LCPP focused, through a series of case studies and reflective activities, on the roles of local peacebuilding organizations during humanitarian disasters. The book *Do No Harm* (Anderson, 1999), is a product of the LCPP.

2

· ·

What Do They Want Me to Do?

Susan Collin Marks and John Marks

A second point of inquiry raises the issue of what exactly the person who is calling is asking you to do. This inquiry is not just about the activities or responsibilities within the immediate proposal, although it is clearly important to assess whether you have the skills required for the request. Fundamentally, this is an inquiry into the evolution and development of defining a role—a relationship to a change process within a context—and finding the resources that might best match the needs being expressed.

We asked Susan Collin Marks and John Marks to provide some advice from their experience on how they develop peacebuilding roles and activities when they receive invitations. They are a husband-wife team who work together at Search for Common Ground in Washington, D.C. Susan, a South African, worked as a mediator, planner, and crisis intervenor during South Africa's transition from apartheid. She traces the lessons from that experience in her most recent book, Watching the Wind: Conflict Resolution During South Africa's Transition to Democracy (2000). *In her capacity as executive vice president of Search for Common Ground, she works as a consultant and facilitator of peace initiatives in many parts of the world. John is the founder and president of Search for Common Ground, one of the most influential nongovernmental organizations in the world working in conflict resolution, with offices in eleven countries. Search for Common Ground tries to minimize parachuting into conflicts and tries to employ a multipronged approach,*

*including extensive use of media to shift societal attitudes. The organiza-
tion has broken new ground in producing documentary television series,
dramatic television series for children, and radio soap opera, all of which
try to promote tolerance and defuse violence.*

*In the lessons that follow, Susan and John suggest that you should not
leap precipitously to the assumption that you are the chosen one when you
receive a call. In fact, the best thing you might do is help the caller clarify and define what is probably needed, brainstorm on options and ideas
to meet that need, and then move to more specific discussions of your
involvement. In other words, separate the process of clarification of need
and identification of resources from your personal commitment. Keep
track of everything you can because this will help when you reflect on the
decision and request later. And make sure you are clear on expectations
as you start the process of commitments.*

·   ·   ·   ·   ·   ·   ·

Lesson 1

Don't trust your memory; write everything down. Develop a shorthand that you will be able to decipher. Be sure to get all contact
details for the person who is calling and the organization and anyone else whose name crops up in the conversation. Check the
spelling of names. Get it right. Susan carries a spiral-bound note-
book with her at all times; it is her informal journal and log, dated,
then kept in chronological order as the pile grows on a shelf in her
office. She can look back to conversations months or years ago and
recapture them quite easily from this scribbled but invaluable
record. John recommends sending e-mails or faxes to the caller con-
firming understandings.

*On the other end of the line, the information and ideas coming from the
caller seem endless. We are writing down everything she is saying and trying to listen for the questions we need to ask so that we understand what
is really going on and why she is calling. Pages fill up with our shorthand*

that we will need to decipher later. We mustn't miss anything; her actual words will help decode what she really wants and remind us later about nuances missed earlier. The fact is that our memories are far from perfect, and we need to have a record of understandings.

Lesson 2

Ask questions and more questions. Don't get into solutions until you have the story straight. Resist even thinking about your possible role or actions at this point. Clarify the issues as best you can, gently bringing the conversation back to the story if it starts wandering off into next steps. When you feel you have a reasonable grasp of the story, then you are ready to ask, "What do you want us to do? How can we help you?"

Now that we have discussed who the caller is, determined whom she represents, and ascertained that this is an appropriate entry point (see Chapter One), we need to know what she really wants us to do and be. We need to find out if we have anything to offer her and those she represents or if another person or organization is more appropriate.

She is calling, we find out, because she has run out of solutions, or because she has attended a training course or read a book and understood that the conflict has engulfed her. She feels the need for help from an outsider, a third party, someone not connected to the events and the people who are overwhelming her community or country. Perhaps she recognizes the signs of imminent violence and wants to prevent it. Or maybe she hopes that we will come in to explain to the other side that they are wrong, that they have to stop the violence.

The desperation in her voice is real. And so first we spend time on her story, creating a coherent narrative of events, people, failed peace attempts, and dangers. She is reaching out. This call is about possibility, and so when we think we understand the story, we steer the conversation to why she has called.

She may say that she needs help this minute because often these calls come as a last resort, when everything else has failed and tragedy is looming.

Or she may say she wants to call a conference to which we will come and speak about alternatives and then collaborate on a way forward. She probably thinks that as outsiders, we would bring something special to the conflict, or that perhaps we have some technique in our toolbox that would be helpful. Does she know what she is asking for, and can it realistically be applied to her country? She may say that she needs us to do work we have done in other places—the radio programs, the women's centers, the peace education for children—so that she can somehow help build a sustained peace.

Lesson 3

Ascertain whether it is really a crisis or just that this person has come to the end of her tether in the long, hard grind of ongoing conflict. It is very rare that you can help in a crisis because in that situation, the people who can best help are those who understand it: the culture, the country, the language, the history, the issues. You might be able to help find someone nearby to help. For example, you might be able to alert an agency already on the ground—perhaps a relief or development organization. The caution is to resist the pull to jump on the next plane and go and try to help unless you have existing longer-term relationships. Your heart will weep with her, but experience suggests that it is unlikely that you can be effective. This is one of the hardest acts of discipline for a peacebuilder, but jumping uninformed into a crisis can cause more harm than good.

We have to resist taking responsibility for a situation just because we have received a call. We have to remember that we are not indispensable. There will be another solution even if we don't take on this responsibility. This is one of the most important lessons for a peacebuilder to learn.

As we continue talking, both she and we begin to see the wisdom of thinking through what role would really be useful for us to take on. We help her clarify what outsiders can realistically offer in her culture and in this situation. What else has been tried to date? What resources exist locally or regionally that may not have been tapped? What can she and her organization do? What kind of intervention, if any, could make a difference? Our intuition works in tandem with our analytic faculties.

Lesson 4

Peacebuilding requires us to align our heads and our hearts. We need to pay respectful attention to instincts and judgments. Asking, "Does this feel right?" is as important a question as the calculation of our experience in relation to the needs. Intuition is based on experience. If you have little or no experience in this setting, then make it a goal to find a mentor or more experienced person who knows this situation or others like it. Ask that person what he or she thinks. Create an intentional reference group—one explicitly set up to help provide you insight and understanding about the setting.

A conflict that turns violent usually leaves the realm of the rational and the intellectual. We respond only with our heads at our peril because we will miss the point. Conversely, if we follow our own irrational longing to help and damn the consequences, we miss a further point. Balance is key.

Slowly we start to hear a different story—the one that emerges when the pain of conflict is momentarily put aside. We brainstorm options for intervention—with the understanding that this is still not necessarily our intervention—to come to some kind of short list of what might help. She thinks that the divided community would come to a meeting to talk about the issues with a sympathetic stranger more readily than with just each other. She believes they would be willing to engage in deep introspection not because they want to, but because they have had enough. She hopes that the moment is coming, perhaps very soon, when they might be prepared to seek a solution.

Lesson 5

Clarification of need is not the same thing as commitment for us to intervene. Creative work may point to skills and expertise other than your own.

She says that in fact there are some nongovernmental organizations that could support an intervention and the peacebuilding work that would follow. But that will take time. She thinks it is going to be a long-term process; we will need to make a commitment to engage for months, if not years, ahead.

Lesson 6

Understand that the conversation is progressing to a decision point and know that if you are preparing to say yes, you are making a commitment that must be kept. It will require resources—money, energy, time, tenacity, action—not on your timetable, but to meet the needs of the people in conflict. Effective peacebuilding requires a long-term commitment. You cannot expect to make a difference if you only parachute in for a short period of time. Are you prepared to make the necessary commitment? Are you willing to give up other activities, family time, and vacations? Can you balance the demands that this commitment will inevitably make on you and your family with your own very real needs?

We ask hard questions about her support base. Can she raise funds for this intervention, funds that would not compromise it? The rich industrialist may be offering as much money as is needed, but if we use his money, will it compromise the intervention? Will the other group suspect a hidden agenda? Or does she need us to find funds? Will potential funders trust their money only to international players? Is that why she is calling us?

On the ground, will there be transport, interpreters, and places to work? Can we access e-mail from there? Are there electricity and water? Can we as Westerners function in the conditions she has to endure?

Is what she is asking possible to do? Does it have a reasonable chance of success?

Lesson 7

We each have to define our parameters for this work. We need to get clear about how much we need to earn, how much time we are prepared to offer, and how much physical and emotional stress we are willing to endure. We need to confront our own safety needs and think through the limits of personal danger we can withstand and still be effective. We need above all to be realistic about who we are and what conditions we require to be our best, and not attach ourselves to someone else's star.

For example, Susan is a South African and very comfortable in the bush because she grew up with it—and often in it. John is an American, with less tolerance for hardship. So when we have to go to some desolate outpost, Susan has better coping mechanisms. John, with his U.S. Foreign Service background, can navigate the halls of power with more ease and sureness. We both do some of each, but we try to maximize our comparative strengths.

It emerges that the possibilities are quite numerous. Our caller has read Susan's book about the South African peace process, Watching the Wind *(2000), and thinks that the community would be willing to consider creating a committee that brings together all the stakeholders. Even the police will come, she says, and the traditional healers, as well as the politicians, although the extremists are unlikely to engage at this point.*

She agrees that a series of training workshops for this range of stakeholders could be appropriate. She knows that the mayor is an ally and that he would welcome conflict resolution training in the schools. He might spearhead this for the region.

We discuss some resources that might be helpful, and we offer to send some useful publications and contact information for other conflict resolution organizations in the region and abroad so that she is aware of a range of possibilities.

Lesson 8

Collaboration helps people make good decisions and creates a basis for cooperation rather than competition.

We finish with an action plan:

- *We will arrange a time to talk again when she will confirm that the community agrees to the intervention and wants it and we will confirm that we want to get engaged.*

- *She will take our conversation to her constituency and get their approval for our intervention. Ideally, she will send a letter of invitation, signed by the appropriate stakeholders, requesting our presence. The letter will include an agreement of support with interpreters, venues, and other details. This information and the affirmation of local commitment to our intervention will help us decide if we can or want to engage.*

- *We will discuss this conversation with our organization, family, and peers to consider if or how to proceed. We will send her a letter outlining the possible activities we have discussed, fleshing out what they would look like, what local support they would require, how they might fit together into a coherent plan, and what other resources, specialist knowledge, and information would be needed. This letter will help her and her constituency decide if they want us to intervene.*

- *We will check in with other organizations working in the region to find out what is already being done to ensure that we wouldn't duplicate or overlap with existing activities or programs. We will also touch base with various authorities as appropriate to ascertain the advisability of getting involved and any consequences that we may not be aware of. We will, in broad terms, do our homework.*

- *We will explore funding possibilities.*

- *We will send the various publications and other resources that we discussed.*

Conclusion

The conversation started with a huge emotional outpouring, and we have ended up with concrete next steps that will help us decide whether to intervene. This may take a number of conversations over a period of time. We do not pretend that we have represented an exhaustive repertoire of issues to be addressed; we have merely tried to give a sense of the many points that must be considered. These are the kinds of things we need to know, clarify, and discuss before we jump into a conflict situation.

Working with conflict is rarely a linear experience. Our work calls on us to work consciously at many levels simultaneously, listening, processing, and acting with our heads, hearts, and gut in sync, and to seek the balance between them. Then we can be what is needed and do what will work, because we will be attuned to the different levels that inhabit every conflict, and every human being, including ourselves.

3

. . . .

Who Else Is Working There?

Louise Diamond

There is another inquiry hinted at in the first two chapters that presents a particularly important aspect of international peacebuilding. This is the "Who else?" question. At first glance, the answer may seem obvious, but the closer you examine it, the more you realize that the complexity of this inquiry takes us to some of the core but perhaps least practiced values endorsed by the field at large: coordination and cooperation. As the field has grown and as financial resources for peacebuilding activities have increased, so too have competitiveness and lack of synergism.

A conceptual and practical leader around this concern has been Louise Diamond. Cofounder and now president emeritus of the Institute for Multi-Track Diplomacy, Louise and her colleague John MacDonald have written, advocated, and practiced approaches for developing coordinated efforts at peacebuilding that link and create synergy with sets of people and activities. Louise, currently living in New Hampshire, has a global portfolio and worked for decades in many zones of deeply rooted, or as she calls them, conflict-habituated, systems. Her most recent book, The Peace Book (2001), outlines a series of suggestions for making peace work practical in everyday life.

From her experience, Louise suggests that a first step in any process is to develop the ability to think and act in a systemic way, recognizing that what will do is not an isolated action but one that will have an impact on the immediate point of contact and the broader web of relationships

and processes. Her advice is never to go into a new setting without con-
sulting with others who have been working there ahead of you on their
views, suggestions, and counsel.

· · · · · · ·

B y now, you've gathered information about the conflict situation, the culture, and your possible point of entry into the system. You've considered what your unique contribution might be.
Now it's time to examine how your intervention might relate with
other peacebuilding efforts already in play in this particular conflict setting.

From my more than a dozen years of experience as a practitioner in places of deeply rooted conflicts, I have pulled out five
general principles that are helpful in building bridges across the
entire system.

Guideline 1: Think and Act Systemically

The conflict situation you are entering is complex, and so is the
peace process you will be part of. You will be engaging with a system of interactions involving people from many sectors, both within
and outside the country. I use the term *multitrack diplomacy* to
describe a systemic view of the peace process. It means that people
from all walks of life can be peacebuilders—indeed, they must be if
the peace is to viable and lasting.

You will become involved in an intricate tapestry of interwoven
social, economic, historical, psychological, political, and intra- and
intergroup dynamics, with a myriad of players. Within this setting,
your particular intervention is not an isolated activity. It relates to
other things that are happening—or could be happening, or will be
happening, or should (or shouldn't) be happening. In short, whatever you do will become part of that system. If you can be conscious
of the larger whole during the entire process of planning, deliver-

ing, and evaluating your intervention, you can be more effective as a peacebuilder.

This means that you need to look at what you are being invited to do not as a separate, stand-alone activity, but in terms of where it fits in the past, current, and future configuration of peacebuilding initiatives. It also means you need to think about who else you can partner with, who are your natural allies, and what existing networks you can be part of.

Here are some useful questions to ask:

- What, if anything, like this has already been done? What is being done currently? By whom? With what results?

- How does this initiative fit in with the larger picture of what else is happening in this situation, even and especially activities that seem quite different from mine?

- How can I cooperate, formally and informally, with existing efforts and interested parties?

- If my intervention is successful, what will be the likely impact on the system as a whole? On various elements of the system? On the people who have invited me in and their immediate constituents? On me?

In 1991, I was invited by a Greek Cypriot woman to come to Cyprus and make a film about the longing and possibilities for peace as seen from both sides, Greek and Turk. I determined immediately that this was not a contribution I could appropriately offer, but that I could and would be willing to go to Cyprus and explore what intervention might be suitable. I did that, and after talking with various people on both sides who had already been involved in some activities of bicommunal dialogue, a new invitation came: Could I offer training in conflict resolution?

That was something I knew I could do and I thought might be useful in the system, because it could be applied in a wide variety of intragroup and intergroup situations on the island. It would also introduce a new way of thinking about conflict in a system that was habituated into a strongly adversarial us-versus-them culture. In other words, I determined that offering training in conflict resolution could make a worthwhile contribution to the whole system and not just to the individuals who enrolled in the program.

I also talked with my local counterparts to determine what would happen if we were successful. They saw that such a program, though totally unofficial and geared toward private citizens, could have a potential impact on the political process, affect public opinion, and change the basic nature of the relationship between the two parties in Cyprus. A training in conflict resolution would obviously not be simple at all, but it could be (and proved to be) a catalytic influence on the larger system and its multifaceted peace process.

Initially, I explored the history of citizen peacebuilding in Cyprus. I learned about initiatives that had been taken in the 1960s, 1970s, and 1980s and their outcomes—both the successes and the challenges. That gave me some valuable information on unique sensitivities in the system and things to avoid at all costs—a lesson that I was to find extraordinarily useful over time.

I talked with both Greek and Turkish Cypriots who had participated in these previous activities and also with the third parties who had led them. From that round of consultations, I was able to place our program of training in conflict resolution in a larger context of ongoing citizen peacebuilding efforts and to draw on existing resources, both within and outside Cyprus.

Guideline 2: Build on Existing Resources

Perhaps the conflict setting you are entering is virgin territory, meaning that no outside person or group has yet made any intervention—

but I doubt it. Even if this were so, in all likelihood there are local actors who have already been involved in some kind of peacebuilding work.

Whatever has gone before you has left traces in the system. There are people who share certain values; who have acquired basic skills or essential information; and who know how to operate within and between the interstices of the various factions, structures, and parties. There are special relationships established, simple or elaborate methods for getting things done, and allies in various places of influence already identified. These are invaluable resources for your work. You do not want to start over again. Where the groundwork has been laid, you want to build further.

As I did my first rounds of fact finding in Cyprus, I identified one third party who had most recently been involved in bicommunal work, Ronald J. Fisher, a professor at the School for International Service at American University. Before my first trip to the island, I called Ron, identified myself and my intentions, and asked about his experience and for his help. He was extremely generous in responding to all these requests. He not only gave me names and telephone numbers of his contacts in Cyprus, many of whom went on to become the core group of our new initiative. He also gave me information about the system and its players that was to prove invaluable.

Ron and I took this cooperative approach even further: over the years, I included him on the staff of many of our projects in Cyprus, and he has included me in his. We share information regularly and help each other in various ways when appropriate. Although each of us maintains our own unique approaches to working in Cyprus, we remain steadfast resources for each other, and our different efforts support and complement one another.

When my organization, the Institute for Multi-Track Diplomacy (IMTD), had the opportunity to do leadership work with youth in Bosnia and Herzegovina, we spoke with our friend and colleague Jamie Spector, who had helped create a network of youth organizations there, Nesto Vise. Rather than try to create a way to reach out to youth in all parts of the country on our own, it made sense to partner with Nesto Vise, which already had a widespread set of relationships with existing youth groups.

Nesto Vise became our local partner for the Youth Leadership Adventure program, which is now going into its third year. By this time, it has developed the capacity to manage the program on its own, and IMTD is no longer needed to keep it going.

You also need to be looking out for potential partners and allies. Ask yourself these questions as you consider others:

- Who in the system can help your intervention succeed?

- Who already has resources in place that can both save you valuable time, money, and effort and provide services that will complement your endeavor?

- Who do you need to help secure your credibility in the system and safeguard your participants from backlash?

In our work with business leaders in India and Pakistan, we made strong alliances with chambers of commerce on each side. In our work with Israeli and Palestinian educators, we allied with a local organization seen as highly credible by both sides. In our work in Bosnia and Herzegovina, we developed good relationships with various relief and development agencies.

In our work in Cyprus, we made sure to maintain excellent relations with the U.S. and other governments that shared a special interest in the peace process there. Our connections with the U.S. embassy in particular proved invaluable when we wanted to invite highly influential players to our programs. Ambassador Richard Boucher made the invitations personally and welcomed participants to receptions at his home and elsewhere. We also partnered formally with another U.S.-based organization, Conflict Management Group

(CMG), realizing that together we had a far greater range of professional and economic resources to bring to the situation than either of us had separately.

Guideline 3: Practice Professional Courtesy

The example of our partnership with CMG illustrates another important point about collaboration and courtesy in our field. We teach cooperation, so we need to practice it as well, even and especially when we may feel the urge to compete for what appear to be limited resources.

Both CMG and IMTD had done work in Cyprus, when a Request for Proposals was put out that was clearly based on both of our work and both of our approaches, which were quite different. The two organizations saw immediately that competing for the funds would not serve any useful purpose, but that by collaborating, we could model that value in our field, provide our clients and beneficiaries with a wider range of resources, and increase the learning opportunities for all involved.

Once an individual or group has done extensive work in some conflict system, they deserve the respect and courtesy of those just coming in to the situation, for several reasons. First, you don't want to replicate what has already been done. You also don't want to step on anyone's toes and inadvertently mess up a work in progress. Finally, you want to expand the available resources as much as possible and open the potential for new and collaborative endeavors.

Twice, third parties came into the work in Cyprus without consulting us and drawing on our years of experience there. In the first situation, an outside group totally new to Cyprus called us at the last minute for recommendations for the right people to involve in its project, which had already been funded without anyone on the team ever setting foot on the island. We cooperated with them, only to discover that their ignorance about the situation actually put some of our friends—and by extension, all peacebuilding efforts—at risk in their own communities.

In the other situation, a high-powered and well-funded third party came to a country in which IMTD had a strong presence and set up what they hoped would be an intervention with great potential to influence the highest political players. They chose the people for their project without consulting us. Had they done so, we would have strongly advised against a particular individual they selected to put at the head of the whole endeavor. We knew, from our own experience with this individual and from the wisdom of the people in his community whom we had worked with for many years and built strong bonds of trust with, that he was likely to sabotage the whole event. He did, with a great loss of time, effort, face, and credibility, not to mention money and hope. All of that loss could have been avoided.

By way of contrast, here is an example of a positive case of professional courtesy. When Search for Common Ground (SCG) had the opportunity to set up a children's television program in Cyprus, they contacted me first to let me know what was happening. They were concerned not to inadvertently get in the way of anything already in motion, and they wanted to build a good, collaborative environment. In this case, there was little overlap in our projects, and we wished each other well. The model that this set for all the players was significant. Several of our friends in Cyprus have asked us if we know SCG and their project, and we are able to vouch for them and show our support for them, modeling the value of multi-track diplomacy in action.

Guideline 4: Do Your Research

We've established that it is vitally important to connect with others working in the system you are about to enter. The first step in finding these others is to ask local contacts in the system about

other peacebuilding initiatives. Ask about activities that are similar to your intended intervention but also about those that
are quite different. Your local partners will undoubtedly know
about both local organizations and outside groups working for similar goals.

Next, ask around the professional conflict resolution community
in North America and Europe. If you know (or have heard) of even
one practitioner in that community, contact that person. Don't be
shy about approaching someone who doesn't know you. It happens
all the time. I get many calls from people about to do projects in
places where I've worked, and I'm always grateful they bothered to
make the connection. In some cases, wonderful collaborative opportunities can emerge.

You can also check in with some of the major university programs in peace and conflict studies (American University, George
Mason University, Notre Dame, the School for International Training, and Eastern Mennonite University, to name a few). They are
likely to have projects in various places of deeply rooted conflicts,
as well as information about those peace processes, and can usually
direct you to a good place to start. Another possibility is to call one
of the larger nongovernmental organizations associated with the
field of conflict resolution and ask for recommendations. And you
can contact some of the major foundations that sponsor this work
(examples are the U.S. Institute of Peace and the Hewlett Foundation) for information on who's doing what.

Finally, there are Web sites and databases for individual organizations and networks involved in the field of international conflict resolution that you can explore. Try especially the Applied
Conflict Resolution Organizations Network, an alliance of many of
the major organizations doing this type of work, and International
Alert, one of the largest European organizations involved in peacebuilding around the world. You can also input various key words in
an Internet search engine to find resources on the Web.

Guideline 5: Explore Local Resources

Do not assume that the only or most important peacebuilding players for you to contact are outside the system. On the contrary, the ones that most matter are the local actors themselves, both individuals and organizations.

I could not have made that statement with the same strength ten years ago. Over the past decade, there has been an explosion of peacebuilding efforts that have trained local people and catalyzed the creation of numerous home-based nongovernmental organizations. The funding for peacebuilding in places of deeply rooted conflicts is being directed more and more at local peacebuilders, and for good reason. They have themselves experienced both the traumas of the conflict and the transformations that come from being engaged in the peace process. They know their system better than outsiders do; they know what is needed, what is possible, and what won't work. They know who to invite in, who to keep informed, and who to avoid politely. In many cases, they have been well trained and mentored by North American or European third parties. Not only are the local peacebuilders more informed, but they have more at stake.

As you consider your intervention, you might ask not only what local players you should speak with about what is already happening, but you might also ask yourself, Should I be doing this intervention at all, or should it be in the hands of local peacebuilders? If you determine that you do have a unique and valuable contribution to offer, you might consider partnering with a local group, to ground the work in the reality of the particular system you are entering.

After a hiatus of several years, I am about to reenter the Cyprus system, but this time from a completely different point of view. I see a need for developing a new approach to leadership that spans the spectrum of society—leadership that can lead effectively for change, for reconciliation, for democratization, for being a healthy partner in the global community of this century. Yet rather than creating the project myself, I am speaking to local organizations that have a natural interest and experience in leadership development. I am sharing my ideas and listening to their ideas, and encouraging them to move forward if they wish, offering myself as a resource to them. I am especially inviting them to lift up the expertise and wisdom that already exists in the system and build their programs on that base. In this way, I am looping back in to Guideline 1: think and act systemically.

Looking at how I can make a true and lasting contribution to the entire system and to a viable and sustainable peace process, I need to recognize that I am ultimately an outsider and that the people who live in this setting—who wish so desperately for a better life for their children and grandchildren—are the true leverage points for change in the system. I can be a catalytic agent, but my suitcase goes both ways: I can come into the system, but I will invariably leave it. Knowing this, I am seeking out those who are central to the change process, to see and support what they are doing to make a difference.

Conclusion

Conflict-habituated systems require interventions of all kinds and from many different perspectives. When we know how our part fits in the larger whole, we start to build the very bridges that are missing in a deeply rooted social conflict situation. Peacebuilding is all about reestablishing the human and systemic links that have been broken. Not the least of our contributions is to model in action what we tout in theory: we are all in this together.

4

· ·

Where Do I Fit In?

John Paul Lederach

The preceding chapters give a good sense of who we are working with and the range of people who may already be carrying out peacebuilding activities. But how do we assess where we fit within that picture and whether the activity we are requested to do is the best thing to be doing? The question of fit is not just about whether we are capable of doing what we are being asked to do but whether this fits the larger picture of what is needed.

John Paul Lederach addresses this question from the standpoint of developing an understanding of the strategic fit. John Paul has worked for more than twenty years as a mediator, trainer, and peacebuilder in a wide variety of conflicts, from Somalia to Colombia. He is professor of international peacebuilding at Notre Dame's Kroc Institute and the founding director of the Conflict Transformation Program at Eastern Mennonite University. He is known for his writings on international and cross-cultural work; particularly well known are his elicitive approach to peace education and the book Building Peace: Sustainable Reconciliation in Divided Societies *(1997).*

From his experience, John Paul suggests that creating a strategic fit will require you to consult and reflect not only on the activity but, more important, on the change process the activity is aimed at achieving. You need to discover your added value in a careful and intentional manner.

· · · · · · · ·

R eceiving an invitation to a new setting can easily feel over-whelming and at the same time exciting. How do you know whether this is worth doing and how it contributes in a construc-tive way to peacebuilding in the setting?

The key to this process of assessment is to develop a strategic fit. *Strategic* means that you have done enough assessment so that you are clear about how your role enters and supports the development of a broader change process and that you bring added value, avoid-ing duplication and replacement of local resources. The assessment requires complex inquiries. To develop the strategic fit, here are some suggestions I have found useful.

Get a Sense of the Larger Picture

An important starting point in any new initiative is to get a sense of the larger picture of what is happening in relationship to peace-building in the country where you have been invited. There is more than ample room in almost all situations for a wide variety of activities and initiatives. However, it is important to recognize what has gone on before you get there and how the proposed activ-ity fits constructively into change processes that are needed in the broader setting.

I usually start with a simple tool: a pyramid that looks at three levels of actors and activities in peacebuilding work, including ways in which they are vertically and horizontally connected (see Figure 4.1). At the highest level is what is commonly referred to in the media as the peace process. This phrase, more often than not, is making reference to an official level of negotiations between well-known and visible leaders representing the government and poten-tially a series of opposition movements that have been in conflict. The middle-range level often involves activities of national networks and organizations and international nongovernmental agencies—sets of people who may well have contacts and relationships with the official process but are more likely to be engaged with the development of the civil society. At the bottom level are sets of people who are working with local grassroots and community-level initiatives, often connected to a particular geographical area within the setting.

The usefulness of a snapshot of what might be happening at these different levels is that you can locate yourself and the organizations that you might be working with and understand how they relate to other initiatives within the setting. Earlier rather than later, it is important to understand the range of contacts you may have and that these are interdependent with other things happening in the setting. You want to avoid a view that suggests you are working in isolation or that you have the key process and activity. Recognize the complexity of different levels and where your process fits in the larger picture. It is extremely important from a strategic standpoint that you understand that you are entering an existing system with an established web of relationships and linkages. I start with an understanding of who I am working with, where they are located, and what other things may be happening.

The questions raised in Figure 4.1 are aimed at creating an initial orientation that is useful for locating your work in this system. At the most visible level, it can be helpful to ask not only what is known about the highest-level official processes, but, more important, what is known about the web of connections and relationships that links these processes to other levels and what the potential gaps are in supporting them toward constructive outcomes. At a midrange level, the key is to think about national networks and the institutions and agencies that may be promoting peace-related initiatives. From your standpoint as a newcomer on the scene, this kind of ongoing inquiry is critical in order to recognize potential gaps in the work and avoid duplication of efforts. At the grassroots level, where ultimately in everyday life people are affected by the decisions we make, the inquiry is oriented at holding up two questions that seemingly are contradictory but in fact are not. These questions form a paradox, different and mutually dependent. What

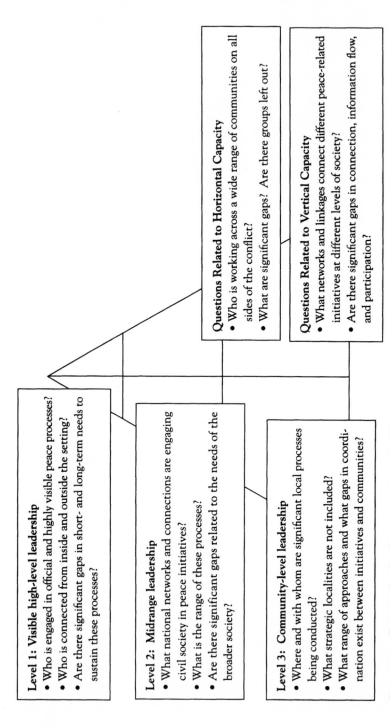

Level 1: Visible high-level leadership
- Who is engaged in official and highly visible peace processes?
- Who is connected from inside and outside the setting?
- Are there significant gaps in short- and long-term needs to sustain these processes?

Level 2: Midrange leadership
- What national networks and connections are engaging civil society in peace initiatives?
- What is the range of these processes?
- Are there significant gaps related to the needs of the broader society?

Level 3: Community-level leadership
- Where and with whom are significant local processes being conducted?
- What strategic localities are not included?
- What range of approaches and what gaps in coordination exist between initiatives and communities?

Questions Related to Horizontal Capacity
- Who is working across a wide range of communities on all sides of the conflict?
- What are significant gaps? Are there groups left out?

Questions Related to Vertical Capacity
- What networks and linkages connect different peace-related initiatives at different levels of society?
- Are there significant gaps in connection, information flow, and participation?

Figure 4.1. Getting the Big Picture in a Peacebuilding Process.

are the community's most immediate pressing needs? What are the hopes and aspirations of the community for change in the intermediate and longer-term future? The kind of process and initiative that you are engaged in must continue to ask these questions and seek, whenever possible, the response of community-level members rather than exclusively those who say they speak on behalf of communities.

The kind of information you begin to get back from these inquiries creates a matrix of response that will provide you with a much better sense of the bigger picture, how the activity you are engaged in contributes to constructive change, and where your role may be best situated.

Focus on the Change Process: Consult Early and Often, and Be Transparent

This second suggestion requires a set of inquiries for moving from the bigger picture down to the specifics of the work. It bears repeating that there is nothing that replaces the hard work of seeking the advice and thoughts of a wide variety of sources and people about your potential role and the activities proposed, particularly if this is the first time you have entered the country.

To move toward a strategic fit, your primary point of inquiry should not be the specifics of the activities proposed. Focus instead on the change processes that the activities are promoting. Put consultation on the change process first and consultation on the activity second. People have a natural tendency to put the specifics of the activity first and hold fast to this order. Keep asking about the change process: What is the purpose and hoped-for change we are seeking to promote?

Obviously, your primary contact for exploring the nature of the change process will be the people who have invited you. Be explicit about asking them who else is working on these kinds of approaches, and seek an open connection with those organizations or representatives of their networks who may be accessible to you directly.

Remember that the purpose of consulting is to listen, and listen carefully. Listen for misgivings. Listen for counsel on what has worked and what has not worked. Listen for the names of people who have gained experience and know about the situation. This is a continuous process, not one that is done exclusively at the point of entry. I believe that a major weakness in our overall capacity as a global community of peacebuilders to help many of the situations where we work has been our inability to coordinate and learn from each other and to be explicit about how our activities are related to desired change.

The purpose of transparency is to set a tone of cooperation and trust. In some circumstances, your invitation may well be conditioned by the need to work quietly and confidentially. Early on, ask your colleagues about the nature of confidentiality, and be sure to respect their requests and guidelines. At the same time, it is important to explore how a good process of coordination can be accomplished within the broader needs of the settings. You cannot control or demand that others immediately trust and are transparent with you, but you can ensure that you create a tone of work and quality of relationship that promotes trust and transparency.

Remember that in settings characterized by long patterns of violence and division, suspicion and mistrust are mechanisms for ensuring personal security and survival. Loose lips do sink ships. Nevertheless, my experience suggests that much of our lack of coordination comes not from our need to maintain confidentiality, but rather our competitiveness and desire to protect our territory among peacebuilders. I believe there is a need to seek broader cooperation, understanding, and coordination among people who are working on different but ultimately interdependent activities promoting conflict transformation and peacebuilding. This can happen only to the degree we start with attitudes and commitment of seeking advice, sharing ideas, and honest transparency about our work. Set for yourself a simple peacebuilder goal and discipline: being a model of cooperation, support, and encouragement.

Assess Your Value Added, and Recognize the Limitations of Your Role

The third important suggestion in developing a strategic fit is the ability to define your value-added and recognize the limitations of your role. The preceding chapters offered solid advice about clarifying your role and establishing good connections. What I want to add here is a further note about limitations.

I have found rather consistently in many situations characterized by deep social divisions and violence that it is easy to see all kinds of things that need to be done, from immediate emergency help with friends you will make to a myriad of opportunities that seem to show up daily, demanding attention and creative response. These opportunities and demands are coupled with what we might call the subtle cloud of guilt. In settings where there are huge, immediate, and pressing needs, we can easily be caught up in a whirlwind of the need to do something. The reality is that in these situations, no one person can do it all. Almost on a daily basis, you will find you need to choose the issues, demands, and opportunities to which you can and cannot give energy and attention. You will need a point of reference. This is the purpose of a strategic fit. This will not be easy to determine, and there are no preset answers. However, it will be much harder if you have not thought about it intentionally beforehand.

My advice is twofold. First, with your primary partners, establish your priorities and be clear about what it is that you bring that others may not bring. This is your value added. Perhaps you are a trainer who has worked with victims of violence and can help facilitate an education program for school counselors. Or you may have skills in developing consensus-based processes for public policy decisions. In other words, you have skills, experience, and knowledge that can help fill a gap in the overall system of things needed for constructive change and specified in an activity. Be clear about the range of this value added, which should remain your point of focus. Make sure to ask what your partners perceived your value added to be for them. Just being an outsider is not enough. Just having access to resources is not enough, and it will usually create unrealistic expectations.

Second, knowing that these situations are dynamic and ever changing, do not be surprised if your well-laid plans are disrupted. You need flexibility and a capacity to adapt. However, when you are faced with the need to make choices and change original plans, do not be swept away with a feeling that you need to do something. In fact, the best advice may be the opposite: "Don't just do something; stand there." In other words, remember to take time for a careful assessment. Give yourself and your colleagues an intentional period to reassess. Return to the core reasons and added value of your participation and presence and ask yourself, "What is the best use of who I am and what I can do, consistent with what we hoped to work on when I first came?" Taking this time, even if it is only a few minutes, can help reframe the moment back toward the larger picture and the specific things that may be most useful for you to do.

The key to this process is recognizing that you have something to bring but also limitations. You cannot do it all, and you will not be as useful in a strategic sense if you are hopping from one thing to the next driven by a sense of guilt that something should be done. Be intentional about your value added, and be flexible in how that might play out when changes happen. But make sure you do it with purpose and intentionality in a process of consultation.

Avoid Duplication

You have a responsibility to assess whether your work and activity are duplicating something already initiated by other people and underway. There is probably no greater weakness in the system of peacebuilding than when the same activities are taken up by different sets of people, particularly outsiders with resources, demanding the attention of leaders and communities to accomplish and repeat the same goals. It depletes resources, frustrates people in the setting, and often leads to a feeling that it is being done for the outsiders' benefit more than clarity of vision from within. In the worst-case scenarios, peace has become an industry with no strategic change capacity and purpose. You cannot control all the things happening, and you cannot control that others may duplicate what you are doing. You can be intentional and clear about whether your role and activity is value added or a duplication.

First and foremost, ask yourself whether what you are being asked to do could be done just as well by someone from within the setting who has similar skills. The most important thing to avoid is that you replace the in-setting resources simply because you are coming from outside or because you have financial resources. Commit yourself to a second peacebuilder goal and discipline: do everything you can to empower people from the setting to take primary roles and responsibilities in support of long-term change in their own homeland. If you find you are in circumstances where the people and skills are available but it is not as safe for them to do the work as it is for you, or they will not be seen as legitimate as the outsider providing this role, then make sure you explore the possibility of team and team building to carry out the activity.

Second, start with the question of whether the process of change promoted by the activities you are asked to do is being taken up by other people, organizations, or networks. We return to the idea of a change process. What are we trying to change? Who else is interested and trying to create similar kinds of change? When you place the focus on change rather than the immediate activity, you will find that your questions are less threatening than proposing the activity itself and lead to a wider array of people and initiatives to consult. At a second level, you can reassess whether the kind of activity you might be engaged in complements and helps build the change process, or whether it duplicates and even may set back existing efforts. Often when you are clear about the goals of change, you can find more strategic ways to think about the specific activities and how to create a web of connected people and initiatives that support the change rather than a flurry of activity that duplicates and has little impact.

Conclusion

How you fit in requires more than just an answer to whether you can do what is being asked. Finding the strategic fit requires a process of inquiry and assessment that is your responsibility and is best done in simple steps:

- Get a sense of the big picture and how your contribution is located.

- Make sure you are clear about your value added.

- Focus on the goals of the change process before you determine the specific activities.

- Avoid duplication of activities unless they are strategically connected to the change process.

- Make sure your role empowers the overall system and local resources and does not replace someone who could do it equally well from within the setting.

Part II

. . . .

The Context

The Geography of Protracted Conflict

As you begin to develop a better sense of the big picture related to the request for your participation, you will come face to face with the question of what you do and do not know about this whole setting: the people, the conflict, and the culture. This leads us to a second set of inquiries critical to the assessment and evolution of preparing a decision and possible entry: What do you need to know about the geography of the protracted conflict setting? Geography is a metaphor that indicates not only place but the history, context, and evolution of the conflict and the cultural meaning structures that are part of the makeup of the people and their setting.

You know you have developed a set of professional skills, approaches, and understandings about conflict and peacebuilding, but how do these relate to this particular setting? And exactly how much do you need to know about the conflict and the setting in order to make an informed decision? When you talk to your friends or family about the invitation, inevitably someone will have just seen a flashing report on CNN that fighting broke out again last night, and they will ask you, "Is it safe to even go there?"

You can break this perplexing aspect of preparation into a series of questions that help you think about what you need to know and how you might fill in your knowledge gaps when time and decisions are pressing. This part of the book opens with an assessment of how much you need to know about the conflict and setting and what questions may be most important for you. Shared electronic knowledge resources and approaches to finding what you need are readily available in quantity, but you need to determine what is most useful to you and how to get to it. We place a significant emphasis on the issue and concern of crossing cultures, including what research suggests and practitioners have found useful. Finally, we provide some practical advice on how to assess and prepare for your safety from people who are seasoned travelers in conflict zones and have researched the growing body of knowledge about security issues from the perspective of international nongovernmental organizations working in violent zones of conflict.

· ·

5

How Much Do I Need to Know?

Christopher Mitchell

Our starting point in Part Two is the simple yet daunting question of how much you need to know about the history of the conflict itself and the setting where you will be going for peacebuilding. This poses a certain paradox. On the one hand, ignorance sets the stage for making bad decisions that might be counterproductive, or even dangerous or disastrous. On the other, none of us will ever master all the details and nuances of the complex histories and the ever-changing day-to-day evolution of conflicts.

We asked Christopher Mitchell to draw on his rich experience of both research and practice in conflict resolution initiatives that cross more than three decades. Chris, trained as a social scientist in Great Britain, conducted some of his early research in the 1960s on the conflicts in the Horn of Africa. He currently is teaching at George Mason University's Institute for Conflict Analysis and Resolution. He has helped develop the theory and practice of the field, particularly working with different forms of second-track diplomacy, the unofficial work that supports governmental diplomatic efforts. Most notably, he has contributed significantly to the development of problem-solving workshop initiatives. In those activities, he has initiated and conducted dialogue and mediation work in Northern Ireland, Cyprus, the Basque country, and the Caucasus. His Handbook of Conflict Resolution *(1996), coauthored with Michael Banks, gives solid, practical advice on the development of the analytical problem-solving workshop approach.*

Drawing on his experience of working in so many different conflict zones, he answers the question of whether a peacebuilder needs an encyclopedic knowledge of the setting before deciding to enter and take up activity: you need to know "just enough." Chris suggests that you start by knowing yourself and then setting the goal of a lifelong process of learning. This most experienced of social scientists and conflict intervenors says the learning never ends. Here, he sets out some key questions to keep in mind as you begin.

•   •   •   •   •   •   •

One essential query for anyone contemplating intervention into a complex protracted conflict is how much to know before initiating any direct contact with the adversaries or attempting to influence their behaviors, attitudes, or relationship. How expert should one become before trying to take up the role of go-between, purveyor of good offices, facilitator, or mediator?

This is clearly a difficult question to answer and varies from situation to situation. However, a few rules of thumb, gained from experience, can be framed.

Guideline 1: Know Yourself

One of the most important guidelines is the fundamental requirement for third parties to know themselves before they begin to undertake any intermediary project. There are at least two aspects to this guideline. The first applies more to individuals who are going to be personally and directly involved in the enterprise, and the second concerns their background and that of their organization in relation to the particular conflict and the parties involved in it.

At the personal level, before becoming involved in any intermediary process, be fully aware of the theories and values that you take into the conflict. Literature from our field suggests the values that make a good intermediary and help make successful intermediary initiatives: a willingness to allow the adversaries to shape their own solutions, a belief in the effectiveness of a nondirective process, and a commitment to involving the voices of disempowered or unheard stakeholders in the forging of any solution. Less attention has been paid to the theories about conflict sources, processes, and sustainable solutions that intermediaries inevitably carry with them throughout any process of resolution. Nobody can escape having such theories, even when they take the form of untested—and sometimes unconscious—hunches. John Maynard Keynes is once said to have remarked, "Those practical men of business who have no time for speculative theorizing are usually the intellectual victims of some long since discredited economist."

In our own field, it seems more than likely that intermediaries' ideas about human nature itself—about whether sovereignty has to be treated as an indivisible concept or can be regarded as something more flexible, about the basic origins of social conflicts, about the viability of sundry solutions or the best means for reaching those solutions—will influence how individual intermediaries approach a particular conflict, as well as what initial information they seek about that conflict.

Mix in some elements of intermediaries' backgrounds and values, and one has to acknowledge the need for some pause for self-reflection on the part of potential intermediaries before deciding what information to seek about an ongoing conflict. For example, any intermediary whose own background involves experience as a member of an ethnic or racial minority—or, conversely, as a member of a culturally and economically dominant group—needs to ask what effects this background might have on the way he or she envisages any situation that could be defined primarily as a struggle for ethnic identity or independence rather than as a problem of political decentralization or a search for nonviolent stability. An intermediary whose ideas have been influenced by Marxist theories might differ in intellectual understanding and practical approach from one brought up to believe in the beneficial outcomes of global free market capitalism. How one views the viability and inevitability of the unified territorial state as a form of political organization must surely affect the way in which an intermediary prepares intellectually to intervene in a conflict over the survival or disintegration of one such state.

The second aspect of the self that intermediaries need to reflect on is the nature of themselves and their parent organization and how this might affect the way in which they will be viewed and, hence, received by the parties involved in the conflict. White middle-class males from North America or Europe are likely to be viewed very differently from their own self-image when they offer their services as "disinterested intermediaries" in conflicts involving Latino elites and indigenous campesinos in a Latin American country. However, intermediaries who have constructed their own self-image as benevolent and nonexploitative facilitators, helping local parties to overcome their problems, often forget this.

Intermediaries should ask themselves simply where they come from, in the broadest possible sense, and how this background is likely to be viewed by those involved in the conflict, before considering what might need to be done to establish credibility in the field. At a practical level, ask yourself: Where do I come from, and what do I bring that will influence how people will view me? How might that affect my credibility?

Guideline 2: Learn Just Enough

What needs to be known about the conflict in question before venturing into that field? Every conflict resolution manual starts with this analytical query and follows with a long list of suggested questions that need to be answered in order to understand the problem and its history. My own answer to the main question is to propose that, initially at least, intermediaries should learn just enough. By this, I mean that the whole intermediary enterprise should be regarded as a continuous learning process. Revising one's picture of what is going on and what has gone on before is never finished. The main source of information should be those people—decision makers, elites, grassroots constituents—who are involved in the conflict and who see and interpret it through particular lenses that may seem distorting but always determine parties' actions and beliefs.

"Just enough" therefore implies that an intermediary's preliminary analysis should be sufficient to enable intelligent questions—often of the "Why?" variety—to be asked, so that basic information is continually amplified, gaps filled in, contradictions and discrepancies noted. It also implies that intermediaries should not set out initially to become experts on the conflict they are attempting to help to resolve, but to know enough about the main outline of events and turning points to ask probing questions. An innocent—but not an ignorant—eye will produce queries that help to reveal the adversaries' histories of the conflict, which will usually be structured in a narrative rather than analytical form, and the latters' theories about why it occurred, which will usually be couched in terms of fault and blame.

I use the plural form *histories* here because it is usually the case that an agreed history of the conflict is unlikely to exist. Rather, various adversaries will have their own versions of what happened and why. These sometimes coincide or overlap, but often they do not. As a process of resolution continues, intermediaries will find that one of the great difficulties for a third party is to have adversaries recognize that there exist legitimately different, and sometimes opposed, versions of what happened, and that although they may agree about the validity of particular facts or events, their evaluations and interpretations may differ. One key task for intermediaries is to have parties in conflict agree that this is an inevitable and acceptable feature of protracted conflicts that can be dealt with by acknowledging that such conflicts always give rise to varied perceptions and interpretations, especially of motivations underlying actions.

Guideline 3: Ask Key Questions

Learning about the various histories of a particular conflict is frequently a secondary matter to discovering whether those involved agree that a conflict does in fact exist. It is hardly unknown for one party in what to outsiders certainly looks like a conflict to deny completely that there is one that needs to be addressed in some fashion.

Often a first analytical task for any potential intermediary is to check to see whether all parties agree that they face a conflict, or whether one side feels that the situation is best characterized as something else—for example, a matter of maintaining law and order or simply the result of a few malcontents who are interfering with an otherwise satisfactory relationship. There is often a tendency for elites or those benefiting from a status quo—what Norwegian peace researcher Johan Galtung characterizes as "top dogs"—to deny that they are actually involved in a conflict that needs to be resolved. There are still those in the Unionist community in Northern Ireland who persist in the view that the situation is merely one of a minority of the minority disobeying the law: hence, the solution is for that law to be effectively and properly enforced. Any preliminary analysis would seem to involve at least finding the answer to one fundamental question, as the answer helps to determine basic third-party strategy from then on:

- Do those involved agree that they are engaged in a conflict that needs to be confronted and a solution found?

If this question is answered in the affirmative, then a number of other basic questions follow. The simplest preliminary list helpful at this initial stage of any intervention involves nine basic queries, often summarized by the mnemonic SPITCEROW:

- What do the parties see as the *sources* of this conflict?

- Who are the core *parties* to this conflict?

- What are the main *issues* in this conflict, according to those parties? What are the underlying issues?

- What have been the major forms of behavior or *tactics* that the adversaries have so far employed against each other?

- What have been the important *changes* (turning points or thresholds) in this conflict?

- What have been the major ways in which the conflict has *enlarged* over time (new parties, for example, or new issues)?

- What other third parties have already played *roles* in efforts to end this conflict and with what effects? What other roles have third parties (such allies, patrons, and relevant audiences) played?

- What range of possible *outcomes* from the conflict has been envisaged so far by those involved in the conflict?

- How do the adversaries envisage *winning* the conflict, and has this changed markedly since the conflict began?

Many of these are fairly obvious, basic questions to ask about any conflict at the start of an effort to help in its resolution and need no comment. Others need some further explanation. The query about other third parties, for example, has become increasingly important over the past decade as the number of potential intervenors has increased geometrically and the practice of conflict resolution has become more widely accepted. Anyone contemplating becoming involved in almost any protracted conflict throughout the world needs to get used to the idea that somebody will almost certainly have been there beforehand. Moreover, they may, or may not, have had a beneficial impact on the conflict and may, or may not, have left a positive view of conflict resolution (particularly by so-called outsider neutrals) in the minds of the local parties. More thought and analysis need to be directed toward what Susan Allen Nan (1999), director of the Alliance for Conflict Transformation in Virginia, has called the complementarity of resolution initiatives, with the aim of making sure that intermediary processes help and reinforce rather than undermine or interfere with one another. Hence, a key initial issue for any potential intermediary is whether there are others currently working on the problem with whom a new initiative might interfere. If it turns out that there are, then this information should add to any proposed initiative the further, and major, task of coordination.

Some of the basic questions lead to other subquestions that can be researched in the initial stages or left until contacts have been made with the adversaries and a deeper exploration of the conflict begun. The list of preliminary questions can be endless, and intermediaries need to decide for themselves which and how many need to be answered, at least tentatively, before embarking on the next stage of the process. Which queries are deemed important, and thus crucial to any initial analysis, will depend on an intermediary's theories about what causes a conflict and what keeps it going. Some plausible assumptions focus on the influence of intraparty divisions within adversaries, the stability of leaderships, and the possibility that key stakeholders in the conflict are not immediately apparent to a cursory survey. Hence, apart from trying to discover basic information about the parties to a conflict and key decision makers at various levels within each of those parties, there are long-term benefits from discovering answers to a range of less obvious questions, such as those concerning the internal structure of the adversaries:

- Are the parties structured hierarchically or collectively, and how internally cohesive are they?

- How vulnerable are the various leaderships to internal criticism, dissension, or revolt, and to what degree does their stand on the conflict legitimize or delegitimize their role?

Similarly, there are questions that need to be answered about likely obstacles in the way of a settlement, including these:

- How are the costs of the conflict distributed within the adversaries, and who might benefit from its continuation? This is the spoiler problem.

- What might be done to alter the goals or cost-benefit schedules of factions that might benefit from continuation?

A more familiar approach is to try to obtain an accurate picture of what those involved think the conflict is about, but even here it is desirable to pose something more than the standard queries about issues in conflict or parties' bargaining positions:

- Is this a conflict in which the continued prosperity or even existence of one or the other party depends on the conflict's continuation?

- Are there important stakeholders in the conflict whose interests and needs are not obviously represented by the currently salient parties?

Finally, some questions obviously arise about the dynamics of the conflict and the relationships of the parties, both before they became adversaries and also what these might be in the future:

- What resources are the adversaries expending on the conflict, and in what ways are these equivalent?

- What, if any, was the preconflict relationship of the adversaries, and is a solution of physical separation feasible in this conflict?

Ultimately, of course, the answers to these questions will depend on when they are asked and by whom, but as a safety net, a final query might serve to remind analysts and intermediaries of the importance of the histories of the conflict for both understanding it and affecting it in some way:

- Have the answers to any of the above questions changed markedly over time?

Conclusion

It would take a major effort at investigation to obtain satisfactorily accurate information on all of the topics posed in this chapter in the initial stages of any third-party initiative. As a very preliminary step, then, some more basic data should be sought, but it also seems important that intermediaries should continue to try to obtain a more accurate and inevitably more complex picture of the conflict. I always suggest that while the intermediary process continues, a tracking map of the conflict be kept and continually revised and updated as new information becomes available.

6

How Do I Get Good Information
in a Short Time?

Heidi Burgess and Guy Burgess

We live in the information age. The ability to find and disseminate infor-
mation is available in unprecedented ways and quantities. This is a
tremendous resource for peacebuilding, in terms of what is available about
a setting and the connections possible to people and networks developing
initiatives in those settings. But as many of us know, information over-
load, knowing what is most useful, and ensuring the quality of and verac-
ity of the sources become significant challenges.

Guy Burgess and Heidi Burgess codirect the Conflict Research Con-
sortium at the University of Colorado, where they have been developing
on-line conflict resource programs since the earliest days of the Internet
and currently direct CRInfo, the consortium Web site. Both have been
trained, worked, and teach in the fields of conflict transformation and
peacebuilding. Their book Encyclopedia of Conflict Resolution *(1997)*
has brought together many of the basic concepts, schools of thought, and
practice for the field. Their recent efforts to create a coordinated set of
linkages for the electronic connections of networks, organizations, and
peace- and conflict-related information Web resources represent a com-
mendable application of the values of cooperation to the newly emerging
Internet community.

To get good information, Burgess and Burgess suggest, will require a
little homework on your part to define carefully what you need; once you
have done this preliminary investigation, you can find tremendous
resources to help you assess key questions in making your decision. Take

to heart their warning that information availability does not automatically translate into quality and that you must have an ability to recognize that perception and information are linked to the heart of the conflicts. When you acquire some tools and persevere in your search, the world can be at your fingertips in a meaningful and useful way. Check out the electronic links they provide in this chapter and the links in the References at the end of this book.

•   •   •   •   •   •

I magine that you are a reasonably accomplished labor-management facilitator and public policy consensus builder on issues of cultural diversity, working out of a base in a town that lies at the junction of Anglo, Hispanic, African American, and Native American cultures. Let's say you live in our home state of Colorado. You are also something of a world traveler. You've just heard from two friends, companions on several of your international journeys, who called to report on their recent research trip to the Guatana Highlands, a small and relatively lush mountain range on the border between Bacomba and Muru. Although the highlands are currently located in Muru, the border is in dispute with Bacomba, which also claims the region. On arrival, your friends found their research overwhelmed by an ongoing crisis that was rapidly sliding toward widespread and, quite possibly, violent civil strife.

They report that in their conversations with local friends and colleagues, the message was unmistakably clear: the Guatana Highlands are in desperate need of help. Since your friends knew that you had enjoyed your vacation in the Guatana Mountains and had been thinking about extending your practice to other countries, they decided to give you a call.

According to your friends, the situation seems to represent a catastrophic deterioration in the long-running conflict between the region's two principal ethnic groups: the richer and more powerful Tokata, with stronger ties to historical colonial powers, and the more populous Kanta, who are indigenous to Muru. Neighboring Bacomba is much more predominantly Tokata. The immediate focus of the crisis is a strike called by the Guatana Coffee Workers Union (GCWU) to protest layoffs and pay cuts by the Coffee Producers Organization (CPO), which has controlled the area's principal export since colonial days.

CPO feels that it simply has no choice. The worldwide collapse in the market for coffee has left it teetering on the edge of bankruptcy. If it can't maintain its competitive position, there won't be any jobs. CPO management views the strike as a plot to ruin them financially and force them to leave the country. They are in the process of hiring replacement workers and security personnel to protect their facilities from sabotage.

The GCWU and strikers view believe that CPO is attempting to break their union and deny them their legitimate share of the company's profits. More important, they see the situation as a chance to mount a meaningful challenge to more than a century of social and economic domination. It is this broader issue that has brought in support from the Kanta Freedom party.

Your friends have given you the names of several people who are working with an informal coalition of community leaders looking for ways to address the issue fairly without sliding into a large-scale violent confrontation. You need to decide what to say. But first, you need to develop a much better image of exactly what's going on. How can you do this using Web resources?

Things You Need to Know

The first key to successful background research on the Web is asking the right questions because if you don't have a clear sense of the questions that you need to ask, it is unlikely that you'll find the answers you need. Here is a checklist of things to find out before becoming involved in a conflict situation:

- The basic social setting in which the conflict is occurring: the geography, religion, history, culture, demographics, and economy

- The contending parties, their formal representatives and spokespersons, and coalition partners

- The nature of the long-term underlying conflicts that divide the parties

- The focus of the immediate dispute (for example, a strike, election, or public protest)

- The contending parties and their image of the situation and how the various parties' images of the situation vary

- The recent history of the conflict, whether similar problems have occurred in the past, how they were handled and what ultimately happened, and whether the same people or groups are involved this time

- To what degree the conflict has escalated, whether violence has occurred, and if so, how much and what kind

- What future events are anticipated and whether the conflict seems to be intensifying or diminishing in intensity

- The geographical lay of the land and where to find good maps of the area's transportation system, economic infrastructure, and natural environment

- What conflict-handling and violence-limiting institutions are present (for example, legal and political systems, the police, the military, or the church) and what they have done or are doing to address the situation

- What other conflict management efforts are ongoing or planned, who is involved, and how the people involved can be contacted

- How similar problems in other areas have been handled, what worked and what didn't, and what lessons can be applied to this situation

- Whether there are people or organizations involved in similar efforts elsewhere who could make a contribution here

- The general information on strategies for dealing with such conflicts that is available

- Where to find information about travel arrangements, fundraising options, translation services, and local communications services, including Internet access

Sources of Information

Traditionally, all of this information would be found by direct communication with the parties. A potential intermediary would need to travel to the region and talk with many people on all sides of the issue to learn exactly what was going on. Although such face-to-face communication is still invaluable and will have to occur before any intervention can possibly be started, it is now possible to get a jump on obtaining some answers by doing research on the Internet and, to a lesser extent, in a good research library. Although such research will not be as firsthand as that which can be obtained by going to the site in person, it provides a way to gather a great deal of valuable information very quickly, which enables potential intervenors to assess whether their intervention is likely to be accepted and helpful. It also enables third parties to learn enough background information about the conflict that they will be able to ask intelligent questions once they get there.

Armed with the above list of needed information, your next step is to decide what information resources you want to search. Table 6.1 offers a useful guide to available resources, along with information about searching options and the advantages and disadvantages of each resource.

Two basic types of search tools are provided in Table 6.1. First, there are the general-purpose search engines (like Yahoo.com and Google.com) and library cataloguing systems, which are usually available on-line. There are also specialized search engines and Web supersites focused specifically on the conflict resolution and peacemaking fields (like crinfo.org and www.incore.ulst.ac.uk, oneworld.org, and usip.org).[1]

The general-purpose tools such as Yahoo and Google catalogue millions of Web pages, print publications, and other resources. They offer services that in a sense attempt to index the whole of human knowledge. By trying to be all things to all people, the services are forced to do a fairly superficial job of cataloguing relatively low-profile and specialized fields like peacemaking and conflict resolution. As a result, there are many resources that they are likely to miss, and their cataloguing systems are unlikely to capture the many nuances of the field. They are also capable of delivering information overload on a grand scale. Still, these systems provide access to newspapers, books, journals, magazines, newsletters, Web pages, and directories of people and organizations that might not be found elsewhere—at least not nearly as quickly.

Specialized Search Engines

Also available are specialized search engines and Web supersites focused specifically on the conflict resolution and peacemaking fields. Of these, CRInfo is likely to be especially useful since it systematically seeks to include in its databases resources from other specialized and general sources. CRInfo provides the same kinds of tools as

Table 6.1. Resources for Background Information.

Resource	Advantages	Disadvantages	Searching
In-print books	Easily available within a few days or weeks Provides more in-depth information Generally higher quality (more effort goes into writing books than newsletters, monographs, or news stories)	Moderately expensive Popular books can be hard to get quickly through libraries Specialized books are often unavailable Because of publication lags, the material is usually somewhat dated Often limited to commercially profitable information Usually offers only a single perspective	Easily searchable through on-line bookstores like amazon.com, conflict supersites like crinfo.org, library catalogues (many of which are available on-line)
Web sites (often with reports, monographs, newsletters, and other informative material)	Extensive information now being posted by all sides of most prominent conflicts Generally free and instant access Often very up-to-date Many official governmental and nongovernmental reports available	Highly variable quality because of the "vanity publishing effect" Quality information with significant income potential is often published in book form and may not be available Quality sites sometimes charge for information	Easily searchable through conflict supersites like crinfo.org, Web search engines like google.com, search engines like metacrawler.com and researchville.com

Continued on next page

Table 6.1. Resources for Background Information, *continued.*

Resource	Advantages	Disadvantages	Searching
On-line newspapers	Extensive worldwide coverage available daily Generally free and instant access News stories from many different social and cultural backgrounds available Newspapers offering alternative perspectives also available	Reporters have limited time to research stories Coverage confined to events considered newsworthy Tends to emphasize coverage of confrontations over concilia-tion efforts	Links to on-line newspapers available from sites like yahoo.com Many conflict-related stories available from crinfo.org
On-line newspaper archives	Quick and comprehensive way to research recent history News stories from many different social and cultural perspectives available	Has the same disadvantages as current newspapers Coverage limited to the past ten to twenty years depending on source Significant charges for archived articles Not available from all newspapers	Searching easily available from newspaper Web sites listed by sites like yahoo.com
Academic journals, popular periodicals	Generally available through research libraries Journals tend to have in-depth analyses Popular periodicals may also have useful information	Single copies of journals hard to get Older articles may be available at research library or through on-line services like jstor.com Journal articles may be of more academic than practical interest	Academic journals searchable through research library services like jstor.org Popular periodicals available through services like findarticles.com

Out-of-print books, old journals and newspapers	Available only through research library collections, interlibrary loan, and used-book bookstore networks (which are increasingly computerized)	Information likely to be too dated to be useful (useful historical information is usually picked up by more recent publications)	Searchable through library catalogue systems (many of which are Web accessible)
Networking	Web searches are a great way to identify and make initial e-mail contacts with others working on related conflict problems, as well as people and organizations in the area	Still requires personal contact if at all possible	Start with Web search and use contact information to start process; supplement with direct personal contacts and networking

the big general-purpose systems; the difference from the others is that it focuses exclusively on conflict in peace-related books, articles, newsletters, reports, Web sites, and organizational and individual information. By working with a much smaller body of information, it does have limits. For more general information, as well as detailed information on highly specific conflict situations, it is better to consult the more general search systems.

Search Tips

Given the relative advantages and disadvantages of the various tools, you will probably want to use them all.[2] For example, you might try to find a couple of books on the general social and cultural history of the Guatana Highlands. You would also certainly want to review recent news stories from the conflict from numerous perspectives, while also monitoring news stories as they appear. You can start by typing in a few key words into a text box on each Web site's search form. For example, you might start by searching for information on Guatana, Bacomba, Muru, Tokata, Danta, CPO (the Coffee Producers Organization), Kanta Freedom party, and GCWU (Guatana Coffee Workers Union). This is likely to result in fairly lengthy lists of possible resources.

You will probably be initially overwhelmed with large numbers of hits that are completely unrelated to the Guatana crisis. For example, you might find a great deal of information about a new car called the Tokata. The simplest way to get around the problem is to find entries that are clearly on topic and then click on the "similar pages" link. (You can scan the resulting lists repeating the process again and again.) You can also look for buzzwords or formal key words that describe your topic more accurately and uniquely. For example, you might find that virtually every article on the conflict makes some reference to either the late Mimmi Fukato, who won a Nobel Peace Prize for her earlier efforts to resolve conflicts in the area, or the Guatana Partition Agreement, which established the region's borders.

Thus, one key to making any search system work is an understanding of the vocabulary that people use to describe the information that you're looking for. You should expect to find significant numbers of people who use words in different ways than you do. Thus, the first step is to figure out how to translate your vocabulary into the vocabulary that others use. You might also find that *Muru* is an uncommon English spelling. An alternative and quite widely used spelling is *Murhu*. Opposing parties are likely to refer to key aspects of the conflict using entirely different words. For example, the Tokata often refer to the Guatana region as the Medroh. Failure to pay attention to these vocabulary differences can leave you with just one side of the story.

In many cases, it will also be worthwhile to use the advanced or power search features that most quality search systems make available. Here, you can use boolean logic to search (Guatana OR Medroh OR Muru OR Murhu OR Bacomba) AND (conflict OR dispute OR strike). You may also be able to browse or search by key words. With Yahoo, you could, for example, select *regional*, then *countries*, then *Muru* (or *Murhu* or *Bacomba*), then *society and culture*. In CRInfo, you can do the same thing with a set of resources specific to conflict resolution. You can search for the same keywords using Robot Search (which searches the full text of all catalogued Web sites) or you can use the Power Catalog Search, which is a more focused search system that tends to yield fewer but better-quality results.

As you find quality resources, you can save the Web links to those resources on your Internet "bookmarks" or "favorites" lists. You can also save or print useful resources while ordering publications from on-line or neighborhood bookstores. Remember that the Internet is accessible worldwide. Although there is considerable variation in Internet access, there are often viable options for connecting to the Internet even in remote regions of the world.[3]

Overall Strategy

Probably the best place to start your background investigation would be with a search for encyclopedia-type information on Guatana, Bacomba, Murhu, Tokata, and Kanta. Although you can get this information from traditional print sources, on-line searching is likely to be faster, easier, and better. In addition to providing general background information on the conflict, this exercise will also identify a large fraction of the more detailed key words that you might wish to search. For example, you can expect to find the names of key cities, political leaders, and notable geographical features that are used to describe the conflict (like river names).

Next, you might try something like the national and regional section of Yahoo. This section provides an astonishing amount of information on any part of the world, including, for example, lists of on-line newspapers, cultural information, links to government agencies, local e-mail directories, travel information, and information about communications and Internet access. You can next look at on-line newspapers from Guatana, Bacomba, and Murhu, as well as from other Tokata and Kanta countries. You might want to start with newspapers published in your native language and then move on to foreign-language newspapers to fill in obvious information gaps. The key is to find news sources that are looking at the conflict from all perspectives.

You might then do a systematic search for organizations involved in human rights and peacemaking efforts in the area. Although this is unlikely to yield a complete list of such organizations, it is likely to identify a number of well-connected organizations, such as the Kanta Rights Fund or the Guatana Reconciliation Project, which can provide you with the information that you need to start exploring the network of people working on the problem. E-mail, telephone calls, and faxes to contacts in these organizations can yield information about the activities of each organization, along with suggestions for others who should be part of your contact tree.

You can also use the Internet's free translation services (such as http://babelfish.altavista.com/) to find foreign-language versions of your key search terms. You can then use the same services to perform initial translations of any pages that you might find. Although these automatic computer-generated translations leave much to be desired, they should still be good enough (when combined with accompanying graphics) to let you make an initial determination about whether a particular page is likely to be useful. For example, a foreign-language search might yield a number of pages on Guatana. Your initial automatic translation might quickly reveal that many of the pages involved the adventure resort business in the Guatana mountains about which you had already know a great deal. Still other pages might pertain to a recently discovered dinosaur fossil. In the midst of these obviously inappropriate pages, however, you are likely to find references to genuinely useful material, such as a previously unknown ethnic reconciliation project. You might then decide to contact a local translator or one of the Web's many human-based translation services to translate the pages. The nuances involved in conflict-related materials are subtle enough to make reliance on poor-quality translations dangerous.

Evaluating Results

The key to a search is patience. You have to be willing to deal with a fair amount of information overload. There is no good mechanism for automatically sorting through available information and providing you with a succinct summary of only the truly valuable and reliable information. It is also important to be able to read between the lines. A great deal of valuable information is buried in materials that are being made available for reasons not directly related to the conflict. For example, information on economic news, tourism, and area cultures is likely to yield valuable insights.

It is also important to consider the quality of the information. Because posting information to the Web is so inexpensive, it is common to find poor-quality, unreliable information that may appear, on the surface, to be perfectly reasonable. To guard against this, gather and cross-check information from multiple sources. It is also prudent to consider the motives of those who publish information. If there are conflicts of interest, consider these conflicts in evaluating the information.

It is also important to stay focused on your conflict mapping questions. There is so much information available that is easy to spend endless hours uncovering an impressive array of information that may be fascinating but probably will not give you the information that you really need.

Conclusion

Using the tools described in this chapter, you should be able to develop fairly quickly an image of the peacemaking opportunities that exist and the contributions that you might be able to make. You should also be able to find the information that you need to start integrating your activities into the larger network of people working on the problem.

In the days before the Internet, it was common to settle for inadequate information at this initial exploratory stage. There wasn't much of an alternative short of spending an enormous amount of time and money doing research. Today, with the Internet, you can get an amazing amount of information very quickly and at very low (or even no) cost. Although information alone cannot solve conflicts, it certainly gives intervenors a valuable first step.

Notes

1. In this chapter, Web links are presented in a shortened format. For example, to reach a link presented as "crinfo.org" you should add "http://www." and type into your browser's (Internet Explorer or Netscape) address window, "http://www.crinfo.org". For Web sites that do not follow this pattern, we have included the entire URL (Web address).

2. The examples listed here are based on the chapter's fictional Guatana Highlands case and will not yield real results from real search engines. You can apply the same basic principles to any actual case that interests you.

3. Information about global access issues is also available at www.crinfo.org/going_on.

7

· ·

What Do I Need to Know
About Culture?
A Researcher Says . . .

Kevin Avruch

Culture is about the very processes by which meaning is constructed and negotiated. You will constantly be interacting with the subtle and not-so-subtle meanings and values attached to the content and history of the conflict, social interactive patterns of people, and responses to and interaction with your very methodologies in all the work you do. At a minimum, this requires that peacebuilders make explicit and more intentional their own cultural values and biases and develop a capacity to see those in other settings as they relate to the constructive transformation of conflict.

We approached Kevin Avruch, a professor of anthropology at George Mason University, to compile important lessons about conflict, peacebuilding, and culture that can be garnered from the academic and research literature. Kevin has authored numerous books on this subject in the field; his most recent is Culture and Conflict Resolution *(1998), which outlines some of these ideas in more detail.*

Kevin suggests that although it is impossible to master all there is to know about a culture, it is extremely important to pay attention to at least two critical elements. First, reflect on your own biases and cultural bases, particularly as they relate to your professional work and the approaches you use. Second, become inquisitive about the ways people make sense of things. He has added some useful thoughts and advice about stereotyping and culture.

· · · · · · · ·

The Azande are an African people living today in the Southern Sudan, Congo-Zaire, and the Central African Republic. It was mostly the Sudanese Azande whom the British anthropologist E. E. Evans-Pritchard lived among in the mid-1920s. Near the beginning of his exhaustive study on Azande natural philosophy and beliefs, Evans-Pritchard tells a story about a collapsing granary:

> In Zandeland sometimes an old granary collapses. There is nothing remarkable in this. Every Zande knows that termites eat the supports in course of time and that even the hardest woods decay after years of service. Now a granary is the summerhouse of a Zande homestead and people sit beneath it in the heat of the day and chat or play the African hole-game or work at some craft. Consequently it may happen that there are people sitting beneath the granary when it collapses and they are injured. . . . Now why should those particular people have been sitting under this particular granary at the particular moment when it collapsed? . . . . We say the granary collapsed because its supports were eaten away by termites; that is the cause that explains the collapse of the granary. We also say that people were sitting under it at the time because it was the heat of the day and they thought it would be a comfortable place to talk and work. This is the cause of people being under the granary at the time it collapsed. To our minds the only relationship between these two independently caused facts is their coincidence in time and space. We have no explanation of why the two chains of causation intersected at a certain time in a certain place, for there is no interdependence between them.[1]

Evans-Pritchard goes on to say that "Zande philosophy can supply the missing link." The Zande know that termites ate away at the supports, and the people were sitting under the granary to escape the hot sun. But why did it collapse at that particular moment on top of those particular people? "It was," Evans-Pritchard writes, supplying now the Zande explanation, "due to the action of witchcraft. If there had been no witchcraft people would have been sitting under the granary and it would not have fallen on them, or it would have collapsed but the people would not have been sheltering under it at the time." For the Azande, "Witchcraft explains the coincidence of these two happenings."[2]

Much of the remainder of Evans-Pritchard's large book is an attempt to make Zande belief in witchcraft—as well as its etiology, diagnoses, and treatments—seem not at all superstitious, in the manner of a dismissive and ethnocentric Westerner, but on the contrary entirely rational and logical given the first or underlying premises of their overall cosmology, as well as their notions of the nature of social power, misfortune, and liability. It is an example of what we might today call alternative rationalities or theories of causation. The collapsing granary also serves to introduce a problem faced by many who venture into cultural worlds not their own: the problem of confronting other beliefs and other minds and asking, "Is *this* the way they think?"

The Zande case is striking because of the dramatic and exotic nature of witchcraft in Western eyes. But usually differences in the way people in other cultures think do not present themselves in such an emphatic way. When they are subtle, they can easily be missed unless one attends to the whole notion of difference carefully. For example, when two middle-class Americans meet socially for the first time, a likely first question is, "What do you do?" When two Moroccans meet, a much more likely question is, "Where are you from?" A first inference from this difference might be that for Americans, one's profession, occupation, or job is an important social marker, perhaps even a key constituent of adult social identity. By contrast, in Morocco, one's place of origin, one's roots (*asel*), is an important social and identity marker.

Notice the order of events here. First, we note a difference. Then we make an inference or two about the nature of the difference. What we haven't done is the third part: to think about the significance or consequence of this difference. Does it in fact matter? And if it matters, when and how does it matter?

Not everyone thinks about the world in the same way, and how people think about the world affects how they carry on social conflicts and how they seek to resolve or transform them as well. A relevant sociological maxim here is that what is perceived to be real is real in its consequences.

Culture and Conflict

For more than a century, social scientists and others have sought to characterize the observable differences among peoples of the world—differences in beliefs, customs, norms, and values—by recourse to the term *culture*. What has research on culture taught us that may be of use to peacebuilders?

A prerequisite for conflict transformation work is understanding how conflict is processed in different societies:

- Culture frames the contexts in which conflict occurs, by indicating, among other things, what sorts of resources are subjects for competition or objects of dispute, often by postulating their high value or relative scarcity: honor here, purity there, capital and profit somewhere else.

- Culture stipulates rules, sometimes precise but usually less so, for how conflicts should be pursued, including how to begin and when and how to end them.

- Culture provides individuals with cognitive, symbolic, and affective frameworks for interpreting the behavior and motives of others and themselves.

- Culture links individual and collective identities, providing symbols (some of them deeply invested with affect or emotion) that connect individuals to others "like them" while at the same time separating those individuals from "unlike others." Thus, culture defines social markers for constituting boundaries between collectivities (social groups). This is the way in which culture gets implicated in ethnic, religious, nationalist, or other communal conflicts.

Our first lesson for practitioners is that they learn to appreciate the many roles played by culture in conflict and the potential for management, resolution, or transformation of conflict. Leaving aside purely communication issues for the moment, it is not usually the case that cultural difference is an independent cause of conflict. This argues against the position taken by some, such as Samuel Huntington in his *The Clash of Civilizations,* that such differences inevitably lead to strife between cultures.[3] But although culture is rarely the cause of conflict, it is always the perception-shaping lens through which the causes of conflict (often enough economic disparities and social inequality within a society) are refracted. And it provides for individuals (especially for such activist individuals as ethnic entrepreneurs or nationalist politicians) a reservoir of shared symbols that may be enlisted to constitute contesting social groups.

Given the varied roles that culture plays in conflict, it would seem that any practitioner entering a conflict situation in some other culture with an eye toward transformation or peacebuilding must have a formidable amount of substantive knowledge about the other culture: its key symbols, sacred signs, root metaphors, cognitive schemas, and worldviews, all of these embodied in a potentially "foreign" language and wrapped, often contentiously, around competing versions of narrative history. Does this requirement all but disqualify the novice, and culturally naive, intervention? The answer is, "not necessarily," but it should make you pause and be extremely aware (no matter how confident of one's "process," experience, or virtuosity in one's own native cultural setting) of what you *don't* know.

What Should We Avoid?

It is particularly useful to reflect on the cultural traps and miscues that we should avoid.

Avoid Oversimplification

The first thing is to avoid simplistic notions of culture, to stereotype. For example, it is tempting to think of every society as characterized by a single culture (as in "Mexican society is characterized by Mexican culture") and every person as possessing a single culture—the same one as everyone else in that society ("Juan is Mexican, and all Mexicans believe that . . ."). But this simplification hides the complexity of how societies are organized (by class, region, ethnic, racial, political, or religious group, and so on), as well as how many identities, or cultures, individuals may manifest as members of such different groups (gender, religion, race or ethnicity, occupation or profession, and so on).

Similarly, it is tempting to think of culture as something unchanging or inherently stable, fixed in some formative historical period, as if American culture has not changed since Alexis de Tocqueville's description of it in *Democracy in America,* first published in 1835. But this simplification ignores observable change and instability in the world, and furthermore it suppresses our awareness of an important characteristic of culture as an adaptive mechanism *to* change (and also, as students of conflict know all too well, sometimes as a maladaptive one too). Cultures change as both a response to and a reflection of historical flux.

Finally, it is tempting, especially when looking at so-called traditional cultures, to think that culture exerts a deterministic control over human action, turning people into sorts of robots who act because "such is their custom."

Research into the nature of culture has shown that culture is not as fixed, homogeneous, immutable, deterministic, or uniformly distributed among members of a society as colloquial usage (or nineteenth-century understandings of it) would presume. Each of the simplifications of culture noted above runs the risk of leading the practitioner working with cultural others into the social awkwardness of ethnocentric stereotyping, at least, or more seriously, into process-disabling pathologies of miscommunication.

Avoid Sterotyping

The next lesson for practitioners is to avoid thinking about cultural differences in simple, overarching, and stereotypical ways: to recognize and respect culture's complexity. One way to do this is by a simple word substitution test. Whenever you hear or are tempted to say something on the order of, "Arabs believe that . . ." or, "For centuries, Japanese have thought. . ." or, "When negotiating with Africans . . ." substitute the words *Americans* or *Canadians*. If you then become skeptical of the resulting assertion—for *you* know how many different sorts of Americans and Canadians there are and how diverse and historically contingent their customs, thoughts, beliefs, and so on, are—then you are well on your way to avoiding some of the pitfalls of one-dimensional cultural analysis.

Avoid Thinking of Culture as Prescriptive

It is especially important to avoid making culture into a mechanism for social robotics, something that invariably prescribes or determines individual behavior. For example, one of the things that most surprised Carolyn Nordstrom in her study of peacebuilding and conflict transformation in Mozambique "was the tremendous creativity average people employed in surviving and working to resolve the war."[4] Social scientists refer to this potential for individual creative action as agency. Peacebuilders and conflict transformation practitioners above all must attend to agency, for if they do not, then how could they even begin to imagine working with individual others to create new structures or institutions, in effect new "cultures of peace," out of existing states of war, conflict, or violence?

What Should We Know About Working in Other Cultures?

It bears repeating that by themselves, cultural differences are rarely the sole cause of serious social conflicts. Although such differences may be politicized into public markers of identity or ethnicity and then used to constitute conflictual identity groups, the conflicts themselves are usually over other things: material or symbolic resources, access to centers of power, or sources of self-esteem. But cultural differences may easily exacerbate potential or existing social conflicts, or stand in the way of their transformation and peacebuilding, because they affect the dynamics of communication between cultures. What are some keys to these dynamics?

Linguistic Differences

The most obvious and visible way in which conflicts happen is when cultural differences are crosscut by linguistic ones: when one's interlocutor speaks a different language than you do. In that case, you know you need a third party, an interpreter, to facilitate communication. But purely linguistic translation is only a small part of competent intercultural communication, since culture encompasses far more than purely linguistic domains. To take one example, one can translate the English word *compromise* into Arabic, but the Arabic equivalent carries with it negative connotations of defeat, concession granting, and compromised honor, not usually found in North American usage. To take another example, the whole notion of apology is linked to ideas of status, hierarchy, shame, and deference in many Asian cultures. It covers rather more ground, semantically and socially, than in typical American, Canadian, or British usage. Finally, cultural misunderstandings can occur even when all the parties are native speakers of the same language. Consider the common situation of different perceptions by African Americans and whites of racism in situations or remarks.

Clearly, successful intercultural communication depends on more than a simple one-to-one translation process, for this is not possible. The third party—the interpreter—that you, as a third party, choose to work with must be more than a simple translator. He or she is your cultural broker, your guide. But the more immersed your broker is in the nuances of the culture, the more likely he or she occupies a place or identity within it and thus may be viewed by others as in some way a party to the conflict.

Another important lesson for practitioners is to choose a translator-interpreter carefully, both for this person's overall cultural competence and willingness and ability to act as your guide to local understandings. However, you need to be aware that individuals willing and able to act as cultural brokers often occupy peculiar positions in their own society. And never forget that translations are rarely transparent, for every translation is also an interpretation.

Communicational Styles

Communication lies at the heart of all transformative and peace-building processes. Research on intercultural communication has identified a number of basic cultural orientations that affect communicational styles and become problematic when individuals with different styles interact.

The most common orientation is called *low context* versus *high context*. Low-context communicators favor direct and unadorned speech: the meaning is in the message and, as Americans might say, "What you see [or hear] is what you get." By contrast, high-context communicators favor indirection. Much of the meaning in any statement lies in nonverbal or paralinguistic channels, such as body language or gesture. Full meaning is rarely to be found explicit, in unadorned speech. Meaning is implicit. Information in high-context settings, rather than being simply exchanged, as in low-context ones, is implied or must be inferred.

Communicational problems arise when "low contexters" meet "high contexters." The "lows" may regard the "highs" as duplicitous, untrustworthy, or inscrutable: "Why don't they say what they mean and mean what they say?" Highs often enough regard lows as simply bullying, brutish, and uncouth—more concerned with the bottom line and today's agreement than with nurturing overall solidarity and a long-term relationship.

Individualism and Collectivism

Many researchers believe that these communication styles reflect deeper underlying orientations, particularly between individualist and collectivist cultures. Individualists value independence and are oriented toward achieving outcomes with objective, equitable, interest-based decision making. They tend to be egalitarian and are comfortable with social interactions cast in a competitive mode. They have little concern with face.

By contrast, collectivists value interdependency and are more concerned with the success of the process in sustaining valued social relationships than in achieving efficient outcomes. They are less comfortable with openly competitive display. More oriented toward hierarchy and authority, issues of face—keeping, gaining, and losing it as a result of social encounters—come to the fore. For collectivists, an ideal third-party process (say, mediation) is not necessarily a formal one carried out by objective, procedure-bound outsider-neutrals (the individualist's ideal) but may be a more informal or guided one, carried out by socially situated insider-partials—respected elders, for example, or religious authorities.

Cautions and Conclusion

These distinctions uncovered by research in intercultural communication (there are others too) are useful to keep in mind when working in cultures other your own. And like many other distinctions arranged as binary oppositions (though virtually all the researchers insist they exist on continua), they seem to explain a lot. But I urge caution in using them, first, because they can all too easily devolve into stereotypes for how "Asians [or Africans or Arabs or anyone else, for that matter] behave," and, second, because when applied, they tend to dissolve away the powerful notion of agency, so crucial to social transformation work. Once again, play the substitution game, and think of how many North Americans you know who are collectivist, sensitive to relationships, face, and uncomfortable with open competition. Many of them are likely to be your colleagues in conflict transformation and peacework, in fact.

But if you need to be cautious in using the results of intercultural research in practice, and the requirements of achieving full competency in another culture (starting with linguistic fluency) seem daunting and impractical, what, in the end, do you need to know about other cultures in order to work in them?

In the end, you need to know deep down that you have a culture as well—several of them, in fact, based on religion, gender, class, profession, and so on, and that you bring them all to social encounters and your practice. You cannot achieve fluency in all the world's cultures, but you can aim for a fluent sensitivity to the power of cultural differences. Some have spoken of this openness to, and awareness of, the world as mindfulness.[5] It is an important component of all reflective and ethical practice. In our context, it means not taking for granted the "common sense" of your own cultural moorings and, for practitioners, not taking for granted that processes or techniques that worked in one setting will work as well in all others. It means being open always to the potential for difference, both dramatic (witchcraft caused the granary's collapse) and much less dramatic (Americans and Moroccans look initially for different baseline social information about one another). These differences often make themselves known in moments when comprehension breaks down, moments of cognitive opacity or misunderstanding. Be open to them. Ask about them, make inferences, and test them. Don't just let them pass. Learn from them. You will be a better, and more respectful and effective, practitioner.

Complete substantive knowledge about a culture not your own is very difficult, perhaps impossible, to achieve. Who can master all the nuances of *apology* in Mandarin or *peace and reconciliation* in Arabic and Hebrew? You can, however, be aware of a number of cultural signposts:

- Know that such nuances exist and are consequential.

- Realize that your own understanding of peacebuilding terms, concepts, and theories is probably not sufficient to the tasks at hand.

- Understand that you can't reasonably be expected to possess full substantive knowledge of the other culture; you need a guide or cultural broker.

- Be sensitive to what qualities or attributions this guide brings to the situation.

- Most important, know yourself. In working in other cultures, in the absence of substantive cultural knowledge, the really indispensable thing is self-knowledge.

Notes

1. Evans-Pritchard, E. E. *Witchcraft, Oracles, and Magic Among the Azande.* (Abridged ed.) Oxford: Clarendon Press, 1976. (Originally published 1937). p. 23.

2. Evans-Pritchard. p. 23.

3. Huntington, S. *The Clash of Civilizations and the Remaking of World Order.* New York: Simon & Schuster, 1996.

4. Nordstrom, C. *A Different Kind of War Story.* Philadelphia: University of Pennsylvania Press, 1997. p. 12.

5. Langer, E. *Mindfulness.* Reading, Mass.: Addison-Wesley, 1989.

8

What Do I Need to Know About Culture?

Practitioners Suggest . . .

Peter Woodrow and Christopher Moore

The previous chapter suggested a number of important considerations that are widely shared in the research literature on conflict and culture. How do we make all of this practical? Are there ways that we can increase our capacity to respond to cultural differences, minor and major? Exactly how do we keep awareness of cultural differences of a group yet not fall into inappropriate patterns of stereotyping? And how can we prepare ourselves for moving into a radically different setting from one that we are accustomed to and have worked in with familiarity?

We asked two practitioners, Peter Woodrow and Christopher Moore, well versed from their own wide-ranging experience across many different cultural settings, to address these questions. Both are currently working with CDR Associates in Boulder, Colorado, an international mediation and training organization. Peter has worked for many years as a trainer, facilitator, and mediator in conflict zones, with peacebuilding, relief and development experience. With Mary B. Anderson (see Chapter Twenty), he coauthored the book, Rising from the Ashes: Development Strategies in Times of Disasters *(1998), addressing some of these questions from the standpoint of humanitarian work. Chris, widely recognized in the field of conflict resolution and mediation, has provided training and direct intervention in more than thirty countries. His book,* The Mediation Process *(1996), is considered the seminal introductory work regarding the work of third-party intervention.*

As practitioners, Peter and Chris provide a concrete set of ideas, attitudes, and tools for responding to the questions we posed above. Their stories and anecdotes illustrate the application of the ideas to lifelike scenarios. They also offer a chart that is helpful for thinking through the impact of cultural differences in a particular setting. Fill it out with your experiences and work settings in mind.

· · · · · ·

Entering a new and different culture can be both exciting and daunting. You might ask, What will these people be like? How will they respond to me? Will they assume that I am like everyone else from my country? How will I understand what is going on? Will there be all kinds of hidden or coded information that I miss or misinterpret? Am I just going to get frustrated?

Culture is all around us. The culture we grew up in has a profound influence on how we see the world and the ways we interact with others. Culture is, in fact, so pervasive, that it is hard for us to perceive it. It is comparable to how a fish views the water it swims in. What is culture? One view states that culture is the cumulative result of experience, values, religion, beliefs, attitudes, meanings, knowledge, social organizations, procedures, timing, roles, spatial relations, concepts of the universe and material objects and possessions acquired or created by groups of people, in the course of generations, through individual and group effort and interactions. Culture manifests itself in patterns of language, behavior, and activities, and provides models and norms for acceptable day-to-day interactions and styles of communication. As Samovar and Porter (1999) suggest, culture enables people to live together in a society within a given geographic environment, at a given state of technical development, and at a particular moment in time.

There is no way to predict how any cross-cultural experience will turn out. However, we can share some of the accumulated wisdom from people who have been working in international peacebuilding, development and humanitarian relief, business, student exchange programs, and even diplomacy. Following these guidelines can increase the likelihood that your cross-cultural experiences will be enjoyable and productive.

Coping with Cultural Differences in New Settings

Following are guidelines for working successfully in an unfamiliar environment and culture.

Work on Your Attitude

More than any specific skill, understanding, or knowledge, your success working in another culture will be shaped by your attitude. Cultivate a sense of humility, flexibility, and respect toward people of the culture you will be working in. The more you can cultivate a sense of wonder and excitement about new and different ways of doing things, the better. Many disastrous interactions are characterized by the opposite attitudes: arrogance, inflexibility, disdain, and fear of difference.

> At first, John was having a terrible time working with community groups in Bolivia. He found himself constantly expecting people to act and respond to him just as his friends, family and colleagues back home did. Finally, after he gave up on that expectation and decided to try to look forward to each new experience of people doing things differently, he started to learn more about local cultural patterns and to enjoy himself. The work went better too.

Know Thyself

One of the most useful ways to prepare for a cross-cultural experience is to understand your own cultural background better. This is actually more difficult than it sounds. You may have to work to discover your own culturally based assumptions, habits, attitudes, and areas of comfort and discomfort. Sometimes these become obvious only when you experience them in contrast to another culture.

Later in this chapter, we provide a chart (Exhibit 8.1) showing some of the variables to think about as you try to identify the central tendencies in your culture, as well as your own personal style. It is also useful to find out how people from other cultures view people from your culture. Their stereotypes may contain some useful information, even if some of the information is incorrect. In a spirit of self-examination, consider whether you practice aspects of the stereotypes, such as getting impatient or saying things too bluntly.

Bill, an American, was on his way to Indonesia. He took out a sheet of paper and wrote down all of the things he had heard about Indonesian culture. On another sheet, he wrote down the images he thought Indonesians probably held about Americans. Among other things, he thought that Indonesians would be extremely polite, somewhat formal, and deferential to elders and people in authority. In contrast, he realized that Americans would be considered almost rude, direct, informal, and more egalitarian in their attitudes. In thinking about his own style, he thought that he would probably be on the more polite end of the spectrum of Americans but also informal in his approach. He was definitely from the "question authority" generation as well and would have to be careful about how he interacted with people in authority positions.

Never Assume Anything

Don't assume that you understand what's going on, even if you are familiar with another culture and language. Hold all conclusions and assumptions lightly; be prepared for surprises and abrupt changes. Develop an attitude of informed humility, with the awareness that there is much you do not know.

Janet's parents immigrated from China to the United States in the late 1940s. They spoke Mandarin around the house and brought Janet up according to strict and traditional ways in an urban Chinese community in San Francisco. Now she has an opportunity to do some training work in China and is very excited. But she realizes that there have been fifty years of change since her parents lived in China. Although she speaks Chinese fluently and knows the underlying cultural norms well, she will have to be alert to the norms of the Communist party and the political context, especially when dealing with government officials. She also senses that she will bring a North American overlay to her Chinese background, especially a need to get things done quickly and efficiently and impatience with delays.

Keep All Senses Tuned

Listen and observe constantly. Pay attention to your own instincts, but check out any conclusions. Ask for clarification whenever you can appropriately do so. Find a cultural informant in the best sense: someone with whom you can discuss the layers of meaning in language, actions, or events. (We discuss how to work with a cultural informant later in this chapter.)

Kevin's trip to South Africa came suddenly, so he had little time to prepare. He had met South Africans before and knew some of the history and politics of the country, but he felt he really didn't know much about the country at a deeper level. Fortunately, he was working with a local partner organization. He found that he hit it off immediately with Nkati, a young graduate student of about his age who had studied for two years in Canada. Nkati's experience abroad made him aware of how North American culture differs from South Africa. Especially during the first month of his time in South Africa, Kevin visited with Nkati frequently, asking him what things meant and why people did things a certain way. Nkati was particularly helpful in explaining how white and black South Africans saw situations differently. Although his consultations with Nkati became less frequent over time, Kevin still sought him out when he got confused.

Develop Patience

In many situations, you will need what seems like extreme patience. Observe the pace of how people behave, interact, and make decisions. Check your own need for speed, quick decisions, and forward progress. Note that the most effective route may not be a straight line but could be a meandering or even circular path. Expect delays for political, logistical, cultural, social, or other reasons.

Sarah was doing research on conflict and its resolution in Ethiopian refugee communities in eastern Sudan. She had received permission from a national government ministry and a United Nations agency to travel to the area and had developed local contacts through a non-governmental organization (NGO) providing relief and development services in the refugee community. However, when she got to the area, she was told she had to seek permission from the local military commander before she could enter the refugee settlement. She made her way with her NGO colleague to the commander's office. It looked like a scene from a nineteenth-century colonial novel. Local farmers, businessmen, and petty bureaucrats all waited in a large outer room, while an officious clerk took down names and the reason for seeking an audience with the commander.

Eventually, Sarah and her colleague were admitted to an inner room (well before many others who had been waiting longer, she noted). People were seated on chairs placed against three walls of the room, while the commander sat behind an enormous desk. Sarah was led to the middle of the room and asked her business. She explained the purpose of her visit to the refugee area. The commander immediately dismissed her reasoning and stated flatly, "We don't allow research in these communities; it's a security situation." For a minute, it seemed that Sarah's long trip and careful arrangements would founder on this man's whim. Then her NGO colleague spoke up and assured the commander that this was not research, but practical work designed to help the refugee leaders, NGOs, and government officials to cope better with a complex situation. After further discussion, the commander finally granted the access Sarah sought.

Balance Relationships and Tasks

Find an appropriate balance between the need for getting things done and the need for building strong relationships. Consider erring in the direction of relationship building (unless you are dealing with Northern Europeans).

Evelyn was in Singapore arranging emergency delivery of food and medicines into Cambodia. She was referred to a Mr. Wong, a respected businessman who, it was said, would be able to arrange for the purchase and transport of the needed items. Evelyn called Mr. Wong's office and explained to him what she needed. He listened politely and then invited Evelyn to have dinner with him. Although this seemed a bit odd to her, she agreed. At the appointed hour, Mr. Wong picked her up at her hotel and took her to dinner at an elegant restaurant and ordered items that were not on the menu. They passed a pleasant evening in conversation about Evelyn's family, schooling, and other international assignments and some about Mr. Wong too. The next day, a young man arrived with a driver, apologized that Mr. Wong was busy, but proceeded to show Evelyn many of the sights of Singapore—places Evelyn had never had time to visit. That evening, Evelyn was invited to Mr. Wong's home, where she met Mrs. Wong and was treated to another wonderful meal.

All of this was delightful, but Evelyn was wondering if she would ever get to talk about the urgent need for food and medicine. Every time she brought up the subject, Mr. Wong politely deflected the conversation, saying that those matters were being taken care of. Finally, after three days of wining and dining, Mr. Wong met with Evelyn at his office and showed her the price quotes he had received for the needed materials and the transportation costs. The prices were better than Evelyn could have hoped for. But she also wondered how Mr. Wong's costs and profit would be figured in. When she asked, he assured her that he would be fine and that it was his pleasure to assist such a worthy venture.

Remain Alert to Subcultures and Individual Variations

No culture is monolithic; every country includes subcultures. Also, each individual exhibits a personal style and is affected by personal history, family background, training, education, occupation, religion, and geographical region. Many countries include hundreds of ethnic groups and languages. You can't assume that everyone from a particular country has the same or even a similar culture.

> Bert was visiting a series of local interethnic dialogue projects in India as the staff member of a funding agency in order to evaluate the progress of the projects and assess whether to continue funding. Most of the projects seemed to be going well, but there were difficult questions about the uses of funds, accounting, and reporting in a few of the agencies. For this trip, Bert had hired an Indian consultant to work with him as a colleague and interpreter. Kumar turned out to be highly experienced, intellectually sharp, witty, engaging, and very efficient. Bert was pleased to have such a colleague to help on this difficult and sensitive assignment. Before leaving for the field, they met to review project reports and documents and to discuss the issues and questions regarding each project. Kumar proved to be insightful and also provided a useful perspective on the difficult conditions in which many projects functioned.
>
> When they arrived in the field, Bert was shocked to observe that Kumar treated project staff with what appeared to him to be incredible arrogance. Although Bert did not understand the language, he could see that Kumar was spitting out questions, ordering people around, and generally acting like a British officer during the raj. The local people responded with what felt to Bert like obsequious defer-

ence, almost bowing and scraping, scurrying around to find the demanded documents, bringing tea, and answering questions with fear and trembling. Bert found himself caught between an educated, upper-class urban intellectual and poorly educated, hard-working rural peasants. Bert suspected that there were layers of caste and ethnic differences too.

Understand Stereotypes

Unfortunately, the world abounds with stereotypes about people from various cultures. The difficulty with stereotypes is that they can form the basis for discrimination, bias, unfair treatment, and unwelcome assumptions about how someone will think and act. However, stereotypes sometimes contain useful information about a society and its people regarding a central tendency or normal way of doing business.

For instance, many societies from the global South and Southern Hemisphere frequently joke about their flexible attitudes toward time, in contrast to the tendency of people from the North to want things to start and end on time. There is some truth in the stereotype; people from many countries of the South do arrive a half-hour to an hour after an appointment and consider that within an acceptable norm. But not all people do that, and those who do arrive late do not do so all the time.

Mary worked hard in Ecuador to plan the six-hour public meeting about the proposed major dam project. She and her two local counterpart facilitators worked on the agenda and developed a full schedule of activities. The meeting was scheduled to begin at 9:00 A.M. Mary arrived at 8:00 A.M. to make sure the room was set up correctly. Finding that the tables and chairs were in the wrong configuration, she started moving them around, wondering where her colleagues were. One of them showed up at 8:50 and began to help finish setting up the room, and the other arrived at 9:10 out of breath and exclaiming about the traffic. Participants began to drift in at 9:30. By 10:00, about twenty people had gathered, and the meeting started. People continued to arrive right up until noon.

Prepare for Different Orientations Toward Competition and Conflict

Cultures vary in their tolerance for the expression of discord and conflict. Members of some cultures place a high priority on building and preserving smooth interpersonal relationships, controlling the overt expression of differences, and avoiding escalatory language or behavior. Others accept that differences exist, allow for direct discussion of conflicting views, value the expression of strong emotions, and tolerate adversarial and even aggressive negotiation behavior. Individuals working with parties in conflict as advisers or acting as intermediaries need to develop an awareness of prevailing conflict norms and behaviors that will calm, escalate, or derail dispute resolution efforts.

Juanita was asked to serve as a mediator for several racial and ethnic groups in South Africa that were working to resolve a contentious issue. Due to her own ethnic background, she introduced a process that inhibited the expression of strong emotions, controlled communications, and minimized advocacy of polarized views. For the most part, the South African participants in the meeting ignored her meeting guidelines; they engaged in vociferous debate, occasionally called names, and uttered put-downs. Many of the group seemed to relish the debate.

Juanita was amazed that no one was offended or stormed out of the meeting. In her culture, participants would not have tolerated some of the language and behaviors and would have called off negotiations. Later, a South African explained that the parties involved in the discussions had been dealing with each other vociferously and directly for years, and although they may not like what was said, they had developed tolerance for it. Also, they assumed that hard debate was the best way to understand and reach an agreement on issues that divided them.

Translating Language and Culture

The vignette about Kevin and Nkati illustrates an important point about the difference between language interpretation and cultural interpretation. Language is a powerful carrier of cultural norms and values and will always be an important tool for understanding another culture. However, comprehending language is not sufficient. Most of us can recall experiences in which we understood our own native language or another language perfectly but did not grasp the deeper meanings of communications, gestures, or actions in the situation. We encounter this phenomenon when we interact with another subculture of our own society; for example, consider a white suburbanite visiting an inner-city black neighborhood or a new employee on his or her first day of work at a new job. Even if you speak Spanish or Swahili fluently, at times you will need cultural interpretation when working in Latin America or East Africa.

A cultural interpreter is someone whom you can trust to provide an explanation of the layers of meaning in words and behavior in another culture. Cultural interpretation usually involves a conversation about the situation: an explanation about the immediate context (if the informant was not present), a description of actions taken, recounting of things said, and then a discussion of possible meanings. Clearly, this takes more time and interaction than translating the words.

A cultural interpreter is an important asset, particularly during the first months or years of working in another culture, but an intermittent need may continue indefinitely. Sometimes a language teacher can perform this task—but not necessarily. You may find a new friend or colleague who can provide this assistance. Some good cultural interpreters will have had some exposure to your culture and an ability to see their own culture in perspective. However, there are excellent cultural interpreters who have never left their local area. The most critical attribute is a willingness to discuss events, words, and possible meanings in a mutual exchange.

Factors of Cultural Difference

People from different cultures respond to situations differently in terms of priorities, emphasis, and modes of interaction. Exhibit 8.1 includes some of the key variables. As an exercise in preparation for working in another culture, you can fill out the chart in the exhibit based on what you already know or can find out about the new culture. You may find it more difficult to identify the attributes of your own culture and personal style. Following are brief explanations of the factors:

1. *Emphasis on tasks or on relationships.* Are people in the culture focused on getting business done, performing tasks, and making progress toward goals, or do they place a greater emphasis on building and maintaining personal relationships? All cultures do both to some extent; it's not an either-or question but a matter of degree and emphasis.

2. *Direct dealing or indirect dealing.* Are people likely to come out and say directly what they need, want, or feel? Or will they hint at it or find a way to communicate through another person? Do people talk explicitly about problems or find an indirect way to indicate a concern?

3. *Expressed emotions or reserved.* How acceptable is it in the culture to express strong feelings, raise your voice, or display anger? Or are people generally controlled, quiet, and reserved?

4. *Quick place, value on speed and efficiency and the short term versus slower pace, value on deliberateness and the long term.* Is this a culture that values speed and efficiency, or do things take place over

Cultural Factors	Central Tendency of Your Culture	Your Personal Style	Central Tendency of the Other Culture
1. Emphasis on tasks or on relationships			
2. Direct dealing or indirect dealing			
3. Expressed emotions or reserved			
4. Quick pace, value on speed and efficiency and the short term versus slower pace, value on deliberateness and the long term			
5. Egalitarian versus value on rank, gender, age, other status			
6. Meaning of yes and no straightforward versus coded			
7. Value on community and group harmony and wholeness versus competition and focus on individual needs			
8. Relationships, roles, and rules explicit, even written, versus unspoken, understood in context			
9. Positional bargaining versus collaborative process to meet interests			
10. Emphasis on privacy and confidentiality versus openness, transparency, and community involvement			
11. Intermediaries as powerful, respected, and known versus neutral, powerless, and unrelated			

Exhibit 8.1. Mapping Cultural Factors.

a longer span of time with due consideration and, at times, an almost ceremonial mode of interaction?

5. *Egalitarian versus value on rank, gender, age, or other status.* How do people view issues of rank, privilege, and other forms of status? Is there higher status conferred based on age, gender, profession, class, caste, race, ethnicity, or any other factor? What are the ways that status is recognized and honored? Or is this a fairly egalitarian society? Even within a more egalitarian culture, are there subtle ways of honoring status differences?

6. *Meaning of yes and no straightforward versus coded.* Do people mean yes when they say yes? Or does yes mean, "I will do my best," "it is possible," or "we will have to see"? Does no mean no, or does it mean, "I can't say yes just now, but try again later" or "I like some aspects of what you propose, but we will have to work further on specific pieces"? This factor is often closely related to the direct-indirect dealing factor and the degree of expressiveness.

7. *Value on community and group harmony and wholeness versus competition and focus on individual needs.* Some cultures place high value on maintaining the integrity and harmony of the group or community. Others are more individualistic and competitive, and the definition of group and individual may shift. For instance, a company might emphasize consensus and unity within the company but compete fiercely with other companies in the community. A closely related dimension concerns the cultural view of conflict itself: Is it seen as a normal part of the fabric of life or an aberration to be avoided or suppressed?

8. *Relationships, roles, and rules explicit, even written, versus unspoken, understood in context.* Some cultures define relationships, roles, rules, and meanings clearly and explicitly. Others depend on members inside understanding the implicit codes within the cultural context. The former are called low-context cultures: the meanings are not dependent on the context. The latter are called high-context culture: the coded meanings are strongly dependent on

understanding the context. A low-context culture is likely to have many things written down in rule books, guidelines, policies, contracts, and the like, while a high-context culture will expect people to understand the rules through the acculturation process.

9. *Positional bargaining versus collaborative process to meet interests.* People in some cultures love the process of give and take, hard bargaining, attempts to overpower an opponent, and the thrill of competition. Other cultures are more prone to work out compromises, seek accommodations, identify and attempt to meet the needs of all groups and individuals, and emphasize collaboration.

10. *Emphasis on privacy and confidentiality versus openness, transparency, and community involvement.* Particularly in the context of conflict resolution processes, some cultures stress treating issues as private matters to be discussed behind closed doors with only those directly concerned. Other cultures view all personal matters as enmeshed in the needs of the community and value dealing with such issues openly and even publicly. Such cultures may also engage a much broader group in conflict resolution, including other family or community members.

11. *Intermediaries as powerful, respected, and known versus neutral, powerless, and unrelated.* Most cultures prefer a particular type of intermediary to help seek resolution to a conflict. There is, in fact, a range of types of intermediaries. In some cultures, the intermediary may be a professional, neutral person who is unknown to any conflicting party and may have little or no ability to assert or enforce a decision. In other cultures, the parties may look for an intermediary who is a respected and even powerful member of the community. Such an intermediary might use moral exhortation, political or social pressure, and even economic coercion to obtain a settlement.

These are only some of the factors of cultural difference. Those described represent a good start for understanding how cultural variations can affect the success of cross-cultural interactions.

Culture as an Aspect of Conflict

If you are visiting another culture to work on a conflict situation, it will be important to understand the relationship of culture to the conflict itself. Conflict often erupts where people from different cultures come into contact with each other and compete over scarce resources. Their differing values, histories, relationships, communication styles, and social structures may cause or exacerbate conflict. Of course, many conflicts are rooted in injustice or discrimination based on culture, often associated with race, ethnicity, language, or religion.

Culture may also provide positive resources for conflict resolution through norms, customs, rites, and traditional methods for addressing conflicts. At times, people from sharply different cultures are able to identify cultural values in common that allow them to begin a respectful dialogue.

Preparing for Work in a New Cultural Context

There are many ways to get ready for working in a cultural setting with which you are unfamiliar. Some of the methods we have found most effective follow:

- Read books. History, political analysis, anthropology, sociology, and other fields can provide good background information. Novels from the culture are a wonderful way to learn more about how people think and interact.

- Look at the "cultural hints" sections of travel guides. Some of these are overly broad (and full of stereotypes), but some include useful information. You can sometimes find helpful books written by people who have lived in the culture for an extended time.

- Seek out someone nearby who is from the culture. Most universities have foreign students and professors from many countries, or you may find a businessperson working in your country. They may be willing to talk with you about their country and might give you some useful do's and don'ts to guide your initial interactions.

. . . .

9

What Do I Need to Know About Religion and Conflict?

Marc Gopin

Violent conflicts across our globe increasingly have been seen through the lens of the clash of civilizations. Look closely, and this clearly engages the issues of religious identity, diversity of affiliation, and belief systems. But how do we understand what role religion may have in conflict? Do we give it a primary importance in all we do, or is it better left to the periphery of our analysis and the exploration of peacebuilding? What if the conflict is about religion and religious identity groups are in conflict? How do we proceed? And will our own religious beliefs, or lack of them, have an impact or influence?

It is not easy to address the depth of these questions in a single chapter, but we asked Rabbi Marc Gopin to reflect on his wide-ranging experience with religion, religious conflict, and peacebuilding. He suggests that there are keys to conflict transformation and addressing the religious meaning structures of a setting with a clear sense of its importance but with an equally clear vision that ultimately it must be understood from within the context. Marc is a professor of conflict resolution at the Fletcher School of Diplomacy at Tufts University. He has worked exten-
sively on conflict in the Middle East and recently completed the books Between Eden and Armageddon: The Future of World Religions, Violence, and Peacemaking *(2000)* and Holy War, Holy Peace: How Religion Can Bring Peace to the Middle East *(2002).*

. . . .

There is no such thing as a protracted and intractable conflict that is exclusively religious, and it is quite possible that there is no such thing as a nonreligious conflict. All protracted conflict embraces the inner lives and cultures of all human beings involved. Therefore, it is safe to say that these conflicts are inherently complex and always caused by multiple factors—among them, power distribution, distribution of scarce resources, class issues, inherited meaning systems and worldviews, psychological conditions, the burdens of history, and the state of fulfillment of basic human needs. But the impact of religious perception and behavior is often overlooked as a hidden factor in conflict.

Religion includes one or more of the following: abiding and venerated personal and communal values, intricate hierarchies of religious social control that claim absolute authority and are that authority in many people's eyes, transcendent symbols, myths and rituals, dogmas of faith, and structures of transcendent meaning. All of these may or may not be contained within written or oral sacred texts.

Research Myths, Symbols, and Religious Practice

Considering how broad the conscious and unconscious influence of religion is on inner life and communal existence in most of the world, it would seem that Western legal and political constructs of separation of religion and state, which have undoubtedly had a beneficial impact on human rights, often lead to a secular psychological denial of the power of religion's impact on most conflicts. At the same time, religion is always only one factor among many.

Your first task as a peacemaker is to identify the interaction of all those factors and understand to the best of your knowledge how religion contributes to the conflict. Clearly, there is a vast range of influence; some people are completely influenced by religion, while others deny any influence. Reading and study, extensive

interviews, and relationship building should be the three activities that help you sense whether and how religion contributes to
the conflict.

Research the symbols, myths, and practices that are most prominent in the conflict. Find their roots. Understand the myths and
values that move people the most in each tradition, and know the
linguistic expressions of this, even if you do not know the whole
language. Listen to the religious and cultural music of both sides.
Try to experience the religious services on all sides, taking in especially the symbols, sermons, and homilies. Study texts emerging
from these experiences whenever you have spare time or are traveling. Go over them again and again until you begin to feel them
inside you.

Keys to Conflict Transformation in a Religious Context

It is your job as peacemaker to be in a position to elicit from the
parties an approach to religion that builds peace and justice out of
the sources of the traditions in question. How can you engage in
such an enormous task? How can you succeed where so many others
fail? How can you preserve your soul from degradation in the
process? Here are some suggestions about your personal style of
intervention and behavior:

- Make frequent gestures of dignity, honor, and compassion to all parties to the conflict. Make these gestures
  even to those who do not deserve it, even to those
  who commit terrible crimes. Do it as long as you do
  not in the process place people in greater danger or
  strengthen criminals who can conceivably be detained
  or deterred in some better way.

- Become a model of listening and compassion.

- In the process, become a model of the receptive side of human experience, in which you demonstrate how to make space for others, for their needs, their very presence, their pain, and their story.

- When you choose to act, become a model of calculation of moral priorities, fully sharing the moral dilemmas that you face as you pass between enemies. Your model of compassion, moral concern, and caution and your skills of shuttle diplomacy can become a model for the parties to the conflict. Ultimately, it is they who must embrace these values and styles of interaction.

- As you experiment with solutions, try to surrender to the details of the situation. Even as you remain aware of the general lessons of conflict analysis and resolution, have the courage to follow paths of the unique situation where they take you. The major limitation on your unique path should be your internal moral compass. Know when the actual solutions that you and others are devising are crossing too many boundaries to be justifiable ways of pursuing peace and justice.

Some Keys to Religion and Peacebuilding

Although every situation varies, it is useful to keep in mind a number of keys that help promote peacebuilding when working with religion and conflict.

One of the most important assets that you have in this work is that a large portion of religious humanity today in principle agrees with much of the agenda of human rights and democracy. It has always been the case, furthermore, that constructive or transformational conflict resolution, or peace and justice, have been ideals of many, if not most, religious traditions. But there is also a deep-seated suspicion in many parts of the world of any Western or other developed institutions. It is beyond my task here to explain why, but what is clear is that it is vital for you and the parties to the conflict to be able to frame the ideas and values of human rights and democracy in deeply religious terms. It is vital that this then becomes the basis for how gestures are made, agreements are framed, and even how education is pursued in these cultures. It is important that you help elicit this from the local communities and that you yourself model this in how you frame your gestures and conversations. It is also the case, however, that you can slip into arrogance and presumption if you are not careful. The key is not to co-opt local cultures but to help open the door for a maximum diversity of expression of shared values. Your job is to model this yourself and also facilitate processes that will allow adversaries to engage in looking for and making explicit their shared values.

It is important for the creative processes of aligning shared values to go beyond education, dialogue, and the framing of formal agreements. Ritual and symbol enter into the heart of a culture in ways that nothing else accomplishes. It is part of your task to maximize the possibility that this will occur, both by eliciting it from the parties and sharing knowledge with them about how this has been done in other places. It is certainly the case that some in each culture are more prone to this form of human communication than others. Generally the more intellectual and Westernized a religious person is, the more prone he or she is to fall back on texts and dialogue and also to be somewhat embarrassed by the deep ritual spaces of his or her culture. But in order for peace processes to be maximally inclusive, you should try to stretch the limits of inclusion by seeking out those religious people who want to pursue peace.

Ethics and righteous deeds are the most important building blocks of deep peacemaking, and religious traditions are rich in these areas. But they are often poor at the extension of good deeds to the "unfaithful," the "infidel," the "enemies of God" (who always happen to be my enemies), and the "agents of the devil." The list of those excluded from ethical deeds goes on. Your job is to help each community engage in interpretative processes that allow for an expansion of the scope of ethical concern and commitment. This is no easy task, and it is often best engaged in not in front of one's adversaries. After all, for many people, this is the most embarrassing part of their religious tradition. They are embarrassed both by the co-religionists who emphasize these texts and traditions and the traditions themselves. The direct challenge to the tradition by a co-religionist is delicate but crucial for deeper understanding. Immerse yourself in the details of this challenge, and help elicit what changes you can.

Dialogue is a problematic moment of human engagement for many reasons. In some ways, it has to be, for it is a re-creation of the conflict without the violence. It also can lead to more harm than good from time to time, especially if it is poorly facilitated. Find out how dialogue for the sake of reconciliation has been done in each culture. Find out what religious frames, laws, and guidelines around the use of the word have improved the chances of the word leading to reconciliation, or at the very least good communication. If you are dealing with more than one religious tradition, you will have to find ways to honor these traditions simultaneously or consecutively. The more comfortable and familiar the dialogic process is and the more that it emanates out of a familiar spiritual form of reconciliation, the better the chance is that the hard talk of negotiation will be softened by spiritual and moral values and goals.

Conclusion

Always remember that religious people are as affected by economics, social structure, and the psychology of war as everyone else. There are violent and peaceful things in all religious traditions, and religious people will selectively view and interpret their tradition based on the way they are coping with conflict. They will elicit what is violent if they are so disposed by personal experience, and they will elicit peace, justice, honesty, humility, acknowledgment, apologies, and compassion if they are so disposed by personal experience. Your task is to help elicit the best possible religious responses to conflict and war. That task requires you to be thoughtful, understanding but not naive, well informed, discerning, compassionate to many on all sides, and humble.

You need to be a role model of everything that you may have occasion to teach, and you must be ready to be a student at every moment as well. Armed with these qualities, you may not always bring peace, but you can feel more assured that you are doing no harm, and that is quite an achievement. Furthermore, in many religious cultures, these qualities will elicit respect, which is critical to your task. Finally, your task is not to stop wars or solve every conflict, which no single one of us alone can do. Rather, your task is to conduct yourself in such a way that your actions, your teachings, and your programs may elicit the best religious values from all parties to the conflict.

10

Is It Safe?

Lessons from the Humanitarian Aid Community

Larissa A. Fast

If you are headed toward a zone of conflict, in all likelihood you are headed for a situation that carries inherent dangers. These are, after all, war zones. Even if the violence is sporadic and isolated, the work you are taking up puts you in contact with people and locations that by their very nature require a personal risk—your own and that of others. As one famous traveler once remarked, "This ain't Kansas anymore, Toto!" What should you give consideration to as you think about entering a conflict zone in terms of safety and security? We asked two sets of people for their ideas.

In this chapter, Larissa Fast, who has a Ph.D. in conflict analysis and resolution from George Mason University, is focusing her doctoral studies on the subject of safety in war zones. She reviews what the international aid community suggests in reference to increasing security for their workers and staff. This chapter focuses on approaches and recommendations from the humanitarian aid community for ensuring safety and security in conflict zones. Larissa has interviewed people from all walks of practice and experience in war zones. She is teaching at Conrad Grebel University College and working for Project Ploughshares in Waterloo, Ontario, Canada, and has worked as a consultant and project manager in international settings for the past six years.

In the past, individuals and organizations working abroad assumed that one's status as a foreigner seemed to offer a measure of automatic protection in countries wracked by violence. This is no longer the case, if it ever was. In recent months, oil workers have been kidnapped in Ecuador, tourists have been murdered in the Philippines, and local peace and development workers around the world have been targets of violence, in part because of their visibility as foreigners. Security issues for organizations and corporations are gaining increased attention, due largely to the tragic and highly publicized deaths of humanitarian workers and others around the globe over the past five years. This chapter emerges out of research I have done over the past two and a half years about the safety and security of nongovernmental organizations and their personnel working in areas of conflict and violence. Much of the research about security relates to humanitarian organizations, but it is useful for individuals and organizations doing peacebuilding work as well.

Humanitarian organizations have concentrated on security issues for their international staff but less on security for their national staff and partners. As a result, the emphasis of this chapter is on security for outside intervenors, though the security of national staff is increasingly a focus also.[1] These insiders are often the ones who have to cope with the extended and dangerous risks of continuing to work in the midst of violence. As Chapter Eleven suggests, it is important to consider seriously the effect your presence will have on those with whom you work in conflict zones as partners, colleagues, and friends. This chapter summarizes some of the thinking and research about safety and security among humanitarian aid agencies and presents a framework useful for outsider peacebuilders looking to answer the question, Is it safe?

What does safety mean? How should peacebuilders traveling to other countries ensure their own safety? Before answering these questions, it is important to define our terminology. Researchers usually distinguish between safety and security, where *safety* refers to accidents and illness and *security* denotes acts of violence.[2] Obviously, the measures we take to ensure our safety from accidents and illness differ from those we take to ensure our security from acts of violence. For both, thinking about prevention is essential. In terms of safety, preventing illness may include being careful about what you eat until your system is acclimatized (for example, avoiding unwashed fruits and vegetables), taking malaria pills in malarial areas or making sure your immunizations are up-to-date, and protecting yourself against sexually transmitted diseases. Preventing accidents is somewhat more difficult, even at home, but you can reduce your level of vulnerability. You may want to check with friends and colleagues in country about what methods of transportation they use and avoid unsafe vehicles and drivers.

In terms of security, researchers have developed a framework that is useful in terms of thinking about security. A group of scholars and practitioners developed a training in security management for humanitarian organizations.[3] Koenraad Van Brabant, a member of this group, expanded and refined the training materials into a book that provides practical advice about how to manage security.[4] (RedR, the Registry of Engineers in Disaster Relief, now provides training for humanitarian organizations based on this framework; see www.redr.org.) Numerous organizations have developed their own guidelines or publications about security (examples are the International Committee for the Red Cross and World Vision) or have begun training their staff in security management. The literature about security remains sparse, and systematic study is rare. Luckily, this is changing; humanitarian agencies are increasingly aware of security issues and are at the forefront of developing non-military security strategies.

What Research Has Found

Several recent studies have focused on security issues for humanitarian aid workers. The first study, conducted by the Center for Refugee and Disaster Studies of Johns Hopkins School of Hygiene and Public Health, identified patterns in the deaths of humanitarian aid workers between 1985 and 1998.[5] The authors confirm the perception that deaths among humanitarian aid workers have increased in recent years. Their study highlights a number of important factors:

- Intentional violence accounts for the majority of deaths (68 percent of the 375 deaths in the study).

- U.N. staff, both program workers and peacekeepers, account for almost half of the total deaths in the study sample.

- No association existed between the age of individual and aid worker deaths.

- Approximately one-third of the deaths occurred within the first three months of the individual's assignment in the country.

The authors caution that their findings are incomplete, in part because of missing records or incomplete information, and they propose that although their study included both national and expatriate staff, national staff deaths are likely underreported. Nevertheless, their report emphasizes the importance of minimizing risk through policy changes, more accurate assessment of risk, and better equipment, planning, and coordination.

The second study, conducted by Oxfam Great Britain (Oxfam GB) and the Small Arms Survey, focuses on the effects of small arms on humanitarian and development work. It summarizes the results of a survey of Oxfam GB staff members from around the world about their perceptions of small arms availability.[6] Of particular interest in terms of safety and security, the findings indicate that the widespread availability of small arms increases the perception of risk for aid workers and civilians alike. Muggah reports that 40 percent of the respondents, from a variety of geographical regions, experienced a "'security incident' involving a small arm: a combination of non-fatal injuries, armed intimidation, banditry and kidnapping at gunpoint."[7] Again, this study contains limitations, but is indicative of the increased vulnerability of aid workers (and others) around the world.

A Security Framework for Peacebuilders

This commonly accepted framework about security for organizations working in violent conflict zones is a triangle composed of three different but complementary strategies: acceptance, protection, and deterrence.[8] Acceptance as a strategy attempts to create and encourage support for programs and activities among local populations and leadership, thereby providing security from threat. Protection strategies aim to protect individuals from threat through the use of active and passive protective devices, developing policies and procedures designed to promote security, and through coordinating security responses of a variety of actors in a country. Deterrence strategies aim to pose a counterthreat, primarily through hiring guards, using military force, or leveraging external deterrent support from diplomatic missions. Proponents of this framework advocate analyzing the context in which you work and then tailoring your security plan to emphasize one or more of the strategies based on your contextual analysis.

Of the three, an acceptance strategy is the most relevant and useful for peacebuilders for several reasons. First, protection and deterrence strategies require substantial human and financial resources to develop the policies and to repair and equip staff with expensive and sophisticated communications equipment. Many individual or institutional peacebuilders lack the resources to devote to these other two security strategies.

Second, the greatest asset of a peacebuilder is his or her relationships, the primary ingredient in an acceptance strategy. If you develop a trusting and respectful relationship with a taxi driver, for example, he is likely to warn you of danger. As Jenner and Abdi advise, your friends and colleagues are important sources of information about safety and security.

Third, peacebuilders, although working at all levels, tend to concentrate on the grassroots level, which implies the need for local support for and acceptance of your work. Receiving and accepting an invitation to work with local peacebuilders confers acceptance on you as an intervenor (see the chapters in Part One).

Acceptance embeds security within social relationships.[9] It implies building trust and encouraging support among those you work with for your work as a peacebuilder or aid worker or human rights monitor. The role you play as a peacebuilder has important ramifications for your acceptance strategy. As a mediator or multipartial peacebuilder, you cultivate relationships and acceptance with a variety of conflict actors. Your relationships are broad, in a horizontal (across conflict lines) and a vertical (across and within the various levels of society) sense.[10] Broad-based relationships provide a measure of protection from all sides. In contrast, as an advocate, you are usually perceived to be partial to one side of the conflict, whether you work with only one side or advocate on behalf of an issue. In either case, advocates often enjoy excellent relationships within one side of a conflict. However, your full acceptance by one side is likely to increase your vulnerability to other groups; you will be seen as part of that side and thus vulnerable to the same threats and risks of others on that side. The most important thing to remember with the acceptance strategy is its dependence on perception: the way the various groups in conflict perceive your role and your relationships across or within conflict lines. An acceptance strategy requires transparency in your actions and motives and a close examination of the strengths and weaknesses of your role in terms of its implications for your security.

Using a combination of the three complementary strategies enables you to address some of the weaknesses of your acceptance approach with protection or deterrence techniques. The second strategy, protection, aims to make you less of a target or reduce your vulnerability. Cell phones or satellite phones, unarmed guards at your residence or office compounds, and alarm systems are all examples of protective devices that reduce vulnerability. Communications equipment, including telephone trees in case of emergency, reduces your vulnerability by providing constant communication. However, protective devices are not always practical or economically feasible for peacebuilders. In addition, they may make you more of a target, both because you have something valuable (like a satellite phone) and because using protective devices sends a message that you have something to protect. In Liberia in September 1994, for example, combatants targeted humanitarian agencies for their vehicles.[11]

Protection also includes policies, or do's and don'ts of being in an unfamiliar place. For example, don't travel alone, look as if you know where you are and where you are going (even if this is not the case), and be constantly aware of your surroundings. In some cases, like varying the routes you take to and from work and home, protection policies or guidelines may be put in place after a security incident. If you are a foreigner, you may decide to notify your embassy or diplomatic mission of your presence in the country. Organizations may decide to participate in security coordination meetings (often sponsored by U.N. agencies) or share information with other humanitarian or peacebuilding organizations in the country.

The last strategy, deterrence, works to prevent attacks. Examples of deterrence strategies are armed escort for humanitarian convoys or the presence of guards at agency office or residential compounds. The presence of guards, armed or unarmed, poses a counterthreat to those contemplating attacks. However, nonviolent methods also have the capacity to deter attacks. Accompaniment organizations, like Peace Brigades International (PBI), use nonviolent deterrence as a primary component of their strategy to protect human rights workers or organizations in countries where human rights violations frequently occur. PBI sends foreign volunteers to accompany human rights workers and organizations on a twenty-four-hour basis for short- or long-term periods. The presence of foreign volunteers demonstrates that someone else is monitoring what is happening to these individuals. In addition, these organizations use international contacts to apply pressure on governments and to mobilize support on behalf of those they accompany. The counterthreat of international opinion and support for human rights acts as a deterrent force that provides security for human rights workers, despite the risks these individuals knowingly take.[12] In general, human rights organizations and other issue advocacy organizations make extensive use of public opinion as a deterrence strategy. Peacebuilders doing advocacy work and with extensive networks of support around the globe can make use of this strategy to multiply the effect of their presence and their peacebuilding work.

Conclusion

The key to making your environment safe is analysis: make sure you are aware of your surroundings, the causes and dynamics of the conflict, the potential threats to your security, and the sources of these threats (see Chapters Five and Six in this book). Thorough analysis, with the help of your colleagues and partners, of the context in which you work and of your role within this context should inform your choice of which security strategy to use and what approaches will be most effective.

Notes

1. InterAction. *The Security of National Staff: Towards Good Practices*. Washington, D.C.: InterAction, 2001.

2. Martin, R. "NGO Field Security." *Forced Migration Review*, Apr. 1999, pp. 4–7.

3. Working Group on NGO Security. *NGO security Training*. Washington, D.C.: InterAction, 1997.

4. Van Brabant, K. *Operational Security Management in Violent Environments*. London: Humanitarian Practice Network, 2000.

5. Sheik, M., and others. "Deaths Among Humanitarian Workers." *British Medical Journal*, 2000, *321*, 166–200. [www.bmj.com.]

6. Muggah, R. *Perceptions of Small Arms Availability and Use Among Oxfam-GB Field Personnel*. Geneva: Small Arms Survey and Oxfam-GB, 2001. [www.smallarmssurvey.org.]

7. Muggah. p. 4.

8. Martin. 1999. Van Brabant. 2000.

9. Working Group on NGO Security. 1997.

10. Lederach, J. P. *Building Peace: Sustainable Reconciliation in Divided Societies*. Washington, D.C.: United States Institute of Peace, 1997.

11. International Committee of the Red Cross. *Respect for and Protection of the Personnel of Humanitarian Organizations*. Geneva: International Committee of the Red Cross, 1998. [www.icrc.org.]

12. Mahoney, L., and Eguren, L. E. *Unarmed Bodyguards: International Accompaniment for the Protection of Human Rights*. West Hartford, Conn.: Kumarian Press, 1997.

11

Is It Safe?

Practitioner Advice

Janice Moomaw Jenner and Dekha Ibrahim Abdi

In the previous chapter, Larissa Fast pointed out the many factors that organizations and individuals working in situations of violence have found necessary to consider, based on research and experience. In this chapter, we move to practical questions, cautions, and tips for people contemplating working in situations of violence.

The chapter authors, Dekha Ibrahim Abdi, a Kenyan, and Janice Jenner, an American, collaborated in working together (and became close personal friends) during a period of violent conflict in Dekha's home region in northeastern Kenya. At that time, Jan was working for an international nongovernmental organization (NGO) and living in Nairobi, four hundred miles or so from the violence. Dekha was a founder and leader of Wajir Women for Peace and later of Wajir Peace and Development Committee, a coalition of citizens' groups, NGOs, and government agencies working to reduce violence and secure a stable peace.

Dekha continues her peacebuilding work in Kenya, following two years as training director for Responding to Conflict, a peacebuilding training organization in Birmingham, United Kingdom. Jan is the director of the Institute of Justice and Peacebuilding, the practice arm of Eastern Mennonite University's Conflict Transformation Program. They continue to collaborate on writing and research projects, and they drink tea together whenever they find themselves on the same continent.

As you will see as you read this chapter, there are no clear-cut answers to the question, "Is it safe?" but Dekha and Jan provide thoughtful ideas to consider.

• • • • • • •

Many of the conflicts that you will be asked to work with have elements of violence, either past, current, or potential. As violence increases, so do the feelings of urgency to intervene, but so does the need for careful consideration before doing so. Plunging too quickly to intervene in a situation of violence, especially in a context outside your own, may end up causing unintended harm. The questions and concerns raised in previous chapters continue to apply in situations of violence but need to be considered even more carefully, since the stakes are higher.

We have worked together in a violent conflict in northeastern Kenya, Dekha as the leader of a very active and effective local citizens' peace movement and Jan as a representative of an international NGO that assisted with the peace effort. Both of us have done work in the context of other violent conflicts. The questions we pose for you to consider come from our personal experiences and the experiences of other peaceworkers whom we know and trust. Although many of these questions are almost impossible to answer completely, nevertheless they are vitally important to consider.

Before You Go

First, you need to consider a number of questions before deciding whether to become involved in activities relating to a situation in which large-scale violence is either a current reality or a strong possibility:

- Is the activity part of ongoing peace processes (for example, humanitarian assistance; diplomatic, U.N., and other peacekeeping interventions; or other peace-

building efforts)? If it is, how will your work be part
of that other work? Violent conflict is not the time
for parachuting.

- Is the activity closely connected to local partners who
  are themselves requesting the intervention? Be wary
  of intervention requests from organizations outside the
  conflict without solid evidence that connections to
  local peacebuilders are strong and lasting.

- Who are the local partners? How much trust do you
  have in the partner organization? Are they whom they
  say they are? Are they advocates, partisans for one side,
  or bridge builders? Do the activities make sense in terms
  of who and what the organization is?

- Why is an outsider needed? Why you? What skills,
  understandings, or identities do you have that are
  seen to be appropriate and helpful?

- Is the specific activity appropriate to the stage of the
  conflict and the intensity of the violence?

- What is the best-case scenario? If your intervention
  is highly successful, what will that mean in regard to
  reducing the violence and establishing safe spaces for
  dialogue and new approaches?

- What is the worst-case scenario? If things go horribly
  wrong with the intervention, will your intervention
  actually cause increased violence? Are outsiders being
  targeted? Will your passport protect you or put you in
  greater personal danger? What are the consequences of
  your presence to your partners and others you interact
  with? Will your presence put them in greater or lesser
  danger?

- What personal risks are you willing to accept? You must be absolutely honest with yourself. If a violent situation seems far beyond your comfort zone, don't decide to go and assume that "it will be okay when I get there."

- What kind of security will be available, and what will you accept? If you are going into a situation where armed escorts are necessary for travel to certain areas, you need to understand the implications of this before you go and decide what your response will be.

While You're There

You've decided to go, you arrive, and you are met by your local partners. Now what?

- Trust your partners. Realize that they understand the situations and the dangers much better than you ever will. If they say, "Stay in the hotel today," stay there.

- Cultivate as many relationships as you can as sources of information and safety. Talk to shopkeepers, people on the street, hotel clerks, and restaurant workers. They'll have intimate knowledge of what's going on at an extremely local level. We've found taxi drivers to be among the best information sources about what's really going on.

- Always keep in mind that as an outsider working on peace issues, your activities may well be monitored. What you say and do may be widely known and communicated.

- In many cases, your Western citizenship may mean that the worst that could happen to you is deportation. The same is not true for your local colleagues: your actions can have a profound impact on their safety.

- Be flexible because situations and activities are likely to change quickly and dramatically. Travel may have to be postponed or cancelled, or workshops may end up very different from what was planned. Again, follow the lead of your local partners.

- Be prepared to spend significant periods of time simply listening to the local peacebuilders. Often the best service an outsider can offer is providing space, time, and an outside perspective for people who are dealing daily and intimately with violence and its effects.

- Keep a sense of humor and a sense of proportion. You cannot take the responsibility for either the violence or for stopping it. Your work may be a part of the many activities and processes going on, but in only very few cases will it be the deciding factor in ending a violent conflict.

After You've Returned Home

Your peacebuilding doesn't end just because you return home:

- Stay in touch with your partners. You have returned to a situation of stability and safety; they remain in the violent situation and need outside contact and support.

- Write up the learnings from your work, including unintended results and activities. Attempt to provide insights as an outsider not only regarding the specific work you did but the overall situation. People who are caught up in the day-to-day realities of violence have limited space and energy for reflection; your insights from a connected outsider point of view can be very helpful.

- Pass on information and items that may be of use to them. Connect them with others who may be able to assist them or provide support in other ways.

Conclusion

Peacebuilders, especially those working in situations of intense violence, don't need outside saviors, cowboys, or martyrs. They need people who will work within their frameworks, will complement and assist their ongoing work, and will stand with them in the midst of discouragement.

Part III

. . . .

So Are You Coming to Help Us?
Advice from the Ground

Before making a final decision about taking up peacebuilding work in a new setting and certainly before arriving if you do decide to go, it might be wise to follow the advice offered in several chapters preceding this part by asking what the role of the outsider is if there are people already working at peace inside the setting. We wanted to push this line of inquiry into your thinking not as an afterthought once you get there, but as an integral part of your thinking as you consider whether to take up the invitation. You will be going to another land, a place not your own. It is the homeland of those to whom you wish to offer help, assistance, or support. In many of these zones of conflict, the people who live there have watched hundreds of people like you come and go, suitcases full of ideas, approaches, and counsel. How does that feel from their standpoint?

It would have been easy to identify a series of recommendations based on the experience of more seasoned travelers, but we opted for a different approach: ask seasoned peacebuilders who are from some of the most well-known conflict settings—Northern Ireland, the Balkans, the Middle East, and West Africa—to offer heartfelt advice to people coming into their homeland in the name of peace. What lessons have been gained? What recommendations would they give you? What do they suggest you avoid at all costs?

The chapters in this part contain advice gained from years of direct experience. Some of it may be hard for you to see as relevant to you, and you may think that it doesn't pertain to you. But be careful with moving too quickly past wisdom that we should carry with us wherever we go.

. . . .

12

A View from Northern Ireland

Mari Fitzduff

Between 1990 and 1995, Mari was the director of the Community Rela-
tions Service in Northern Ireland. During this critical period of the Irish
peace process, she and the Community Relations Service probably had
the widest range of contacts, support mechanisms, and understanding of
the variety and levels of peacebuilding initiatives. She reflected on many of
those experiences in her book Beyond Violence: Conflict Resolution
Processes in Northern Ireland *(1996). Currently, she is director of the*
Initiative on Conflict Resolution and Ethnicity, a resource center of
the United Nations that works with ethnic conflict research and practice
across the globe. As you will see, her advice, in the succinct form of do's
and don'ts, has the ring of authenticity gained from real-life experience.

. . . .

The building of peace in Northern Ireland has been supported,
enlivened, and challenged by the many hundreds of strangers
who have come to our shores to offer assistance and guidance. They
came with their ideas, their disciplines, their values, their Power-
Point presentations, and, in some cases, their funding. They often
helped us when times were tough, distorted perspectives needed
reframing, and we needed to have many difficult conversations with
each other. We owe them much. And it is in that spirit of thank-
fulness, and in the knowledge of the many callings on our time and

capacity still to come, that I offer the following reflections for peace-builders going to a new setting.

Do's for Peacebuilders

Do Be Clear About What You Are Doing: Advocacy Work or Conflict Dialogue Work

Before you start, be clear about whether what you are doing is advocacy work for a particular group or cause or conflict dialogue work, which means agreement—seeking connections between and within groups. Both are valid approaches, but both have a price. Advocacy work can decrease connections and fail to achieve an agreement for change. Dialogue work can increase connections but fail to develop sufficiently to have the very difficult conversations about such issues as power, equality, and national or other allegiances that are necessary for a sustainable solution.

If you are involved in one kind of approach, try to respect the necessity for the other approach. Competitiveness ill behooves us in such situations. Also, remember that in any conflict, there is nearly always one side with which it is more fashionable, more necessary, or easier to empathize, usually because of perceived or proven previous oppression. Outsiders in particular need to be careful not to be too seduced by the apparent simplicities of a conflict.

Do Be Responsible About the Possible Effects of Your Work

If you want to embark on work that is contentious and likely to rouse significant feelings within and between people, be sure that you both prepare and debrief well, providing support where necessary for follow-up work. In Northern Ireland in the early 1970s, some of the intensive group work that happened under the aegis of U.S. intervenors was so confusing to so many local people that it prevented constructive group work from happening for over a decade.

Do Be Clear About Your Values

I remember one workshop when we were visited by a group of conflict experts from the United States. It was early in the 1990s when
they came with their PowerPoint presentations (a novelty at that
time). They were presenting to a gathered group of community
workers from areas of Belfast where Catholic and Protestant communities live on the same streets their ideas about how the conflict
could be solved. Their presentation was impressive. Following it,
there was a pregnant pause, eventually broken by a community
worker, who gently and courteously thanked them for their presentation and the time they had taken in developing it. Then just as
gently, he asked them whether they would be prepared to spend six
months or so of their time with us working on these issues in Northern Ireland and not put the work down as a professional credit on
their curriculum vitae. This time, the pregnant silence was theirs.

Many of us became very adept at this value-sorting process.
Although we eventually came to acceptable terms of engagement
with many of the offers of assistance that were proffered, the offers
that were particularly useful were often those that were given by
those whose values were not merely seen as career gain. The Men-
nonites and the Quakers were particularly valuable. Their values in
relation to conflict resolution have long been historically clear, and
they were often prepared to travel with us for long periods of time,
even residing with us for years.

Do Find Local and Respected Partners

It can be difficult to find partners who are actively trusted by both
sides, but you can usually find someone to whom both sides are willing to give the benefit of the doubt until proved otherwise. You will
know you are working with the relevant people if the people you
reach, the ones who come to you because of your partners, are ones
who can make a difference in their communities or their institutions.

Organizations that already work on and with both sides can be especially helpful, but also working with one particular group (what we call single identity work) to assist their capacity for dialogue may also be useful and necessary at times.

Do Use Credible Status

If you have it, use credible status from either your beliefs or your profession with groups like governments, militaries, and major institutions such as churches. These groups are often floundering with ingrown and limited perspectives and often feel compelled to eschew what they view as outsider advice. But belief speaks to belief, and profession often speaks to profession, and can be heard and listened to more readily. Much of the best work in Northern Ireland was international and comparative: police to police, believer to believer, and business to business work.

Do Offer Opportunities for People to Meet

If you have the opportunity, offer safe, and if possible social, opportunities for people to meet each other outside their usual contexts. The American Consulate in Belfast and the Anglo-Irish secretariat, both hidden in the outskirts of Belfast, contributed enormously by their bravely open Christmas and Independence Day parties; many of those on opposite sides in the conflict could meet at the gatherings. Such meetings would have been impossible to arrange in any formalized or undiluted fashion.

Do Take Protagonists Away from Their Usual Territories

If you have sufficient funding, take protagonists away from their usual territories to weaken their boundaries in salubrious surrounding, with plenty of room for chance conversation and plenty of food and drink (where teetotalism is not a problem). Although this can eventually backfire (if it is done too often, the groups will become blasé and even demanding in their choice of venue), such added incentives can be the deciding factor when difficult decisions are being made about participation by the most significant movers and shakers.

Do Help with Funding

Helping with funding or finding funding when that is an issue makes it a lot easier for many of the groups you may wish to work with. And unless you have thoroughly researched and agreed with key figures in the community and prospective groups, do not seek funding for your own work on the backs of their need unless partnerships have been clearly delineated and agreed to. Do not pay yourselves big consultancy fees and expect locals to work for nothing or with minimal institutional expenses.

At the local level, the driving survival need to achieve enough funding in order to continue work and to develop an organization can leave groups open to the mercy of outside influences and funding interests. Also, be very clear and open about where your funding is coming from and its acceptability as a funding source to the parties.

Do Be Faithful to the Work

Do not run away because you do not achieve immediate success, or your paper has been written, or another exciting conflict venture calls. People appreciate at least a modicum of continuing interest in their cause. So ensure a soft leaving, if such has to happen, and maintain contact if you can. And send the papers you have written on your experience. I often wonder where those hundreds of people are who took so much of my time and never sent on the eventual report, paper, study, or dissertation.

Do Use Experiences and Examples of What Has Been Useful Elsewhere

This is an extremely productive approach. Do not assume that all such examples will be immediately relevant, and indeed, many people listening will take great delight in telling you that such approaches would not work in their particular situation. Nevertheless, offered in an open and tentative manner, such work can inspire new possibilities for reflection and action.

Do Examine Opportunities That Are Not Linked Directly to the Armed Conflict

Particularly in tense political times, providing opportunities to look at, for example, economic investment opportunities or local community development necessities can provide a safe enough topic for people to feel that they can meet in the same room together, itself an achievement in difficult times. Many U.S. business investors, such as those involved in Boston-Derry Ventures (a Northern Ireland–based economic development organization set up to develop business links with the United States), helped such dialogue in Northern Ireland even in very difficult times of violence.

Do Undertake the Work for Its Own Value

Understand that you are unlikely ever to achieve much public recognition for the work you are doing. To be successful, you usually will not be able to talk, and particularly not able to write about it openly for many years. When you do, you can be assured that the participants will contest your version of it, particularly if your work is successful. Revisionism means that others, and not you, will inevitably take the credit. Learn to seek your own quiet credit, and cherish the learning that you have gained that may increase your usefulness in another time and another place.

Do Treat Every Situation as a Learn-Learn Situation

In addition, present the situation in this way to those you are working with.

Do Nots for Peacebuilders

Do Not Think the Work Is About Solutions

Even if you are right, people often have to come to the solutions afresh themselves. We have filing cabinets full of potential solutions, many of them intricately and intelligently crafted. For over thirty years, they have been coming, and many of them would have worked. The problem was not so much in developing the solutions but in getting people to open the filing cabinets together and look at these possibilities together.

Do Not Assume That There Is No Capacity for Conflict Management or Peacebuilding

Many of the communities may well have been struggling to limit the conflict and to create openings for dialogue even in very difficult circumstances. These efforts need to be recognized and validated. In Northern Ireland, we have been subjected to far too many examples of training by people from elsewhere whose work has been sensed to be patronizing and undemanding in its challenge by people working on the ground, often in difficult circumstances that are beyond the experience of many such visiting trainers.

Do Not Assume That the Contestants Are Irrational

Do not decide that it is your job, as an apparently cosmopolitan and thinking person, to help those you are working with to clarify and refine their perspectives and see the irrationality of their ways. The frustration and disbelief of observers is not a particularly useful component to add to the work. Conflicts of an ethnopolitical, religious, or cultural nature are often based on a mixture of emotional and rational motives, and you need to understand and appreciate such realities.

Do Not Pressure Others to Let You Observe in Sensitive Mediations

These potentially sensitive mediations are likely to be difficult enough for the facilitator, with every nuance having to be weighed in the balance. Outside observers often elicit a reiteration of the usual rhetoric or fundamentals from the participants, who often feel they have to market their perspectives and result in wasteful display by the parties. These displays can be much more easily bypassed by the local mediator, who, if he or she is skilled, will already know most of them by heart.

If a local mediator invites you to the meeting because he or she is convinced that your presence will be useful, be sure to clarify your role beforehand with her or him.

Do Not Use What People Have to Say to Damage Them or Their Party Politically

While it is appropriate, if you are shuttling between groups, to convey possibilities on issues for dialogue, any suggestions must be made in such a way that they do not give grist for further damage by the other side, or you will forever be eschewed as a mediator.

Do Not Assume There Is Only One Way to Mediate

Do not be too wedded to a particular way of mediating. Different cultures often need different approaches, and in Northern Ireland, up-front dialogues were much, much rarer than forms of shuttle and other mediation processes.

Do Not Betray Horror at What You Hear

You are likely to be tested on this. Some may want to test you to see if you can understand why they have committed atrocities (for example, paramilitaries who have murdered). A small minority may just want to shock you. If they see you as naive and gullible, they may even embellish their horror stories, both about what they have done and what has been done to them, for the occasion.

Do Not Become a Groupie

For some, and sometimes for women in particular, there is an attraction in being close to an apparently passionate cause and also to men who have been violent in the cause of an ideal. Such activities are often viewed with a great degree of cynicism and often crude humor by observers and by the men themselves in their own unguarded conversations.

Do Not Do This Work If You Believe That You Could Never Maim or Murder

If you believe that the divisions in the conflict are about good and bad people and not about the contexts of exclusion, identity fears, and threats to meaning that can accrue and make conflicts almost inevitable (and that can be accrued, and often are, by governments before they wage war), then this work is not for you. It is only when you truly realize that given a particular context, you too could use, or be very severely tempted to use, a gun or a sword, legally or illegally held, that you can successfully undertake this work.

Do Not Expect That You Can Usually Achieve a Just Agreement

There may have been the rare case of a just agreement, but most agreements, if they are not outright victor-loser situations, are a mixture of pragmatism and politics and often acceptable only because the continuance of war is a worse alternative. The likelihood is that there will be amnesties for state and other militarists, that some will get knighted and others will become ministers of the state. Life moves on, and the victims are left to carry the cost, often for decades after the wars that are over. Stay for a while with their needs if you can; the work does not end when the worst of the violence is over.

Do Not Take Yourself and Your Work Too Seriously

I was much humbled by an experience of my own in the Northern Caucasus region in the early 1990s where we were asked to do a mediation between some fighting Kabardine and Balkar groups. In our innocence, we agreed. We spoke little Russian, but knew enough to know that we were being badly interpreted by our guide. We could sense the aggressive and scornful comments of the groups to each other and about each other. We literally heard the rattle of their weapons under the table. As somewhat bemused mediators, we offered a few inane comments, asked a few basic questions, and heard back badly translated answers. But later that night, we were invited to celebrate the marvelous agreement that had been made between the groups, celebrated with much drinking of the local brew. That was when I first humbly realized that often the mediator merely provides the excuse for the parties to do the work when the time is ripe in their time and by their reckoning.

Do Not Get Addicted to the Adrenaline of Conflict

If you are closely involved with such work on the conflict ground, the work will take you to the edge of what you are capable of, will test and try you as few other disciplines do, and will have you living on the cusp of both danger and meaning for far longer than is healthy for your system. Be careful that you do not end up getting addicted and therefore miss "your war." Such missing can affect your capacity to make a thoughtful response to the next call, in the next place, to become a useful stranger on yet one more bloody battlefield in our still far too violently blighted world.

13

A View from the Balkans

Katarina Kruhonja

At the start of this chapter, Katarina relates a story about how the peace community in Croatia and the Balkans initially sought help from the outside during periods of the worse violence. Many of those people who were the first to respond remain close and valued advisers and friends now nearly ten years later. Katarina herself is highly valued by the world community of peacebuilders, particularly those who have had the privilege to work with her in Europe. She has helped networking between peace and human rights organizations in the region. Her home organization, Centre for Peace, Nonviolence and Human Rights, is committed to postwar peacebuilding and reconciliation.

In this chapter, Katarina suggests that it is helpful to understand that settings filled with difficulties and violent conflict mean that people have many things on their mind, most of them related to survival. Outsiders may want things to move quickly or may not understand when the original proposal shifts given changing conditions. Take time, and know that patience is required, she suggests. You have to build and earn trust.

. . . .

The Centre for Peace, Nonviolence and Human Rights Osijek, my home organization, is widely recognized as a peace organization in the entire area that was formerly Yugoslavia. We work on community-based peacebuilding in war-torn areas of Croatia, in cooperation with the international community and other similar initiatives from the region, which encompasses southeastern Europe, particularly the former Yugoslav countries of Bosnia and Herzegovina, Serbia with Vojvodina and Kosovo, and Montenegro and Macedonia. Ours is the story of empowerment through informal (and, later, formal) networking, cooperation and exchange with both the international and regional peace community. We offer here the lessons we have learned that are useful to peacebuilding practitioners.

Lesson 1: Note That We Asked for Help

In the middle of the Bosnian war, a group of people from a city being shelled and in an atmosphere of total war seeking alternative approaches to the violence sent, through the antiwar campaign, a message to the international peace community: "We need help! We are thinking how to work for peace in a war. Can anyone help us?"

Our appeal was a clear request for practical skills in peacebuilding. That the request was coming from the receiving end is very important. If that is not a case, it is necessary to take time for achieving a mutual understanding of your entrance, even if it is only a fact-finding or exploration mission. I would hesitate to enter this sort of situation without being asked: you might be helpful, but you might also be one of those many people whose coming is an additional burden for local people. You must also be aware that even if you are invited, the changing dynamic of the crisis may mean that your host cannot give you the expected attention or that your particular field of expertise may no longer be a priority.

We were happy, and indeed blessed, with the very first people who responded; all had had previous experience supporting people in crisis. Before setting out, they researched the security situation and were aware of the risks. Their team had people from different fields of expertise that might be helpful to our situation, and they were able to provide a long-term commitment if we needed it.

They also had a supporting network of other persons and organizations that could (and did) provide more help if needed. Through them, we developed long-lasting connections and cooperation with a number of international and regional initiatives.

At that time, we were not aware of all that would come about as a result of these connections. Today, after nine years, this relationship is vivid and fruitful, although completely different from what it was originally. For example, I am going to visit Adam Curle, who was on the initial team, to reflect together on experiences regarding peacebuilding aimed at thinking about a strategy for the future; Traude Rebman, another on that original team, offered to come to contribute to the tenth anniversary of our organization.

Even today, we are learning by looking back on this experience. It influenced our own behavior as we became well-intended helpers too. But what we realized immediately and what was healing and empowering us was their acknowledgment that our intention in seeking peace was legitimate and not unrealistic; that in every situation something toward peace could be done and that our willingness to explore possibilities for peacebuilding was the right step forward; and that we were competent to define what was possible. They were with us to listen and help us in the process of defining these possibilities, reminding us constantly of real but joint resources—what we have and what they would be able to contribute.

When our personal security as peace and human rights activists became an urgent issue, members of the Peace Brigade International came on our invitation. The primary mission of this organization is to act as bodyguards. But what they provided us was seven days of joint analysis of our real level of risk, our strength and weaknesses, and our own assessment of our need for protection. At the end of the week, we decided that we would not give up and could go on without their help. I am not sure that they were aware how much they helped us. I am taking this opportunity to acknowledge it with deep gratitude.

Lesson 2: See the Community and the Organization as Equals and the Authors of the Work

I will highlight two issues. First, peacebuilding is most of all about mutual interactive trust building, learning, and empowerment. Second, at the receiving end of your help, there is not only a recipient but always a messenger as well. The quality of your relationship with her or him will in the same manner influence a number of future relationships. For example, some time ago, I heard from a woman we are working with who lives in a village very much damaged by the war. She said that through our support, she became empowered for cross-ethnic community building, but she was afraid that we would abandon her because she is not strong enough to deal with the new situation: the community recognized her as a peace promoter, with all the controversy that this brings in the war-damaged community. I could understand her because I had the experience of being exposed, being strong and weak in the same time, and being well supported when I needed it.

All that I mentioned are the reasons that the key lesson is to see the community and the organization not just as a recipient of outside help but as equals and the authors of the work. Always keep an attitude of respect in your peacebuilding relationship.

Lesson 3: Expect to Work on Long-Term, Slow Change, Not Just Crisis Solutions

Are you invited to work in what is presented as a calmer postconflict situation? Do not be surprised at finding organizations that seem almost chaotic or rigidly hierarchical. This may be particularly true for transitional post-totalitarian societies.

Setting norms for the institutionalization of postwar peacebuilding is a new challenge requiring explicit attention to the identification and development of various professional and management skills. As we have discussed in conferences, charismatic responses are not sufficient. We need more than just good rhetoric. Keep this in mind. Whatever your primary task or aim is, it will be useful if you find ways to share your management and organizational skills.

Lesson 4: Build Relationships; Don't Just Complete Projects

If you are a young, ambitious student from a Western university who has ten weeks to do practical work in the region, do not expect to get condensed information on your very first day and a pile of material to read overnight. Recognize that information sharing is a process: first, there are brief chats, then longer talks, then friendly meetings. You may feel even neglected because everyone else is so busy. And remember that we are people, not subjects of your research.

Our region has become a very recent case for studying conflict. Furthermore, the awareness by local peacebuilding organizations and their founding agencies regarding the need for research and impact assessment is growing. Therefore, individual outsiders who are invited can be genuinely interested in research. However, this position is quite delicate. Our experience is that the process can be fruitful and empowering but at the same time traumatic, with a real danger of jeopardizing people, ongoing initiatives, and organizations. I am talking from the perspective of a peace activist or grassroots peace organization; local research institutions might have a different experience.

Final Lessons

A few more lessons emerge from my efforts as impact assessment becomes an integral part of peacebuilding efforts:

- Be flexible, and remain people centered. The language barrier is very important, particularly if research is going to be done on a community level.

- In almost all circumstances, things take longer than planned. Build in time for sufficient and ongoing repetition of the question, "Did I understand you well?" and, "Tell me more!"

- If evaluation is to be participatory at different stages within a peace project, internal preparation and capacity building for this approach are very important. The cultural attitudes that support the practice of evaluation in Central and Eastern Europe are quite from those in the West. We expect to be the object of neutral, objective external observation but are less familiar with participatory action research. Therefore, it is probable that evaluation, as well as capacity-building exercises, will be seen as an additional burden to already overburdened peace activists and other workers. These are all reasons for careful monitoring of the effects of the evaluation on the involved team.

- Provide opportunities for validating findings.

- Take language and cultural differences seriously.

- Ask for active responses; silence does not necessarily mean affirmation.

- Create space for discussion, and make sure that internalization takes place. Particularly in the early postconflict period, one has to put people before evaluation; if necessary, the process should be temporarily postponed so as not to harm people and their relationships.

Conclusion

All that has been said could probably be summarized as, "Listen to be able to understand." But do you want to be neutral aiming at being objective? Your specific knowledge, skills, and experience are important, but if you could provide the space where we would feel accepted and help ensure that nobody is excluded from that space, your offer would be precious. More important than neutrality is inclusivity so that everyone will gain deeper understanding.

14

A View from the Middle East

Zoughbi Elias Zoughbi

Once again, the cycle of violence in the Middle East has escalated, dashing many of the hopes for a peaceful transformation that seemed within reach only a few years ago. Throughout these cycles, Zoughbi has been working at conflict transformation and peacebuilding within the Palestinian community and on peace initiatives with Israelis and international colleagues. He is the director of Wi'am, a center for conflict resolution located in Bethlehem. In his capacity as an educator, trainer, peace activist, facilitator, and mediator, he has seen many well-intended people come and go in the past decade. He has worked extensively with international visitors. His advice suggests that our process is not only how to learn about and with people from the setting, but how to unlearn the views that are given about a place, its history, and its people from readily available but inadequate news and information.

I've heard it said, spend two days in the Middle East, and you can write a book; spend two months, and you can write an article; but spend two years, and you will write only a paragraph. This is true and valid wherever you go. Don't rush to write or think you have it all figured out too quickly.

I am the founder and director of a nongovernmental organization; previously, I ran a program dealing with exchange visits and alternative tourism to the Middle East. I have also been responsible for placing volunteers in the West Bank (including East Jerusalem) and the Gaza Strip. The issues raised in all of these places are the same for any person entering a situation outside their home culture, though the details may be different. Here is the advice that I proffer based on my work.

Understand Who You Are

Who am I? is the first question you should ask yourself whenever you go anyplace in the world. What is my identity? What are my identities? Am I an outsider or an insider? Am I a social activist or a politically correct person?

In any foreign country, you are always an outsider. No matter what your attitude and position regarding this conflict or that, you are a foreigner. And no matter what you do, no matter what you represent, no matter what your ideology, philosophy, or principles, you can be part of the struggle, but the struggle is not yours.

Good Intentions Are Not Enough

As a Westerner, you are probably aware of the recent interest in the topic of reconciliation. Almost everyone who comes to the Middle East pushes the agenda of reconciliation. Many have good intentions but a shallow understanding of our situation and little empathy to understand the call of the oppressed for justice.

George, a visitor, promised a nongovernmental organization in Hebron thousands of dollars for a project titled, "Reconciliation: Jewish Settlers and Hebronites." Thousands of dollars will be spent on it if the Palestinians accept the project, the visitor tells us.

This very project, though, is full of insensitivity. In our context, an issue like settlements is thorny. Most Palestinians are asking for a dismantling of the settlements, as well as for the evacuation of Jewish settlers from the land occupied in 1967. The outsider looks at the theme as building reconciliation. But the very project title of the initiative requires Palestinians to deny their historic concerns. The point is that it is offensive to people in conflict to face initiatives that do not take seriously an understanding of their history and situation.

Be Cautious of a Superficial Use of Balance

In our region, the Palestinian–Israeli conflict is often viewed as a test case, a laboratory for human experiments and research. Hundreds of people come here to bring Israelis and Palestinians together, but with little consideration for historic issues, power relationships, and the dynamics of the conflict. The same is true of many other conflicts around the world.

An example from Palestine is illustrative. As a result of the intifadah of 1987–1992, an Israeli rabbi and a leading female Palestinian activist talked about the situation with a group from outside. A member of the expatriate body asked, "What can we do to help those people who were wounded by the Israeli soldiers?" The activist answered, "You can help by building clinics, supporting the hospitals, or even sending the wounded wheelchairs." Here, the Israeli rabbi interjected, "Why not a wheelchair to the Palestinian and another one to the Israeli?" On the surface, the response seems balanced. It is essentially saying, "Both of you are victims." But from a Palestinian viewpoint, the conflict itself is not balanced.

Many outsiders come and look at a situation from the perspective of neutrality. We see this as a very distorting and disturbing trend. Instead of saying, "I would like to have a balanced view," say, "I would like to work for justice for all people and fight against oppression in whatever form it is represented." This goal will take more strength, determination, and time.

The West is used to hearing balanced reporting about situations from many places in the world. Even in the midst of countless human rights violations taking place, Westerners think it is appropriate to mention equal numbers of violations for each party, even when this is not the case. Whenever you go to a foreign country, you should try to be impartial; it's the only truly respectable way to come at a situation. Impartiality is not neutrality, however; impartiality does not turn a blind eye to truth and justice.

Be Cautious About Pushing Your Cultural Values in the Name of Peace

Lots of newcomers focus on issues like gender without understanding the culture and tradition. We have lots of workshops where women represent 60 percent of the group, for example, and they are outspoken, very powerful, and have perseverance and strong commitment.

Then Ruth came and tried to push toward a program of women empowerment using her Western trends and feminist approaches, and imposing it on the locals. We appreciate Ruth and people like her who volunteer to serve the local community. However, it's important to listen to the local people and see what they want and need. Never tell them what they want and need.

Be Prepared for Suspicion

There will be people who will be suspicious because of the very fact that you come from a powerful country in the North. Remember that you are from the North, the source of colonialism and injustice, which has caused a lot of misery and oppression. Despite the fact that many people will differentiate between you as a civilian and the government that represents you, others think that you are responsible for the injustice perpetuated by your country at one time. You might be held responsible for your government's support of the bureaucratic authoritarian regimes in Latin America or the reactionary forces in Africa or the Middle East.

Seek to understand the historic patterns that underpin the suspicion. Don't assume that it is irrational. History is a problematic issue because it is often narration of the victor. You have studied for a longer time than you will spend in other countries. Start unlearning what you learned in the past. It is a process that has a starting point but not an ending point.

Focus on Building Trust

Trust is built with time, performance, and relationships, not just good intentions. Be prepared to take the time and pass the tests that are necessary for you, the visitor, to earn the trust of us, the ones living with the conflict. Be prepared to answer questions about yourself, your motivations, your goals, and to whom you are accountable. In situations of conflict, people need to know whom they can and cannot trust.

Be prepared to listen. People at our end need someone to listen to them. They need to talk, even to nag. You might have heard one story hundreds of times. You shouldn't show boredom or disrespect.

Don't promise a lot. Certainly, never promise more than you can deliver. You need to be clear even if your hosts are ambiguous or not direct.

It is always good to build healthy and straightforward trusting relationships. If you write or interview or are being interviewed, share copies of the final product with the host. Ask questions to inform yourself, but realize how easily you may be misunderstood. Ask questions so you can learn. If you disagree or disapprove of a behavior, form your response as a question, not a judgment. Be inquisitive, taking a learning posture. Reserving judgment is good advice.

Don't come with a negative perspective. Avoid stereotypes, patronization, and condescension; they are not constructive ways for communication. Live as we live: live simply, walk humbly, love kindly, and do justice.

Learning the language is important but not as important as understanding the body language of the people you work with. Celebrate the differences with the people you are seconded to. Respecting their culture, tradition, and religion, as well as their habits, is the surest way to have a successful experience. Appreciating their food and hospitality is essential.

Many places you may visit where there are protracted conflicts are like ours. We are a community-based society. Although there are more trends for individualism, we still believe that the family is a viable socioeconomic unit. If you live with a family or in a home adjacent to a family, you are accountable to this society at large and to the family hosting in particular.

> Alice rented an apartment and shared it with her friend from Boston who was a classmate. One night they had a party, and people from both sexes attended. Some male friends stayed late. You might imagine the negative repercussions and all the negative thoughts Alice's neighbors created and formed. Alice had not realized that what she was doing would not be acceptable to everyone else. She didn't spend enough time listening to her neighbors and friends to see what behavior is appropriate.

If you believe in constructive criticism, practice it in your own country. Since most of the time, your country is responsible for lots of negative things that have happened to the people of the Third World, you shouldn't expect the same level of criticism to be leveled at places your country has helped to oppress. You might be more confrontational; you might be free to talk about any subject, to wear whatever you like, or to move without limitations. You might talk about homosexual rights. This might be a taboo subject for some other cultures and traditions. It's important not to sell out your beliefs, but you should realize that in some places, people are not open even to speak these words. It is always good to be sensitive, respectful, and careful.

Most of the time, people are surviving, not really living. Avoid blaming the people you are working with. You are free to blame your government and your people, but be humble about your knowledge of the country you work in. You might be working at a different pace or better approach. Take into consideration people's sense of time and pace. Avoid being patronizing and condescending.

Conclusion

North Americans working in areas other than their own country or region have a number of challenges:

- The challenge of how to balance the mainstream media and how to embark on an appropriate unlearning process

- The challenge not to preach nonviolence at people and not to convey a delegitimization of their struggle to end apartheid, injustice, occupation, and colonial expansionism and power

- The challenge of helping people shift their attitudes of blame, guilt, and victimization toward collective responsibility

- The challenge of humility and recognizing that you are not the savior of the people

- The challenge not to be overwhelmed or burned out and to find mechanisms and healthy techniques to air out frustrations and approach difficulties with innovation, creativity, and vivid interaction with the surroundings

- The challenge to cope with a different culture and its traditions in an unstable and uneasy environment

- The challenge not to overidentify with the people while standing with them. Remember that their challenges are not identical to your challenges.

- The struggle of living in areas where boundaries and checkpoints are the landmarks. Be prepared to face limitations or even prevention of travel. Your personal freedom may be infringed on.

15

A View from West Africa

Sam Gbaydee Doe and
Emmanuel Habuka Bombande

Some years ago, journalistic reporting suggested that the chaos of the inter-nal and regional wars in West Africa was a model of what was to come in the twenty-first century. The article depicted the human disaster of war and violence in parts of West Africa, but it missed completely any sign of hope in the midst of that chaos. Sam Doe and Emmanuel Bombande and the West Africa Network for Peacebuilding represent precisely the kind of hope that emanates from a people's desire to build a community of com-passion, justice, and care, values deeply embedded in their African tra-ditions and ways of life.

Sam, from Liberia, worked during the war years with conflict reso-lution training, trauma, and healing in the affected communities and in particular with the care and reintegration of child soldiers. Emmanuel, now located in Accra, worked for many years with the Nairobi Peace Ini-tiative, including a decisive process of reconciliation between warring groups in the northern regions of his native Ghana. They start their advice with the art of storytelling.

Wisdom in African Storytelling

The Kpembe-Wura

One of the contentious issues in the complex web of conflicts in the Northern Region of Ghana is a protracted dispute between the

Gonjas and the Nawuris over the traditional ownership of a certain town. The two communities have been adversaries for several decades.

Salaga, an old slave market in the Gonja chiefdom, is a commercially viable town within the Northern Region. As part of his assignment, a Nawuri young man found himself working on a development project with a nongovernmental organization (NGO) in Salaga. Once he was identified by some Gonja youth as a Nawuri, he was manhandled and severely beaten. For these youths, a Nawuri was not welcome in Gonjaland. (This is a consequence of the earlier intercommunal violence in 1994 in the Northern Region of Ghana. The already fragile relationships between the Gonjas and Nawuris worsened as the two tribes fought in the larger interethnic communal conflict.)

The police in the town became paralyzed over how to handle such a sensitive ethnic-based issue. If they applied the law in favor of a Nawuri in a Gonja town, the Gonjas could mob the police depot. Since the Gonja youth understood their action only in terms of ongoing hostilities with the Nawuris, their adversary, the police could not treat the assault on the Nawuri development worker as criminal. Their inaction infuriated the Nawuri community. The demand for justice and the respect for the human rights of all Ghanaians became a loud call within the Nawuri community, as well as within other communities that perceived that they had also suffered similar injustices.

This was where Alhaji Ibrahim Haruna, in his capacity as *kpembe-wura* (traditional ruler, "owner of Kpembe"), came in. He convened a meeting of elders and a cross-section of inhabitants at his palace. He then summoned the offenders, in this case his kinsmen, the two Gonja youth, and the victim, the Nawuri young man, to appear before him. The Gonjas had expected the traditional chief to punish the Nawuri even more since the two communities were not friendly to each other. To their dismay, the *kpembe-wura* talked

about the values of peace and the importance of interethnic tolerance and mutual coexistence.[1]

Referring to an earlier ruling he had made to settle cases of ha-
rassment and assault, he directed the Gonja youth to pay a cow and
the equivalent of thirty U.S. dollars. He explained that the money
and cow would be used as reparation for the victim. This was a sanction on the Gonja youth, but it was also a public demonstration that
he stood for all, including non-Gonjas, in settling such intercommunal disputes when they occurred on his land. He would therefore not hesitate to reprimand his kinsmen or any other tribesman
who committed crimes.

Amid loud murmuring and to the chagrin of his kinsmen, the
kpembe-wura declared that the fine would be paid on a set date at
another public gathering. He was well aware that the youth could
not afford the money and cow they were to bring, and yet he made
it public knowledge that this was an appropriate sanction that could
not be reversed.

At the end of the public sitting, he privately told the district
chief executive (DCE) that he thought it was expedient for both
the traditional chief and the DCE to pay the fine on behalf of the
youth.[2] He assured the DCE that it would be a confidential arrangement between the two of them to help build peace. He explained
that such a public gesture would build confidence with the Nawuris
and lead to improved relationships between the Gonjas and
Nawuris.

Prior to the second public sitting, the Gonja youth were offered
a cow and money to present publicly to the chief. As is customary,
an elder of the community would present the money and cow on
their behalf at the chief's palace. The offenders were not told the
source of the money and the cow. In such cases, it is understood that
the extended families and other kinsmen of the youth might have
made the contributions given the solidarity that exists in African
societies. Once the money and the cow were presented to the chief,

he praised and appreciated the efforts of the youth. In great traditional style, he again spoke to the importance of respect for one another and mutual coexistence for peace and tranquility among Gonjas and Nawuris.

This chief's action stunned the Nawuri ethnic group. The only reason the Nawuri man had gone to Salaga was to carry out an assignment as part of the development project of his NGO.

One of the negative impacts of the conflicts in 1994 and 1995 conflicts was that Nawuris had stopped traveling to Salaga for fear of reprisals by the Gonjas. Their boycott of Salaga reduced the level of commercial activity there. Instead, the Nawuris traveled more often to Tamale, the regional capital, which was much farther away. As a result, they stopped using the Ghana Commercial Bank in Salaga and shifted their commercial activities elsewhere.

Interestingly, this falling activity coincided with the period the Ghana Commercial Bank was undertaking a national evaluation of its operating capacity with the view to closing some of its unprofitable branches. Because patronage of the Ghana Commercial Bank in Salaga had dropped considerably as a result of the Nawuris' refusing to use the bank, it was one of the branches earmarked for closure.

The chief's intervention, however, created so much confidence and trust that Nawuris again started traveling to Salaga, interacting and doing business there. People talked about Alhaji Haruna as a new chief who was objective and accommodating and encouraging all the communities to reach out to one another, respect each other, and live in peace.

With increasing interactions between the two communities, commercial activities began to flourish, and the Salaga branch of the Ghana Commercial Bank was once again booming. The decision to close down the bank was rescinded.

An incident that could have erupted into violence provided an opportunity for increased confidence and improved interethnic relations. Although the dispute between the two communities over

Kpandai lands has not been resolved, mutual coexistence and tolerance resulting from this single gesture of the *kpembe-wura* have improved considerably.

The Women of Mano River

Saran Daraba Kaba is head of the Mano River Women's Network for Peace. In 2000, forty women under her leadership traveled to the border between Guinea and Liberia to intervene in a violent dispute that had the potential to deteriorate into bloodshed and destruction between the Kissi ethnic communities on both sides of the border. Although it was the same ethnic group but in the two neighboring countries, Guinea and Liberia, the level of emotions generated by killings that had taken place as a result of the cross-border war in the subregion was unprecedented.

Imagine forty women sitting on the grass and listening to the Kissi ethnic community on the Guinean side of the border. To the astonishment of the women, the level of anger and bitterness could not allow any meaningful exchange with the elders. Spontaneously, the women decided to sit and just listen. They did nothing but listen. As the elders spoke, their emotions deepened, and they cursed and swore to massacre their own kinsmen on the other side of the Liberian border. At a point where the women could no longer take in the outpouring of violent language and the quest for revenge, they broke down in tears one after the other. Some of them rolled on the grass and wailed loudly, "Where is the future for our children?"

Suddenly all the elders, who a few moments before had been swearing and cursing, also broke down and joined in the weeping. "The blood that is running in your veins is the same blood that runs in the veins of your brothers and sisters on the other side of the border in Liberia. Would you like to kill your own brothers?" the women asked. The elders looked at one another and one by one began thanking the women for their patience and tolerance in allowing them (the elders) to discover reason and wisdom. They vowed that on the contrary, they wanted to reach out to their brothers on the other side and swear an oath that they would never allow government soldiers or rebels to use their territory or kin to inflict further pain and suffering on the two communities. They explained that they had suffered enough and that it was time for the wars in the Mano River Union countries to end. All they needed was peace to go back to the land and farm. They appealed to the women to carry this message on their behalf to leaders of the region.

The Singing Mediator

In the 1980s, Burkina Faso and Mali went to war over the border. Several conferences and mediation efforts were made to end the conflict, but none succeeded in convincing the parties to pursue peace.

The president of Guinea at that time, Ahmed Sekou Toure, invited Presidents Thomas Sankara and Moussa Traore of Burkina Faso and Mali, respectively. In front of the presidential palace in Conakry, one of West Africa's celebrated griots (praise singers), Kanja Kouyate, put on a spectacular performance before the host and visiting presidents.

The performance took on the form of entertainment, but Kanja Kouyate was calling on the two presidents at war to make peace. He did this by evoking their ancestors and appealing to their inherent human goodness as leaders to lead their people out of conflict. Through poetry, song, and dance, he brought out qualities that were a hallmark of a true African leader and challenged the two presidents to look to their ancestors and bring back dignity instead of shame and suffering to their peoples. So emotional was this performance that the two presidents not only shed tears and embraced publicly, but took a solemn oath before the public and witnessed by their ancestors not to return to war.

On their return home, they called an urgent meeting and signed a peace agreement that has never been violated since then. Not only did the war end, but cooperative relations between the two countries have increased dramatically as well.

And Who Are You? A View from West Africa

Imagine an outside mediator trained in one of the best schools in the North with all of the expertise and skills to do the job of mediation in protracted conflicts with a great portfolio as special representative of the U.N. secretary-general or a big power of our world coming in to mediate any of the conflicts in these three stories. Imagine the obvious tension and frustration such an expert could experience. This person's professional training suggests that it is important for all the issues in conflict to be identified and a painstaking effort deployed to find options and the best alternative to a negotiated agreement. But this mediator cannot find any logic in the ways the peacebuilders in these three stories managed these conflicts.

But who is the outsider to impose the meaning and methods on a conflict rooted in the social construct of the people involved? Who has the right to make meaning for another group or to recreate another people? It would be wise to take seriously the statement that "conflict is connected to meaning, meaning to knowledge, and knowledge is rooted in culture."[3]

Lesson from the *Kpembe-Wura*

In the example of Alhaji Ibrahim Haruna, the *kpembe-wura*, it was important to reach out to the Nawuris not only in words and appeals, but also through a demonstrated action that could challenge and change the perception of his people about their neighbors, the Nawuris. Out of such demonstrated action, the Nawuris could begin to see their relationships with the Gonjas differently. Once convinced that a Gonja chief would protect the dignity of Nawuris just as he would do for Gonjas, other issues that hitherto were the reason for discontent, suspicion, and mutual mistrust began to fade. These actions to assure Nawuris that their dignity would be protected led to solutions for the more contentious issues. This would have increased even more rapidly if traditional chiefs were supported and enabled to see and understand their roles as reconcilers. In this example, they become the best intervenors.

The lesson from this first story is this:

Intervenors from the outside must ensure that their actions will not erode the potential of such traditional institutions in dealing with issues that generate conflicts and underdevelopment.

Lesson from the Women of Mano River

Many conflict resolutions textbooks and manuals have chapters on communication that elaborate active listening as a key skill. Although these resources are important, the intervenors in the Liberia-Guinea ethnic dispute—in this case, the forty women—added a new dimension to listening. They listened with their hearts so much so that they were filled with the sorrows, pains, and suffering of the Kissi communities along the national border. Through their tears, the women transmitted the pain and anguish of the community back to the elders, who also discovered an essential element of their humanity that had eluded them.

An intervenor outside of the context of the women would not have responded as these women did. One has to be part of this community to understand that empathy at this point was more important than anything else. Empathy, when it is genuine, connects people with fewer spoken words, but the ultimate aim of dealing with violence remains invariably the primary goal.

The lesson from this story is this:

Well-prepared mediation sessions often miss out on critical cultural dimensions that form the bedrock for bringing people in protracted conflicts together.

Lesson from the Singing Mediator

When Kanja Kouyate sang the praises of the ancestors of the conflicting presidents and evoked the presence of their ancestors, was he also mediating? What has this got to do with mediation? One element that is critical to mediation is the integration and reconciliation of time or events. Understanding the roots of conflicts is a fundamental principle. The *griot* demonstrated what was fundamental to Africans when there is conflict: the relationship. Tracing the root of the relationship of the parties—and not the root of their conflict—takes precedence over all the processes. The *griot* was invited to look into time and evoke physically and spiritually the community to which the disputing nations belong.

The lesson from the singing mediator is this:

Outside intervenors need to take into account the fundamental worldview of the participants in the conflict.

Applying the Lessons

What do these lessons suggest for outside intervenors? One critical area for reflection with partners is how Western concepts for intervention have either strengthened capacities for peacebuilding in Africa or weakened them. Each time any form of intervention does not recognize the existing local capacities for peace, the programs of intervention become short-lived events. Within the context of the African worldview, intervention from outside to resolve conflict is understood as imposed even if there are tolerance and receptivity toward the intervenors.

Second, outside intervention that does not take into account critical partnerships that build and strengthen capacity at local levels does not offer space for communities to become their own peacemakers and thereby consolidate their own culture of peace. Outside intervention that is imposed subtly encourages communities to adopt new cultures for conflict resolution, which in itself creates confusion and eventually feeds into new conflicts. The outsider who comes into any conflict situation with a package to resolve conflicts outside his or her own society is bound to cause more harm than good. Conflicts find their meaning in people's cultures, and it is within those cultures that solutions can be found.

The international community needs to come to this realization. When the United Nations and the great superpowers blundered in Somalia in the 1990s, it was the elders of that land who took nearly six months to bring sanity to Somaliland. Perhaps a humble world could have learned from that experience. Unfortunately, it did not.

In Sierra Leone, for instance, great euphoria was stirred up in 1999 over the setting up of a Special Court, a Human Rights Commission, and a Truth and Reconciliation Commission and the holding of elections when a substantial portion of the country still lacked civil authority. The international community, under the auspices of the United Nations and in cooperation with the Sierra Leone government, wanted to "prosecute persons who bear the greatest responsibility for the commission of serious violations of international humanitarian law and crimes committed under Sierra Leonean law."[4] The Truth and Reconciliation Commission was to "create an impartial historical record of violations and abuses of human rights and international humanitarian law related to the armed conflict in Sierra Leone, from the beginning of the conflict in 1991 to the signing of the Lomé Peace Agreement; to address impunity, to respond to the needs of victims . . . promote healing and reconciliation."[5]

These are laudable initiatives to stop future human rights abuses and discourage others from committing heinous crimes against humanity. Nevertheless, two factors tend to undermine these initiatives. First, they are virtually foreign impositions that seem to have lost touch with the people and culture for which they were established. These initiatives disregard the cultural heritage and symbols of the people, as vested in their chiefs and elders, and the way they handle disputes. The majority of the affected people or victims do not understand these new structures and how they would benefit them. They simply look on and accept whatever comes. Yet the specter of vengeance remains entrenched in the minds of the people since the imposed culture of reconciliation and justice is at variance with theirs. For them, nothing has been done to reconcile them with those who victimized them.

Second, the commitments to sustain these structures are often weak and unsustainable. The international community reacts with vigor and enthusiasm to situations. Although such reactions are most often ephemeral, they raise unprecedented expectations among victims of violent conflicts to the extent that they are psychologically affected when their hopes are dashed. A general state of despondency seeps in, thus creating a crisis of confidence between victims and the international Samaritans.

In Sierra Leone, the issues of funding for the proposed Special Court and the Truth and Reconciliation Commission remain unresolved. Proposed budgetary allocations for the two structures are yet to be obtained. And even if initial budgetary commitments are fulfilled now, given that the court and the Truth Commission will sit for over a year to adjudicate cases and try to make sense out of the excesses of the war, is the international community willing to sustain it for at least three years? Reconciliation is not automatic; it takes time and requires resources to work effectively.

Conclusion

For peace to prevail, the international community has to demonstrate genuine commitment to helping victims of violent conflicts rebuild their lives. These commitments must be fulfilled and on time. Those affected must always be involved in whatever process is being put in place to restore their humanity and bring peace to them. Strangers, however good their intentions are, must be willing to take their cues from the people they have come to assist. They must listen with their hearts and develop a deep-seated commitment to respect and follow the victims in their quest to bring peace to themselves and live in harmony. Otherwise, the people—the victims of violent conflicts—will be suspicious of the good intentions of even genuine strangers who come in to help them end their nightmarish experience. At that point, people will begin to ask, "And who are you?"

Notes

1. Alhaji Ibrahim Haruna recounted this story in a workshop with Gonja traditional leaders that the West Africa Network for Peacebuilding facilitated. The values of peace and lessons for interethnic coexistence came out of the workshops and consultations for peacebuilding in the Northern Region.

2. The DCE in Ghana is the highest-ranking political head at the district level and represents the president of the Republic of Ghana in the execution of his executive functions.

3. See Lederach, J. P. *Preparing for Peace: Conflict Transformation Across Cultures*. Syracuse, N.Y.: Syracuse University Press, 1995. p. 8.

4. Agreement Between the United Nations and the Government of Sierra Leone on the Establishment of a Special Court for Sierra Leone, in *Sierra Leone Gazette*, Feb. 10, 2000.

5. Supplement to the *Sierra Leone Gazette*, Feb. 10, 2000: The Truth and Reconciliation Act, 2000.

Part IV

. . . .

Intervention Matters
From Money to Ethics

The chapters in this part turn to the core concerns relevant to every peacebuilding intervention, whether conducted by insiders or outsiders. There is no avoiding the question of money, from the view of funders to the specifics of payment for work delivered. And there is no avoiding the hard questions of ethics and accountability.

It is important to address this topic early in the process of decision-making preparation. Who is paying for this work? How does that get negotiated? How do foundations and funders think about the support of peace-related initiatives, and what are they looking for? If I take up this request, to whom am I accountable? Are there multiple levels of accountability? Whom will I rely on to make tough ethical decisions once I am involved? Is there a useful framework for guiding those decisions that I should have before leaving? And how will I know if something that I am doing is having secondary and undesired impacts? Is it possible that my good intentions could create harm? How might I avoid this possibility?

These are the intervention matters. And these questions, while perhaps seemingly insignificant at early stages, loom as the most important grounding you may have once an engagement for peacebuilding is initiated and develops.

16

Who Pays?

Money Matters from a Practitioner's Perspective

Bernard Mayer

Money matters are often experienced as unsettling and even unpleasant by most peacebuilders (with such lofty ideals as peace and justice, they wonder, Why are we bogged down in the details of negotiating fees and arguing over payments?) yet remain an integral part of entering a new setting. Very few of us can operate on independent wealth or the extended bankroll of a benefactor with no strings attached. Most of us must figure out a way to pay costs, at least for travel, food, and lodging, and many who work at peacebuilding full time need to make a living. These needs raise intriguing, and sometimes perplexing, questions: Who pays? How is money negotiated? How is this related to settings of significant poverty where many of the worse conflicts are taking place and where resources for even basic needs are under great demand? How do money, influence, accountability, and integrity of work and goals mix and match?

For an initial understanding of these concerns, we turned to Bernard Mayer, who has worked in the field of conflict resolution for more than twenty-five years for CDR Associates as a trainer, mediator, and organizational manager. He has helped design dispute system and training programs for local communities and national governments and has conducted evaluations of peace initiatives and organizations in several countries. His most recent book, The Dynamics of Conflict Resolution *(2000), provides a practitioner's view of the keys to constructive change processes through social conflict.*

* * * * * * *

An American conflict resolution organization had a vision about how to bring peace and civil society to emerging democracies. This vision was rooted in a belief that nations that had recently shed authoritarian governments had not developed the core skills, institutions, and values of collaborate problem solving, citizen participation, and creative approaches to the resolution of conflict that longer-existing democracies had been developing over decades, if not centuries. This organization believed that the approaches of collaborative negotiation, facilitated decision making, consensus building, and mediation that have been taking root in Western democracies could be contextualized and made available to these nations in a way that would be both useful and empowering.

Because of its effective fundraising efforts and its track record of introducing conflict resolution programs in North America and because foundations were interested in helping emerging democracies stabilize, this organization was successful in obtaining several generous grants to establish a variety of conflict resolution training programs and services. A number of in-country organizations and individuals, some of whom had attended seminars in Europe and North America on conflict resolution, were eager to work with this organization. The organization hired several North Americans to train and consult with these partner organizations and to help organize local conflict resolution centers. It used the money it received to provide funding to the local organizations, hire local staff, and fund travel, training, office space, and other services.

The organization's programs grew and were well received, and considerable success could be claimed based on the number of trainings conducted and conflict resolution centers established and on the facilitated meetings and dialogues that ensued. Funders were pleased with this success, so they increased their funding, and the programs continued and grew. Conflict resolution, mediation, consensus decision making, interest-based negotiation, and related approaches and practices became familiar concepts, and many in-country people were trained to be facilitators or trainers themselves—and this

included people from a variety of ethnic backgrounds, among whom
there was considerable tension.

A significant success story? In some ways decidedly—but not
without some significant downsides. Consider some of the developments that went along with this success:

- In-country staff turnover was great. Many of the people
  who left felt that the organization itself was not democratic and questioned, sometimes bitterly, the allocation
  of resources.

- Although considerable numbers of local and national
  government officials were trained, very little changed
  in how government went about doing its business.

- Major conflicts occurred on the international, national,
  and local levels during the course of this project, but
  no one seemed to think of these conflict resolution
  centers as a resource during these times.

- When project funding ran out, very few of these programs were sustainable, able to continue on their own,
  with local funding, or through their own international
  fundraising efforts.

- There was considerable unhappiness about the fact
  that the costs of bringing one American or Western
  European conflict resolution professional for a two-
  week training could fund a local office for a year.
  Furthermore, the fees paid to these consultants seemed
  astronomical by in-country standards, even when
  the consultants themselves were quite well liked.

- Some of the consultants from abroad were greatly
  appreciated and provided important training, vision,
  and support to the local staff, but sometimes they
  did not seem grounded in local circumstances and

appeared more interested in having an overseas experience rather then in providing genuine assistance. Some of the consultants themselves felt that they were more useful as window dressing than as genuine supporters of conflict resolution programs.

- Often, the in-country staff had no clear idea about what the overall budget for the project was, how it was arrived at, how allocation decisions were made, and how priorities were set.

- The American organizational leadership often felt that the motivation of people to attend trainings or participate in a program was purely for money and not out of a genuine commitment to bringing a different and more peaceful and democratic approach to dealing with conflicts.

This is not the story of any one conflict resolution organization or program, but elements of this story could be applied to many well-meaning and potentially worthwhile conflict resolution efforts. With the best of intentions, American and Western European conflict resolution practitioners often create an almost colonial relationship with their in-country partners that can undercut the very basic purpose of their efforts and the values they espouse. When the trap of falling into a quasi-colonial relationship between different organizations can be avoided and a genuine programmatic, administrative, and financial partnership can be established, the power and potential of collaborative approaches to conflict resolution can be unleashed. But when the values of the conflict resolution work are not reflected in the administrative and financial arrangements that govern the program, then the potential impact of conflict resolution efforts is severely limited. The way in which financing is obtained, funds are allocated, and financial accountability is maintained is not a side issue to the potential success of international conflict resolution efforts; in many ways, it lies at the heart of the challenge facing conflict resolvers and funding agencies.

In this chapter, these issues will be considered. Particular use will be made of an assessment of conflict resolution programs in Eastern and Central Europe and the former Soviet Union funded by the Charles Stewart Mott Foundation during the late 1980s and the 1990s.[1]

The Nature of the Challenge

For conflict resolution efforts to take root in emerging democracies or other non-Western countries, the lessons learned in Western Europe and America have to be thoroughly integrated into the context within which they are to be undertaken. Westerners, even if they choose to live in a local country for years at a time, maybe permanently, can be effective only in genuine partnership with local practitioners who know the society, the culture, the politics, the nuances of communication, and of course the language.

The Western partners, however, come with several structural sources of power that make it hard to attain a genuine partnership. They are usually the ones with experience in the kind of conflict resolution processes that funders are interested in promoting. They function without the incredible stress that living under difficult economic circumstances and volatile or unpredictable political conditions brings to their partners. Local partners often look to Western democracies as a model for what they hope to achieve (even if their idea of what these democracies are like is often distorted), and thus they sometimes place too much reliance on the international partner's judgment.

Added to all this, the Western partners often come with connections to funders, knowledge of how to raise money, and of course the funds themselves. Although in-country colleagues may be motivated by a genuine commitment to bringing more effective conflict resolution and collaborative decision-making processes to their societies, they often are dependent on the funds that their Western colleagues bring to secure their basic livelihood. Even with the best of intentions, this can result in a very unequal partnership.

The problem is not just one of values or philosophy or walking our talk. Unless a genuine partnership is achieved in the financial issues, a productive programmatic partnership is difficult to achieve. If, for example, the Western partners suggest that training in conflict resolution might be a good first step in introducing conflict resolution procedures to a region, or if they suggest developing a group of neutral facilitators to help organize and carry out community dialogues, then it is very possible the in-country colleagues will feel obligated to accept these suggestions, even if the time is not right, the approach is culturally inappropriate, or the impact is likely to be minimal. There are many variations about how this might play out, and many in-country practitioners are very able to negotiate effectively, set limits, and guide their Western colleagues effectively. Many international partners are sensitive to these dynamics and work very hard to ensure that an equal relationship develops. But the structural forces and constraints are still present, and even with the best of intentions, this can inhibit the effectiveness of the program over time and create some of the problems outlined in the example at the start of this chapter.

Ironically, in an effort to counteract this problem and avoid using the resources they do have in an insensitive way, Western practitioners may sometimes fail to provide appropriate input and the guidance, or they may avoid asking for the financial accountability that a project requires. There are many examples of considerable funds being frittered away because clear expectations, goals, strategies, and reporting procedures were not negotiated, clarified, and followed.

By no means is this the norm of how international conflict resolution programs most frequently function, but it is almost always a challenge that has to be faced in order to create an effective partnership. It is also an opportunity. By working through the nature of the financial relationships so that they reflect the goals of the project, the values of cooperation and partnership, and the need for financial accountability, the overall purpose of the project can be enhanced, and a genuine new culture of decision making and conflict resolution can be promoted.

A different and in some ways opposite problem related to funding is almost always present as well. American and European money often seems tainted to citizens of emerging democracies. This may be particularly true of people involved in ethnic conflicts or in struggles involving large international corporations. Many conflict resolution professionals who work abroad have had to deal with suspicions about their source of money and their real agendas. People wonder whether conflict resolution efforts are funded by the American State Department, the Central Intelligence Agency, or the Defense Department. They wonder whom international colleagues really report to and why they care about what happens in other countries.

There are two related problems here. One has to do with the suspicions some may have about who is behind a project. The other problem occurs when funders do in fact have a vested interest in how a conflict is resolved or in suppressing the development of certain political struggles. What happens, for example, if a considerable source of money is available from a U.S. government agency or from a large corporation to fund a dialogue about the environmental impacts of a proposed development project? The corporation or perhaps the agency may have competing interests. It may genuinely want to create a forum that will allow all those likely to be affected by the facility to discuss their concerns and arrive at some mutually acceptable approaches to the issue. But it also may very much want to see the facility developed.

This structural conflict of interests is not unique to international settings; conflict resolvers face this in the United States regularly. But when combined with an overall suspiciousness about American and European motives, with genuine concerns about the impact of

American policies and economic investments, and with a long history of exploitation at the hands of colonial powers, this problem takes on an added poignancy. Often, the approaches that contribute to creating an effective financial partnership will also help alleviate people's concerns about the sources of money. Of course, sometimes it is impossible to play an effective conflict resolution role if financing comes from a source that is significantly tainted.

Walking Our Talk with Money

Most of these obstacles can be overcome when funding arrangements can be constructed in a way that reflects the following four principles:

- Transparency: The sources, amount, conditions on, and purpose of the funding should be open to all partners in a project.

- Inclusion: Local partners should be involved as much as possible in obtaining, dispersing, and accounting for the money that is spent.

- Mutual accountability: Partners should be genuinely accountable to each other and to funders for how the funds are spent and accounted for and what is achieved as a result.

- Reality: There are some painful truths about funds: the limits on them, the disproportionate costs of Western staff, difficulties in building in accountability procedures across international boundaries, and the mercurial nature of funders that it is important to be realistic about. A partnership built on unrealistic or naive expectations is just as likely to founder as one built on hierarchical relations.

Transparency

As core a value as openness and honesty may be for conflict re-
solves, we often shy away from sharing information about our funding, salaries, expenses, and debts. Partly, this may be a reflection of
other values we hold about privacy and autonomy. But failure to
share important information about our budgets and funding with
local partners or clients often breeds suspicion, distrust, and inequality. Furthermore, it promotes an inequality, all too reminiscent of
colonial practices, based on our disparate knowledge of each other's
finances. Lack of transparency makes it hard to engage in genuine
joint planning or strategic cooperation. Transparency about financing seems to be a sine qua non for a collaborative approach to international conflict resolution efforts.

But being transparent may not always be a simple or straightforward matter. The differentials between Western European and
American salaries and expenses and those likely in developing
countries is enormous. This is a fact of life, but one rooted in many
of the dynamics that breed both resentment and a desire to emulate
Western societies. When the amount of money allocated to the fees
of Western consultants—even those working for nongovernmental
organizations (NGOs) or universities—administrative overhead
expenses, and the costs of travel is shared with international colleagues, it is understandable that feelings ranging from resentment
to anger to hopelessness are stirred up. After all, the money it may
take to fund one relatively brief visit by Western conflict resolution
professionals to a developing country might be enough to pay for
the yearly salaries and expenses of several local associates who are
likely to be struggling financially.

As a result, questioning the value of the Western partner's contribution is only natural. This can lead to cynicism and resistance to
the genuine contribution Western partners can make. In fact, many
local partners might view their Western allies as primarily useful

as a conduit to international financial resources. Transparency alone will not counter these forces; they are bred deeply into the structural relationships among the societies that we inhabit. In fact, transparency alone, if it is disconnected from other elements of a genuine partnership, can make matters worse.

But whatever the problems that transparency poses, it is essential. The questions that local partners might raise about the fairness of the allocation of resources and the relative value of Western associates are important ones that should be discussed, evaluated, and taken seriously. There are far too many stories about Western associates who parachute in and parachute out of developing countries or conflict-ridden areas without ever immersing themselves in a way that can make their potential contributions valuable. This may provide a valuable experience for the Western consultants but is likely to do very little to make a genuine impact on local conflicts or conflict resolution capacities. Indeed, it can become part of a sense of being colonized that many struggling developing countries experience.

Visitors to areas devastated by recent conflicts such as Bosnia, Kosovo, and East Timor have commented that the countries seem to be occupied, in an almost imperialist way, by NGOs and international agencies. These organizations are often well motivated and may provide essential services, but the cultural costs can be great, and so can the level of dependency and cynicism that results. Therefore, the hard and sometimes painful questions that transparency can raise are also key questions that are central to our ability to empower others to deal with their own affairs and their own conflict, a central goal of most conflict resolution programs.

Transparency is also essential for a very different reason. International conflict resolution efforts often occur in societies characterized by very hierarchical and authoritarian approaches to decision making. There are many consequences of this, including distrust or conflict within local conflict resolution organizations and other important local partners. Suspicions about how a local partner may be expending funds or about the ways in which local partners may be trying to enhance their own personal or political position through their connections with international organizations are commonplace and not always unfounded. Financial accounting and reporting practices that are commonly accepted in Western countries, and the concept of accountability, as we understand it, are not necessarily understood or practiced in developing countries.

Whatever the values one may hold about this, there is no question that the disconnect between international and local practices can be a source of friction and also can pose a long-term obstacle to the ability of organizations in developing countries to raise money on their own from international sources.

For all these reasons, it is important to promote internal transparency within partner organizations, both to assist in creating a more trusting and collaborative set of relationships and help prepare these organizations to be more independent of Western colleagues. Promoting internal transparency is much more difficult, if not impossible, if there is inadequate transparency among international partners.

Inclusion

Western conflict resolution organizations are often very attuned to taking an inclusive approach to the design and execution of projects, but less aware of the importance of taking such an approach to the financial dimension of their work. Since control of financial resources ultimately means control of a project, this is a major obstacle to creating genuine international partnerships. Often, the approach taken is for a Western NGO to research potential funders, develop a budget (perhaps in cooperation with local partners), receive the funds, disperse the funds in accordance with its own accounting practices, review reports from in-country partners, and prepare reports back to the funders. Even if the relationship among the partnering groups is characterized by transparency, this is not a genuinely inclusive approach or one likely to lead to sustainability.

Ideally, all participating organizations should be involved in all phases of the funding activity if a genuine, equal, and sustainable partnership is going to be created. This means participating together in investigating funding sources, developing the initial proposal including the budget, discussing budgeting decisions, reviewing financial statements, preparing reports, and so forth. Genuine equality is often generated most effectively by cooperating on the nitty-gritty (and sometimes tedious) details of financial management.

Technical or logistical obstacles often interfere with a desire for inclusion. For example, the kinds of financial statements or budget details that funders require may be literally foreign to many local partners, or language and location may make it difficult for direct communication among funders and local organizations to occur. But the more we give in to these obstacles, the more we will reinforce structural sources of inequality and the more dependence we will create. It may not always be feasible for local partners to participate in the initial stages of creating budgets or contracting with funding organizations, but the goal of creating local capacity for financial management and direct fundraising is an important aspect of creating international conflict resolution capacity.

As with transparency, the involvement of local partners in all aspects of financial management can create difficulties; decisions about how to allocate funds, account for funds expended, and deal with funding requests can lead to some difficult exchanges. Partnering organizations may have very different ideas and values about how funds should be allocated or how financial decisions should be made. Money is often the arena in which underlying value differences or divergent conflict resolution philosophies get expressed. And all this is often played out against a background in which local partners are facing extreme personal financial stress. With all the other obstacles to generating effective international programs, conflict resolution practitioners may resist taking on this sticky additional area of collaboration. In the end, however, if local partners are not included in financial management procedures, the genuinely collaborative relationships that are an essential aspect to effective conflict resolution programs will not develop, and the goal of sustainability will suffer.

Mutual Accountability

Accountability is a tricky concept, but one that most funders expect programs to live by. Sometimes financial accountability is a matter of law. Funders are required to institute certain safeguards to make sure their monies are used for their intended purposes and to guard against corruption or misuse of funds. But funders also want to know that their resources are being used effectively and productively.

Many of the procedures around accountability that we might consider simply good financial management practices are actually quite culturally specific. For example, our views about nepotism, hiring and firing practices, whether to operate from an assumption of honesty or dishonesty, whether bribery is an appropriate use of funds, or what constitutes bribery are all very much defined by the societal context in which we live.

Consider a situation in which a funder has agreed to support the purchase of videotaping equipment. A local partner is aware of a very good deal on good equipment from a marginally legal source. To obtain this equipment might require paying what we might call a bribe. Furthermore, there is no chance for obtaining a genuine proof of purchase. Since this may not meet certain accountability requirements, this source of equipment may be unavailable, and the alternative might be much more expensive. Buying the more expensive alternative could easily result in a reduction of money available for staffing or salaries. We have to make these choices all the time, but the standards and criteria we bring to these are very much derivative of our cultural background.

In practice, what this often means is that local partners are forced to adapt to the standards and norms about accountability that are foreign to them but familiar to their international partners. Local partners are therefore buying into a set of procedures that they might not naturally accept or see as appropriate except in order to obtain needed financial resources and technical expertise. This is another source of inequality, and it also is an arena in which considerable manipulation or game playing between partners can occur. To some extent, this is an inevitable dynamic, and it is certainly an old one. The money is, after all, flowing in one direction, and accountability and reporting procedures will develop accordingly. However, this does not mean that it should be simply accepted as a given.

One response to this dilemma is to view accountability as a two-way street and to develop procedures that reflect this. For example, at a certain point, it may be important to change the funding practices so that local organizations are directly funded, but with a line item for hiring international consultants as they deem appropriate. Setting up goals and objectives for the actions of international partners, and perhaps the funders themselves, to be assessed in part by the local partners and the different participants in conflict resolution efforts can also help produce a more mutual approach to accountability. There are other approaches to consider too:

- Creating a joint steering committee of different partners to review budgets, expenditures, and performance

- Hiring an outside evaluator to report to all elements of the project on an ongoing basis

- Having a regular review not just of programmatic performance but of funding processes

- Bringing funders together directly with local partners and clients

- Reevaluating fundamental program goals on a regular basis in accordance with the experiences of local partners

- Working with funders to diversify their staff to reflect the societies in which they work

- Periodically bringing together different local or regional groups to provide feedback and recommendations to funders and international conflict resolution organizations

If this approach is to mean anything, then funders and international partners have to be genuinely open to the information they are being given by their local associates. This may occasionally mean changing the structure of the funding process itself. For example, it may be more important to fund organizations than programs, to change accountability requirements that are not realistic or practical, or to alter the details required in project proposals to allow for more flexibility in the face of rapidly changing circumstances. Some funders can accommodate these changes; others cannot. This is one reason for the increasing use of intermediary funders and regranting programs. An intermediary group can take a more flexible approach to funding specific projects or organizations while meeting the more demanding accountability needs of the organizations providing funds to them.

Reality

No matter how committed all involved may be to establishing collaborative financial relationships and working across international boundaries in a respectful way, there are certain realities that cannot be avoided. No service is done to anyone by pretending that these realities will go away simply by good intentions or communications—for example:

- Those who provide money have power over those to whom it is provided. Funders may have needs that make no sense to local organizations but must be attended to.

- Local conflict resolution organizations and practitioners may have a desperate need for financial assistance that may trump their commitment to project goals and that can on occasion lead to the misuse of funds.

- It may be impossible to know exactly how money is really being spent.

- Western consultants or staff generally are much more expensive than local staff.

- There is seldom anywhere close to enough money to meet local needs.

- Different values about conflict, leadership, hierarchy, accountability, and standards of performance inevitably affect how financial decisions are made, how money is tracked, and how programs are evaluated.

- Funders change their priorities and experience changes in their financial circumstances that can easily affect the monies they are willing to make available to local programs regardless of the effectiveness of those programs.

- Funders tend to avoid open-ended, long-term commitments, even when that is exactly what is needed.

Sometimes some of these realities may change; usually they do not. Often, the best we can do in the face of these circumstances is to accept them, be honest about them, and decide whether a conflict resolution effort is reasonable or viable given them. In an effort to sell people on a project (funders or local partners), it is often tempting to underestimate or soft-sell these realities, but they are an essential part of the picture, and it is best that they are faced early, honestly, and regularly.

Conclusion

One of the greatest assets that Western conflict resolution organizations offer to international conflict resolution projects is access to financial resources. We tend not to dwell on this because we prefer to be valued for our expertise, experience, and skills. But there are many circumstances in which our role is defined by the resources we bring with us as much as by our skills. There is nothing wrong with this, but we can easily err by not facing the consequences of this fact. If we really want to promote a more collaborative, democratic, and peaceful approach to the resolution of conflict, then we must address the implications of how funding occurs and the challenges this poses to achieving our deepest goals.

This does not mean being naive and turning over money or control to people who are not yet able to manage this in accordance with the standards that our funders must maintain or who are not yet sufficiently experienced or committed to the goals of collaborative approaches to conflict. But it does mean being very aware of how easy it is for Western conflict resolution groups to reproduce in their relationships with local partners some of the worst elements of colonial or imperialistic political relationships. If we attend to the principles of transparency, inclusion, mutual accountability, and reality, we can deal with this challenge in a responsible and effective way.

In the end, the most profound message we may deliver is our deep belief and commitment to a different approach to decision making and conflict resolution as reflected in how we approach our financial and managerial relationships with local partners and clients.

Note

1. CDR Associates and the Berghof Center. *Reaching for Peace*. Flint, Mich.: Mott Foundation, 1999.

· ·

17

Providing Resources for Peace
Money Matters from a Funder's Perspective

John Tirman

Increasingly, the fields and specific activities related to conflict transformation and peacebuilding are seen as legitimate, important contributions for the well-being of our global and local communities. As the understanding of both the need for and capacity to deliver important services has increased, so too has the resource base from foundations, charitable trusts, and benefactors. If you stay with this work for any length of time, sooner or later you will find yourself approaching and working with funders. As practitioners, we too often think about funding proposals and funders themselves as a necessary but peripheral aspect of our work. However, if we take seriously the advice to think systemically, then we must understand that the procurement of funds, accountability to use them appropriately, and relationship with people and agencies that can provide these resources are integral aspects of the overall change process. How does all this look from the eyes of a funder and the funding world? What are their concerns, hopes, and fears?

We asked John Tirman to speak from his years of experience as a grant officer and the director of a major foundation to these issues. John is the program director for Global Security and Cooperation at the Social Science Research Council. For thirteen years, he served as the executive director of the Winston Foundation, which provided significant funding for the fields of conflict resolution and peacebuilding. His most recent book, Making the Money Sing: Private Wealth and Public Power in the Search for Peace (2000), *outlines in much more detail some of the lessons he provides here.*

In this chapter, John suggests that the best way to create healthy processes between the funder and the practitioner is to develop an actual relationship. Accountability is not just about reporting facts and details; it is about engaging each other with the learning about how change processes and the theory of change are being developed. There are probably no words more important in this relationship than transparency *and* regularity.

•   •   •   •   •   •   •

I worked as a donor for twelve years in two foundations funding conflict resolution and peacebuilding work. From my experiences, peacebuilding poses some unique funding challenges, primarily that the context is unpredictable, there is often a sense of great urgency, and the activities must be adaptable to quickly changing circumstances.

Donors are not well equipped to cope with emergencies and unpredictable flux. Among most private foundations in the United States and public funding agencies in the United States and Europe, the typical amount of time to respond gainfully to requests is three to four months at a minimum. This reflects, not surprisingly, the sizable load of requests, the internal procedures of review, habits of planning, and the like. So for the practitioner who needs to secure resources quickly for an unanticipated set of events, the best advice is perhaps the most obvious: think and plan well ahead for unknown exigencies.

This imperative for financial planning can be pursued in four ways: accumulating an emergencies fund, building ample contingency fund planning into project budgets, cultivating wealthy individuals as donors, and nurturing relationships with all donors that foster trust and confidence and thereby permit unusual requests. These are not easy tasks, to be sure, but they are worthwhile for other reasons as well. The cultivation of individual contributors, for example, is useful because they tend to be less fickle over time than institutional donors. In all such strategies for fundraising, however, one must be mindful of the perspective of the donors, a factor often overlooked in an urgent situation.

Relationship Building with Donors

One concern of donors centers on the familiar image of chasing fire engines. One could see this vividly just after the Dayton peace agreement in 1995, when large numbers of nongovernmental organizations (NGOs) announced their intention to get involved in Bosnia. The opportunity for postconflict peacemaking seemed very ripe indeed: the international community was committing $5 billion for reconstruction, the warring parties were deeply embittered, communities were traumatized and divided, hundreds of thousands of Bosnians were displaced, and other parts of the former Yugoslavia were at risk. I informally surveyed the foundations with international security programs in the United States and found that despite the significance of the challenges in Bosnia, scarcely any were interested in funding the postconflict tasks. Nearly the identical response befell the aftermath of the Kosovo crisis in 1999. Donors not already committed to working in the Balkans were not persuaded that they should suddenly invest there.

Part of this reluctance stems from sound principles: donors want to see a theory of social change at work, as well as a sustained dedication to a particular region or set of problems. In that context, much of what was proposed for the former Yugoslavia did not pass muster. Projects without roots, profound local involvement, or a convincing analysis of how particular activities fit particular circumstances looked flimsy and perishable.

It was not enough, for example, to assert abstractly that Bosnian Muslims and Croats in a bitterly divided city like Mostar should start dialogues and thereby resolve their differences; a long history of trauma, inequality, and discrimination had to be addressed first, as well as citizens' legitimate fears about their safety and indeed the integrity of the reconstruction process itself. Without detailed knowledge of the local conditions, the history, the economics and sociology of the antagonists, and the language, and without a long period of trust building, mechanisms such as dialogues stood little chance of even convening much less accomplishing anything. Yet many conflict-resolution NGOs believed that processes that might have worked elsewhere could be transferred, like so many auto parts, or, as one person told me, "Bosnia needs a heart transplant, and we are the surgeons." In the face of this naiveté, this basic lack of knowledge, it was not surprising that many funders balked.

The same standards hold for conflicts that don't earn headlines or bombs from the North Atlantic Treaty Organization. Does the organization proposing an intervention have a comprehensive understanding of the region? Does it have experience and a diverse circle of collaborators in the area? Has it been invited in, and if so, by whom and for what purposes? Are the methods the organization has used in the past applicable to this new situation? Is it sensitive to the cultural and social dynamics, as well as political conditions? These are the kinds of questions that will guide most donors' considerations of a request for funding. They impart a fundamental interest not just in skill or technique, but also in familiarity and knowledge. Changes in the on-the-ground situation—sometimes catastrophic changes—are less likely to be troubling to donors if they feel that the organization's original mission has sufficient rigor and flexibility built in. Difficulties are much easier to cope with when intervenors are knowledgeable, experienced, and connected.

A second set of evaluative tools a donor will use centers on the quality of the performance of a grantee. The results of conflict-prevention work are notoriously difficult to assess. Even when a situation worsens, the organization may be doing very useful work, and even when a situation improves, the performance of the organization may have nothing to do with the outcome. Unlike many foundation-supported activities in education, advocacy, and institution building, conflict prevention cannot be judged solely by events or intended consequences. Most donors who take the risk of funding such activities will understand that, but the grantee has to work with the donor to establish guidelines for evaluation.

If, for example, the politicians in a particular country beset by civil war are isolated, stagnant, and unable to see new ways to use their authority to end the war agreeably, then an organization might take delegations of legislators to other places where similar problems were addressed, giving the political leaders new ideas, tools, and hope. The situation may nonetheless deteriorate, but the organization should still be able to articulate why this was important (here, good analysis and a theory of change are essential) and prove how useful the trip was for the politicians. Performance can be assessed independent of larger events. Capacity building, forging new channels of communication, linking to the international community, strengthening civil society, and creating independent media: these sorts of activities can be regarded discretely. If they track well with a donor's sense of what works, then an organization's performance is appreciable even in confusing and rapidly changing circumstances.

Like the concerns about fire engine chasing, performance is a bedrock canon of making grants. The donor must have confidence in the organization, and this is earned through performance. And just as one must show a sustained commitment to a region and a profound depth of understanding about a particular conflict, one must also be able to demonstrate competence. For each of these requirements, the NGO seeking support must work assiduously over months or years with the donor. There is simply no substitute for familiarity. Ideally, the relationship should include extensive conversations of strategy, theories of change, and knowledge of particular situations.

Discussions should be two ways, enabling the donor to impart some wisdom and gain some ownership of the project. It should include visits by the donor to see the work of the NGO and visits by field staff, board members, and others apart from the executive director to the donor. Particularly insightful internal memos, testimonials, and other occasional missives should be sent along. Transparency is a must; practitioners should obviously take care to shield sensitive documents or conversations with people at risk in the region of conflict, but donors must have as extensive access as possible to these details and will observe the vow of *omertá* (confidentiality) that guides all private foundation business. (Public agencies are less reliable in this respect.) The measure of transparency will conform to the general comfort level that has been established.

The point is simple but somehow rarely fulfilled: build as close a professional relationship with the donor as possible. Neither superior nor obsequious be; treat him or her as an equal in every respect.

In short, what donors want are past performance, proven skills and knowledge, a tested strategy for change, and transparency.

This relationship building, based on these qualities, is sound fundraising advice regardless of the grant seeker's endeavor. But it is particularly fitting to the problem of mounting resources quickly in emergencies.

Engaging in Sound Financial Planning

Let us return to the four suggestions for financial planning mentioned at the beginning of the chapter. When the telephone rings, the problem of money should be at least partially solved by having employed one or more of these fundraising strategies. The best of these is the accumulation of money precisely for the unexpected. As every nonprofit manager knows, this is far easier said than done: core funding, with no strings attached, is the hardest to come by. Most donors want to pay for projects only, as if the costs of the organization's infrastructure—office, accountants, fundraisers—were free. Projects are exciting and productive; overhead is not. This fallacy afflicts almost all donors, including some of the most knowledgeable. One way to address this ingrained habit of favoring project over core support is to create a reserve fund category and convince donors that this mechanism is integral to your organization's performance: a reserve fund is the incubator in which new ideas can be hatched.

Project money alone does not enrich that common space where staff can think anew about the organization's mission. Indeed, such a fund should be designed to support several different kinds of endeavors: learning, reflection, imagining, and skills building as communal activity. It can be called a venture capital fund or some such moniker that signals its expectation of a long-term payoff, and it can be part of a larger fundraising effort to provide stability and a more permanent platform for operations (such as purchasing a building). However it's pitched, a fund that equals about 10 percent of the annual budget (and is distinct from a reserve fund for more basic cash flow needs) should provide for the occasional imperative to act quickly on behalf of a new situation for which there is no project support.

The emergency fund, or venture fund, is the most direct means to the financial independence needed to act swiftly. Two similar devices are worth mentioning. One is to build contingency into virtually all budgets, and to do so amply, adding 10 percent or so to project budgets in addition to seeking standard overhead costs. Explanations would, of course, parallel those one would make for a discrete fund. Building contingency into an operating budget is a perfectly legitimate fiscal tool. It may in fact be easier to raise money this way than to appeal for a separate allocation for a venture fund, but not every donor will go for it.

The second fundraising device is to cultivate individuals of wealth who are interested in the issues you address. This kind of fundraising is grueling, taking years to build a donor base of any significance. But once achieved, such a list is relatively easy to keep active, and the donors provide loyalty and flexibility that institutional funders rarely exhibit. Individuals can be approached quickly for an emergency allocation, they are more readily persuaded by that sense of urgency, and they often like personal involvement. Taking them on a fact-finding mission, for example, is a way to draw them into the organization's work. Often, these people have skills that can be helpfully discharged as well. Put them on your board of directors, and make them an integral part of that level of responsibility and action: boards tend to be inert objects unless the executive staff provides momentum, but even then a board needs a spark plug to come alive, and wealthy individuals typically provide that sort of energy because they want to join to do something useful. As they become more involved, they will prize the utility of the venture fund. They will also be effective advocates (as other board members should be, too) with foundation officers in raising contingency funds. If board members are contributing to the venture fund, then institutional donors will be more amenable too, not only because the first dollars are the hardest to raise but because of the commitment those contributions demonstrate.

Having that fund established and in the bank is preferable to raising it on short notice. As organizations mature and prove their usefulness, donors will be more likely to see the logic of such a venture fund, although educating donors on the necessity of providing core support is a lifelong endeavor. Here again, the relationship with the donor is vital. Bankrolling a venture fund is an act of confidence and trust. Whether the request is presented as part of a long-term plan or as an emergency, the relationship already established is invaluable.

If money is needed for an immediate undertaking, then the case for making the grant must be presented with clarity and depth. It is not enough to say a situation is pressing, people are dying, or refugees are fleeing. However heartrending, such pleas rarely hold sway with institutional donors. Instead, the appeal must be made on the basis of the other qualities donors typically admire: that you are knowledgeable, that your plan of action (even if only fact finding in the beginning) matches the needs of the situation and your organization's proven capability, that the situation itself seems appropriate for the kinds of interventions at which you excel, and that there is substantive and legitimate local partnership.

These requirements imply an ability to mount a case quickly and convincingly, and that turns on some rather basic leadership skills. Can you articulate how your organization works? Can you mobilize talent quickly? Can you discriminate among different conflicts and how that affects needs on the ground? Do you know enough to make a sound judgment about a new situation or have mechanisms in place for acquiring and synthesizing reliable, in-depth knowledge?

Conclusion

Creating the kind of organization that can be mobilized swiftly to respond to emergencies in troubled, faraway places is a multi-dimensional challenge. Mounting financial resources is just one piece of that, however indispensable, and should be understood as a mechanism dependent on other performance-driven qualities: well-trained staff with diverse skills, a knowledge base refreshed by experience and new learning, and articulated and tested theories of action. With these fundamentals in place, the arduous chores of cultivating donors will be more successful, less onerous, and suitably poised to respond to the most urgent and unexpected events.

18

To Whom Am I Accountable?

Howard Zehr and Clement M. Aapengnuo

Once there is initial contact and a request has been made, a relationship develops with a range of people, organizations, and networks. Thinking systemically about your entry requires you to recognize these connections and relationships at local, national, and international levels. As you negotiate entry and subsequently the delivery of work, consider to whom you are responsible and accountable. Is it exclusively the people who have asked you to come? Is it those who might be affected by your work or recipients of the efforts? Or is accountability to whomever is paying for your services? How you develop your sense of accountability will have everything to do with whom you include, seek advice from, and ultimately make decisions about the direction of your work and even when it is appropriate to say yes or, more important, choose not to do something. How in a complex international setting do you think about creating a structure for being accountable?

We posed these dilemmas to Howard Zehr and Clement Aapengnuo. Howard, a professional photographer and dedicated activist in criminal justice, is widely known as the leader in the conceptual and practical development of the restorative justice movement in North America, now extended to initiatives all over the globe. Currently teaching at the Conflict Transformation Program at Eastern Mennonite University, he has traveled extensively and worked with the initiation and support of restorative justice programs in more than a dozen countries. His book Changing Lenses (1995) has marked the development of a whole new field of work in justice and peacebuilding. Clement works as the coordinator of the Northern Ghana Peace Project, a joint project of the Catholic Diocese of Damongo and Catholic Relief Services.

Howard and Clement suggest that accountability is a foundational concept because it takes us to the heart of recognizing that our actions have intended and unintended consequences and that we are responsible for thinking about and through what those may be and how they affect people. They propose that this requires a reference framework of people that is clear, regular, and connected particularly to the communities that will be directly affected by our action. Their suggestions may significantly affect how you think about responsibilities and about whom you seek counsel from and to whom you report.

. . . .

When we are called into a situation, a community, a particular project, to whom are we ultimately responsible? To those who invited us in? To those who are funding the project? To the people affected? In short, to whom are we accountable, and what does this accountability entail? In this chapter, each of us offers some reflections, and then we make some joint suggestions.

Why Accountability Is Important (Howard)

Accountability has become a big issue for me, in part because it is a major issue in my field. Although I teach in and operate from a graduate Conflict Transformation Program, the focus of my work is in restorative justice, and in that field, accountability is a foundational concept. Accountability in restorative justice involves encouraging people—offenders, but others as well—to be aware of the impact of their actions on other people. It also emphasizes that actions affecting others often generate obligations and responsibilities. In restorative justice, the primary obligation falls on the shoulders of one who does wrong, but attention must also be given to obligations that community members might have toward offenders, victims, or one another. Both the theory and practice of restorative justice, then, have made me acutely aware of the importance of accountability. I have learned that I need to be aware of and take responsibility for the impact of my actions, intended as well as unintended.

The literature of criminal justice reform has convinced me that all social interventions, however well conceived and intended, have unintended consequences (Zehr, 1995). This will be true for relatively new fields like restorative justice and conflict transformation just as it was when mediation or prisons were introduced. It is true for our individual interventions; we may achieve what we intended, but there may also be results—obvious or latent and hidden—that were not intended. As the restorative justice movement has developed, some of these unintended consequences have begun to surface, reminding me again of my responsibility to be aware of the effects of my actions. In fact, it suggests that I have a responsibility to look for and take account of those unintended consequences, not just wait passively in case they happen to surface.

In addition to restorative justice, I teach and work within the field of qualitative research, and in this field, too, accountability has been an increasingly important theme. Race and gender studies as well as feminist critical theory have radically changed the relationship between researcher and subject (Denzin and Lincoln, 2000; Kvale, 1996). Qualitative research emphasizes that our subjects are no longer raw material to be exploited but research partners to whom we have obligations and commitments. Postmodernism has accentuated that relationship by helping us to understand that the knowledge that emerges from such research is constructed in context during the interaction, with both researcher and subject playing a part. Since knowledge emerges from interaction, the biographies (including gender, race, and culture) of both subject and researcher play a role. By emphasizing obligations to subjects, then, my research work again highlights the importance of accountability.

A more personal dimension to my concern about accountability arises from my religious background. I come from the Anabaptist community, a religious tradition that developed during the Protestant Reformation around the idea of the church as a priesthood or community of believers. In my tradition, this has meant that we look to the community to help us discern direction rather than operating purely individually. It has also implied that when we are in positions to affect others, we ought to have others looking over our shoulders. These practices have been somewhat eroded over the years, but they have been central enough to my religious tradition that the idea of accountability has been deeply embedded in me.

Based on experiences and perspectives such as these, I offer the following observations or assumptions that call for attention to accountability:

- When we intervene, we have an obligation to be as conscious as possible about the impact of our actions and to take appropriate responsibility for the consequences. This includes unintended as well as intended results.

- As an outsider, there will be definite limits on how comprehensively we can understand the situation we are in without the help of insiders.

- Regardless of our intentions and of how consciously we work to overcome them, our actions will be guided in part by who we are, and this includes predilections and biases that come from our gender, culture, and personal histories.

- When we are in positions of influence, all of us need others looking over our shoulders, providing not only support but also discernment and critical feedback.

All of these observations suggest that we need to be deliberate about addressing issues and structures of accountability when deciding to be involved.

What Does Accountability Entail? (Clement)

As a project coordinator of a peace initiative in northern Ghana, I often ask myself, "To whom am I responsible? To whom is the project responsible?" Put in broader terms, when you are called on to do peace work, intervening as an individual, organization, or government in a conflict situation or developing a peace education program or process, to whom are you accountable? The donors? The executing organization? The academic, cultural, religious culture, or philosophy of the sponsoring organization or funder? The people, the beneficiaries of the intervention?

And what is the measure of success? When can you say you have achieved your aim or goal, whatever that goal may be, and how will you measure it? The achievement of the goal is often seen as a mark of the success of the intervention, but is the goal a meaningful one? Training two hundred peace activists may be quantifiable and verifiable, but it does not necessarily mean peace is achieved. So what are appropriate goals, and who determines the goals and criteria for success? In short, to whom am I accountable, and what does this accountability entail?

The plethora of peacebuilding activities in the world in general and in Africa in particular raises many questions of accountability. Most of these activities and programs have their origins in relief and development organizations and are funded by them. These organizations are waking up to the reality that one cannot do relief and development work without peacebuilding. Many have fully integrated peacebuilding activities in their programming, while others treat peacebuilding as an appendage to their programs. Either way, they are funding peacebuilding programs within the development and relief framework, and in this framework, development projects are physical, visible, and quantifiable. Consequently, they speak of achievable and measurable goals and timetables, often using a project period that is three to five years with renewable cycles. Peacebuilding becomes a project and not a process.

In such an environment, there are multiple accountabilities: the donor, organizational structures, local partners, and, we hope, the people being served. Accountability to the people should be for the purpose, direction, and outcome of the intervention. The intervenor is a catalyst and not an expert who has all the answers. Priorities and perspectives of the people should inform the decisions made at all levels. They must participate in program-level planning. They must develop their own indicators of progress and be involved in monitoring, reviewing, and evaluating what progress has been made with programs. The insights, priorities, and other learning gained through these process become a basic part in planning, making decisions, and reporting at all levels.

This accountability to the people is not just a buzzword when it comes to peacebuilding, because the people for whom the intervention was made have to live with the consequences of that intervention. They must therefore be involved in deciding how things should go. They are indeed the stakeholders, and it is to them that we are accountable. This holds us accountable to them for the quality of the intervention. In fact, a key measure of success lies in the ability of the intervention to engage the people concerned: to involve them in such a way that they themselves initiate a process they can own, that will help them solve their problems, and that will ensure that subsequent problems and conflicts are dealt with without having recourse to an external intervention. Ironically, the success of the peace work is in working oneself out of business.

Accountability must first and foremost be to the people in the conflict. Has this intervention in any way helped them resolve their problems? Has it in any way helped the community put in place a system or process that will ensure sustainability? Can the parties claim ownership of the process? How involved have they been in the whole process? How much creativity has been allowed?

Any external intervention in a conflict situation, if it is to succeed, must work at empowering the parties in the conflict to work together to find a lasting solution. Any ready-made and well-packaged intervention by specialists from outside is unlikely to be helpful. Yet the parties in a conflict are often so engrossed in the conflict that they are unable to come up with viable options for solving their problems. However, given time, space, and resources, the people in the conflict themselves can find lasting solutions to their conflict. In the local language in Ghana, Dagari, we call this process "allowing the monkey to bathe its child." It means that the process may be very time-consuming and unpredictable, but the outcome will be the best as far as a sustainable peace is concerned.

Unfortunately, these communities do not have the financial resources to initiate and see the process through. In most cases, they are in the conflict precisely because of limited resources. Accountability to organizations and donors includes ensuring that the funds made available for the intervention are appropriately used. Government, religious, and organizational policy, procedures, and goals should not be the parameters used for accountability in such interventions.

In terms of monitoring, process indicators are more important than outcome and impact indicators. Here again, the communities to which the intervenor goes should determine the process, outcome, and impact indicators for themselves. This requires that the community be part of the planning process, determining what they need and how they want to measure their achievements. The intervention them becomes a response to their need, and only they can determine if that need has been met by the intervenor's activities and donor funding.

Key Questions for Intervenors

These observations suggest the following key questions that an intervenor should consider:

- To whom will you be accountable in this project? The inviting person or organization? Funding sources? Your peers in the academic or practice community? The people you are serving?

- Will you have multiple accountabilities? If so, what is the priority of accountabilities? Do any of these accountabilities potentially conflict with one another? How will you handle these conflicts?

- How is success to be measured? Who has determined these measures?

- What lines or structures of accountability already exist for this project? Which may need to be established for this particular project?

The bottom line is this:

- How can you maximize your accountability to the people you are serving?

- How can you make your accountabilities as clear and transparent as possible?

- How can you contribute toward a solution that is sustainable and owned by the community?

Some Suggestions for Practice

Following are some suggestions for putting these principles and concerns into practice:

- Establish written criteria and priorities and a set
  of questions that will guide your decisions when you
  are called on to intervene. I (Howard) have such
  a set posted over my telephone and consult it each
  time an invitation or opportunity arises. These change
  over time as my own priorities change. For me, they
  include questions like these: Do those being called
  on to present or intervene include women and people
  of color? Are crime victim groups involved? (The
  second question is an effort to be accountable to an
  important group of stakeholders often neglected in
  the field of justice.)

- In each situation, think consciously, and discuss
  with the parties involved your lines of accountability and potential conflicts of interest and
  accountability.

- Work with the parties toward clarity of goals and
  measurements. Why are you being invited in?
  What are the goals? How will success be measured?
  Who has determined these measures?

- Make sure you have a circle of accountability and
  support for this work within your own community.
  These can be quite informal, but we should try to
  make this as conscious and deliberate as possible so
  that these people know the expectations and feel free
  to serve in this way.

- Find ways to make yourself accountable to the population you are serving, even if is not always practical to
  do so to the actual people involved. Ways of doing this
  include establishing feedback groups and identifying
  mentors from the community or a reference group
  representing the community.

As an example from my own (Howard's) experience, in recent years I have completed several documentary projects resulting in books. These have used interviews and photographic portraits in an attempt to bring to awareness the realities of two often-neglected groups: life-sentenced prisoners and victims of severe criminal violence. I have tried to maximize my accountability to these groups while at the same time maintaining an appropriate degree of independence. To do this, I had reference groups from each population who looked over my shoulder by giving advice and reading manuscripts; these were people who worked in the field or had similar experiences but were not included in the project. In addition, in the latest project, I invited my subjects to give feedback on the edited text to make sure they were correctly represented.

Here are some more general suggestions that we have found to be important:

- Work consciously to create an environment in which feedback, both positive and negative, is solicited and safe. Ask people to tell you when you make mistakes. Try to monitor yourself, looking for signs of defensiveness, and ask your feedback group to look for such signs as well.

- Be as transparent as possible about your motives and the things you do.

- In addition to your accountability structures, seek out what the literature of research often calls encultured informants: people who are in the community or intimately acquainted with the community who can serve as guides and provide additional feedback.

- In these situations, expect to be tested, so carry through on your promises and maintain confidences.

- As much as possible, try to be one with them (for example, in lifestyle) while in the community. This doesn't mean you should try to be something you are not, but at least don't seek special privileges and don't stay in the fanciest accommodations.

- Don't take yourself too seriously. I (Howard) remind myself that what I can do is always quite limited, and the world wouldn't be much different if I weren't here. I take seriously naturalist and activist Edward Abbey's call to be a half-hearted fanatic.

To take accountability seriously may sound somewhat frightening and burdensome and does add a layer of complexity. It is well worth the cost. You are more likely to do work that is meaningful and helpful to the people involved, and your own satisfaction and learning will probably be greater as well.

· ·

Is This the Right Thing to Do?

A Practical Framework for Ethical Decisions

Wallace Warfield

From a first point of contact until the completion of work, peacebuilding will pose a series of complex decisions, many requiring a quick and urgent response. How will you make those decisions when, at the spur of the moment, you may be required to decide on something that can affect the direction and quality of work and relationships? Is it possible to develop a frame of reference for making ethical decisions that is responsive to complexities of issues in volatile conflict settings, yet adaptive to the dynamic pace that much of peacebuilding requires?

We asked Wallace Warfield to think through his experiences and approach to these questions. Wallace teaches skills and theory at the Institute for Conflict Analysis and Resolution at George Mason University and has worked as a practitioner in community and international conflict for more than three decades. His early work came in the context of race and community conflicts with the Community Relations Service in the United States. Two of his more recent articles are "The Potential for Local Zones of Peace in Moving from Civil War to Civil Society" (1997) and "Reconnecting Systems Maintenance with Social Justice: A Critical Role for Conflict Resolution" (2000).

In an interesting paradox of different but related ideas, Wallace suggests that you must be explicit in creating a frame of reference for ethical decisions and pay careful attention to your intuitions. In fact, make sure your ethical framework gives you permission to stop and listen to the tug of your doubts and check them out before going onto decisions. As he

*illustrates with an example from his own experience, even a few minutes
of reflection can make a big difference in the life of good decisions and
appropriate process.*

·   ·   ·   ·   ·   ·   ·

A ll forms of conflict resolution, whether in the guise of training
or a more direct form of intervention, present dilemmas for
the practitioner at one time or another. The dilemma could be as
straightforward and unadorned as when one party to a conflict does
not show up for a mediation session or as impenetrable as two
groups unable to free themselves from deeply embedded identities.
Ethical dilemmas present a special problem because they deal with
principles and values that defy simple solutions and remain ambiguous in an evolving field lacking well-defined boundaries.

In this chapter, I define ethics and what constitutes an ethical
dilemma, suggest a sample of ethical dilemmas that confront the
individual conducting international peacebuilding, and, then, drawing from my own experience and those of colleagues who have done
this work for a number of years, propose guidelines in the form of
model building that practitioners new to this part of the field will
find useful.[1]

Defining Ethics and Ethical Dilemmas

In any professional endeavor where individuals are engaged in a
practice that has the potential to harm others, a concern about
ethics exists. In a very general sense, ethics can be considered a set
of guiding moral principles that define the rightness or wrongs of a
course of action. However, for this discussion, what is needed is
a definition that speaks to the circumstances surrounding a form of
professional practice. With this in mind, we can think of an ethical dilemma as a situation in which the practitioner is faced with a
doubt about how to act in relation to personal and professional values, norms, and obligations.

In the field of conflict resolution, various attempts have been made to define ethical parameters for a diverse field of practice. Following membership approval of ethical standards of responsibility for third-party practitioners in 1986, the Society for Professionals in Dispute Resolution later published a document that by using an array of exercises, sought to establish ethical parameters for the practitioner.[2] Here, the emphasis was on impartiality (maintaining a nonbiased stance with all parties to the conflict) and confidentiality (upholding the private nature of mediated discussions).

In another discussion, researchers asked to what extent it was ethical for a mediator to superimpose her or his sense of outcomes on what the parties desire in settlement.[3] For example, in a conflict contextualized by a history of disempowerment for one or more of the parties, but where the presenting issues are framed in terms of monetary settlements, should the mediator push for a social justice outcome?

An ethical dilemma that emerges in the conduct of a peacebuilding intervention is a conflict within a conflict. There is the conflict setting the practitioner seeks to intervene in, presumably involving opposing parties. This is conflict of an intergroup nature. However, an ethical dilemma is also a form of conflict because the practitioner may find that her or his contemplated actions are incompatible with criteria and standards established by the profession. And as noted above briefly, any field (in this case, the field of conflict analysis and resolution) attempts to establish ethical parameters that guide practitioners. The dilemma is created when a practitioner is about to engage in an activity that in some intuitive way he or she feels is right for the situation and is aligned with personal ethics, but contravenes one or more of the field's ethical standards. Or perhaps a practitioner's values and the more abstract values canonized by the profession are in alignment, but the activity the practitioner happens to be engaged in is divergent. In this sense, an ethical dilemma is very much an intrapersonal conflict. When an ethical dilemma of this sort is imposed on the subject matter conflict, it can become the dominant concern.

Any number of factors acting in combination creates the potential for an ethical dilemma in international peacebuilding. Rather than attempt to create an exhaustive typology of these issues, I offer a few as illustrative examples. The point, after all, is to set the stage for a prescriptive model that can be used in a wide variety of circumstances.

Culture

Conducting peacebuilding in an international setting lends an added dimension to ethical dilemmas because it introduces factors that have a different significance from interventions that take place on the home turf of the practitioner. For example, more than likely, the initiative will be taking place in a locale with culture groups unfamiliar to the practitioner. Ethical perspectives are social constructions that vary across cultures. A certain behavior occurring in a conflict situation may seem inappropriate, even disturbing, to a practitioner. That same behavior or situation may be seen as quite appropriate and justifiable to individuals or groups who come from a different culture.

Exposing Users to Greater Risks

International peacebuilding, whether in the form of training, problem-solving workshops, or some other intervention, often takes place in settings marked by significant power imbalances. Conflict resolution in the most celebrated democracy can be viewed as a threat to the regime. Threat escalation increases in states where the political culture is less than fully democratic. In these systems, the dominant regime may see itself as the mediating influence between competing groups within civil society. In this sense, the regime acts as a broker between such groups, rewarding, punishing, but ultimately controlling an exchange process between itself and these groups to serve its own political interests. An external intervention that affects this arrangement can be viewed as a threat to the regime. Should a practitioner who is aware of this do the intervention anyway? What if the intervention exposes the users to physical risk? Are ethical concerns satisfied as long as the practitioner knows the user accepts the risk?

Conflict Intervention Under the Guise of Training

Much international peacebuilding takes place in the form of training nationals in various aspects of conflict analysis and resolution. In this field, training has become increasingly popular and taken on a dimension unto itself. Trainers may have some sense that users are facing a conflictual situation; however, the mechanistic nature of a lot of conflict resolution training has a tendency to make conflict abstract, divesting it of personal meaning. In many international scenarios, conflict is not an abstract; it is an all-too-tangible reality. In these settings, there is no bright line between training and a more direct form of intervention, particularly in an ongoing conflict situation. Is it ethical for external practitioners to portray themselves in one guise when in fact they are operating in another?

An illustration to highlight the last two points might be useful here. Several years ago, I was a member of a team of conflict resolution specialists who traveled to Moscow to conduct a series of training workshops with Russian scientists, academics, and environmentalists on methods of responding to environmental conflict. None of us was Russian speaking, so virtually all interactions were handled through translation. One day, after the formal training sessions were over, a Russian participant asked us if we would like to visit a site in a community where the government was planning to construct a new power plant that would supplant a smaller and older one. The government's rationale for building the plant was that additional power capacity was necessary to handle the energy needs of a growing immigrant workforce. Residents of a community on the outskirts of Moscow were protesting the construction on the grounds that the older plant was more than adequate to produce the needed energy. A larger plant would increase the risk of pollution, and there were no plans for necessary safeguards.

We all hopped into a car thinking we were about to embark on an interesting but harmless field visit. Instead, we were driven to a home in the suburbs of Moscow where waiting for us were a half-dozen local activists, including a local political representative. We found ourselves drawn into a discussion about strategic options in the guise of interest-based negotiations. In reality, we were four foreigners on an intervention team who were engaging in a form of advocacy for one side in a conflict and, at worst, pursuing our own agenda—in a country not fully withdrawn from its cold war discourse and possibly leaving community representatives to deal with negative externalities.

In an attempt to extract ourselves from this uncomfortable situation, we indicated that we really wanted to see the plant before returning to Moscow. "But of course," our hosts replied. "In fact, we'll join you." We hapless American trainers and our entourage then descended on not just the plant but the plant manager as well. Once we were there, the local residents confronted the plant manager with their protest, not too subtly indicating they had American experts to back them up. We were now thinking we were one telephone call away from jail and probable expulsion from the country. Somehow, we managed to extract ourselves from this ever-thickening ethical dilemma and amid a flurry of anemic excuses fled back to Moscow, looking over our shoulder all the way.

A Model for Responding to Ethical Dilemmas

As unsettling as ethical dilemmas can be when conducting international peacebuilding, the distress can be significantly reduced through a form of reflective practice called model building. Model building is the process of constructing frames of reference that will allow the practitioner to develop multiple rationales for what is occurring or what could occur. The process encourages the practitioner to move from an overreliance on short-term contingent observations to a deeper understanding of anticipated or unfolding events.

As suggested by the examples, some ethical dilemmas are generic to the nature of the work and therefore have the capability to be anticipated and planned for. Many others however, occur without much advanced warning. Consequently, building a model for ethical responses requires a two-track approach: deductive and reactive. The model envisions the practitioner's responding to an ethical dilemma in four stages: pause, reflect, share, and determine options and select.

Stage 1: Pause

Whether you are in the planning stages of an intervention or in the midst of it, pay attention to the inner tug of discomfort. Pause before plunging into the next set of activities. Take a time-out by calling for a break in the activity or simply shutting down your own participation momentarily and ask yourself what you are feeling. You may have identified an ethical dilemma. Obviously, it is easier to pause on the planning or preintervention end than it is when one is in the midst of a situation, but there are ways of accomplishing this on the ground as well.

Stage 2: Reflect

This is more than a detached factual observation of a series of unfolding events; rather, it is a form of reflection that is intended to give meaning to an act or pattern of activity being observed. Here, the practitioner is trying to determine how the activity has meaning for his or her sense of ethics. Reflect on how your personal and professional values may have changed since the last time you examined them. Most of us spend more time honing our applied skills than we do thinking about our ethics. Yet as conflict resolution and peacebuilding venture into more complex social dynamics, new ethical concepts will continue to arise to challenge preconceived beliefs. For example, the arming of rebel groups in civil war zones to ensure the delivery of aid to entrapped civilian populations was not on the ethical landscape as recently as the mid-1990s.

Stage 3: Share

You have paused and reflected, and think you have identified an ethical dilemma. Should you just sit on it? No. The longer the delay is, the more entrenched or complicated the dilemma becomes. Events gather momentum; new dimensions in the form of additional characters with accompanying agendas come into play; the legitimacy of the practitioner's platform begins to deteriorate; and eventually, the practitioner is pulled further and further away from the intentional plan with the risk that it will be ultimately abandoned.

Whether it is taking place in the relative luxury of the planning stage or on the ground, sharing is perhaps the most difficult part of the model-building process. Sharing means a process of externalization and assessment with more than one pair of eyes.

More than likely, you will be conducting the intervention as part of a team. We know that teams are forms of small group relationships where individuals bring claiming and maximizing values to an endeavor. That is, individuals working in groups are torn between competing with others in pursuit of self-actualizing objectives and collaborating for the benefit of the group.[4] If you are the junior member of a peacebuilding team, for example, your instinct for self-preservation may instruct you to sit on it, rationalizing that you will raise it at a more convenient time, or the situation will simply go away. But share you must.

The ethical concern is the higher value, and you owe it to yourself and your colleagues to put it on the table. Besides, others may have a similar concern and for one reason or another are hesitant to raise it. If the dilemma arises in the midst of an intervention, as awkward and unprofessional as it may seem to pause, reflect, and share, it doesn't begin to compare to how one feels when an ethical dilemma is left unattended and the situation inexorably deteriorates around you.

Stage 4: Determine Options and Select

Model building is designed to strengthen the application of best practice. As with any other good construction, the purpose of each stage is to set a platform for the stage to follow. Obviously, it is possible to encounter an ethical dilemma and plunge directly into a response. However, if the practitioner is on the ground, this is likely to magnify the dilemma rather than resolve it. Most ethical dilemmas that emerge in international peacebuilding are seldom clearly delineated, and except in the most blatant scenarios, most of us are not instantaneously in touch with our ethical schema. Pausing, reflecting, and sharing allow practitioners to get in touch with their core values, which are often obscured behind the ego of applied skills.

At stage 4, the practitioner is trying to determine what choices are available to prevent the situation from deteriorating further. The first three stages have enabled you to name the ethical dilemma. Choice is informed by three factors: (1) how strongly you hold the personal value at stake, (2) how sharply it diverges from the value held by the general profession, and (3) your knowledge of what others have done in similar situations. Your selection will be determined by how you scale the indexes of each factor and weigh them against each other. For example, if you hold a particular ethical value highly, as does the profession, and as far as you know, very few practitioners have departed from the norm, the selection of choice response will be relatively easy. On the other hand, if your personal value diverges significantly from the profession's and (as far as you know) practitioners adhere to the professional ethic, then your selection of a response is going to more difficult.

How might this apply to the Moscow scenario? From the perspective of my personal value, while I recognize that the concept of neutrality has application in a range of conflict settings, I hold a higher value that the best negotiations are conducted between adversaries who have interdependent symmetries of power and opportunities to change conditions. From the vantage point of professional values, the practitioner team not only lacked neutrality; we were involved in an undeclared form of practice, engaging in advocacy consultation with one side in a conflict—a form of practice generally frowned on except in the most contingent of situations. This was a departure from our stated purpose for being in the country, which was to conduct training with a broad group of individuals focusing on no particular conflict.

At this point, one might be persuaded by the inconsistencies of practice known to take place around this particular ethic to go with a narrow assessment of the personal value over the professional. However, our intervention activated a higher ethical value that resonates with all three choice factors, and that is to do no harm. As external actors, we put the township residents at increased risk of possible retaliation by the reigning political powers. They may in fact have been cognizant of the risk, but that did not remove our responsibility for acknowledging this sooner than we did.

It seems there were at least three points where model building could have mitigated the ethical dilemma. When first informed of the opportunity to go on site, we could have paused by assessing the suggestion more carefully and pushing the interpreter for more detail. Second, finding ourselves at the residence and meeting with the protest group, what would have been the harm (absent some minor embarrassment) in the practitioner team's asking to be excused to meet privately, allowing us the opportunity to discuss our concern and then in the spirit of transparency raise the concern with our hosts? Finally, in the same spirit of transparency, we could have avoided compounding the felony by demurring the field trip once we realized what it was going to entail.

Conclusion

The difficulty in writing about ethics in professional practice is providing prescriptive guidelines that do not come across as neat, rational actor formulas best applied in game theory rather than in the chaotic reality of an intervention. Yet to rely on the intuitive seat of one's pants or divine intervention is not a preferable alternative. Model building will not guarantee that the international peace-builder will invariably arrive at the right ethical decision. Ultimately, whatever the response, it will reflect the subjective judgment of the practitioner. Model building applies a disciplined cognitive approach that can mitigate the worst outcomes of an ethical dilemma.

Notes

1. For an interesting example of this, see Lave, C., and March, J. *An Introduction to Models in the Social Sciences*. New York: HarperCollins, 1979.

2. In 2000, the Society for Professionals in Dispute Resolution merged with two other prominent dispute resolution organizations and uses the transitional name Association for Conflict Resolution.

3. Peachey, D. E. "What People Want from Mediation." In K. Kressel and D. J. Pruitt (eds.), *Mediation Research*. San Francisco: Jossey-Bass, 1989.

4. For a good discussion of this, see Lewicki, R. J. "Group Decision Making as a Problem Solving Negotiation." In D. A. Lax (ed.), *The Manager as a Negotiator and Dispute Resolver*. Washington, D.C.: National Institute for Dispute Resolution, 1985.

20

Can My Good Intentions Make Things Worse?

Lessons for Peacebuilding from the Field of International Humanitarian Aid

Mary B. Anderson

One of the most perplexing aspects of peacebuilding is that we too often find that our good intentions have consequences that we did not intend. It is not possible to control everything that happens in and around our work, but is it possible to increase our capacity to recognize, from the entry point on, how and when we can avoid unintended consequences and improve our ability for constructive impact and spin-off of our work?

This question has been at the core of Mary B. Anderson's work over the past five years. Mary, president of Collaborative for Development Action, is a development economist by training, though much of her recent work has been in the arena of how outside intervention in the form of humanitarian aid, development work, or peacebuilding intersects with settings of protracted, violent conflict. Her research initiative and book, Do No Harm: How Aid Can Support Peace–or War *(1999), has set a standard for the international humanitarian aid community. She currently is engaged in a parallel initiative on how conflict transformation and peacebuilding contribute to these same change processes.*

Mary, in outlining several lessons learned from the international aid community applied to peacebuilding, suggests that one of the keys is the recognition of the patterns emerging from settings of deeply rooted conflict. She says that even small decisions, like deciding to hold a seminar in English for logistical reasons, can affect who will participate and the impact the effort might have on the ground. She believes that it is possible to improve our ability for constructive impact and avoid unintended consequences.

· · · · · · ·

Peacebuilding and humanitarian assistance are closely related though separate fields. Many of the values, dilemmas, and lessons from either field are applicable to both.

In humanitarian assistance work, when people's lives are at risk, the decision for humanitarian workers is not whether they should or should not provide help. The imperative of humanitarianism is clear: when people suffer a crisis that leaves them unable to survive without external support, those who are in a position to help have the right—and obligation—to do so. The question, then, is how to help. Furthermore, as aid agency staff have become increasingly aware of the ways that well-intentioned outsider help can inadvertently worsen suffering and reinforce the likelihood of future crises, the answers to the "how" question are neither automatic nor routine.

Each of the elements of this question—such as how to identify who will be served, how to deliver goods and services, how to decide which local groups to engage as partners, how to arrange the logistics of work—involves processes that can undermine existing local capacities among those who suffer, thus weakening their abilities to cope even further, and feed into and worsen the circumstances that first put them at risk. Correspondingly, in each of these areas, would-be helpers have numerous options. Experience shows that some approaches to providing assistance in crises can meet the immediate dire needs of those at risk and at the same time leave them stronger, more secure, and better able to manage the future that follows their survival. Other approaches may meet the first need only but also increase the probability that those helped will soon be facing the same emergency again. These effects, particularly the negative outcomes, are greatly intensified, and the consequences more critical, when the crisis that prompts a humanitarian response is warfare.

How Does Good Work Go Wrong?

In humanitarian assistance programs, certain specific patterns have been identified by which good work—that is, work that is successful in saving lives and alleviating suffering—nonetheless also feeds into and reinforces conflict. The direct negative effects occur through the resources transfers that aid entails. That is, when external resources, such as food, medicines, and shelter supplies, are introduced into a resource-scarce environment where groups are in conflict with each other, these resources can represent wealth and power. To a significant degree, fighting among groups is about wealth (as a means of effective fighting) and power (as a result of effective fighting). Thus, many of the potential negative impacts of aid arise directly from the types of resources offered and the ways that they are offered.

Aid's goods can be, and often are, stolen to support armies or to purchase the necessities of warfare such as weapons. Aid agency decisions about who should receive goods always have distributional effects, favoring some groups and leaving others unserved. When the recipient group and the excluded group exactly match the subgroups that are in conflict, the aid is perceived, by these groups, to be improving the wealth and power base of one over the other. The result inevitably is a worsening of the relations between groups. Aid's resources always affect wages, prices, and profits. When certain groups in conflict benefit while others do not, as for example, when those engaged in making wealth from the divisions created by warfare are hired to provide delivery services for aid's goods, the impact is one of reinforcing incentives for warfare. Aid provided in environments of scarcity can substitute for local resources that could have supported civilian survival, thus freeing up those internal resources to be used in the pursuit of warfare. Finally, the delivery of aid's resources legitimates some activities and actors and delegitimizes others, and these impacts can also reward the pursuers, and beneficiaries, of conflict rather than those who work for peace. These five impact patterns—through theft; distributional impacts; market effects on wages, prices, and profits; substitutional effects; and legitimization effects—show up across a variety of conflict areas and are experienced by a range of agencies providing many types of aid.

Avoiding Negative Impacts and Supporting Local Capacities for Peace

Knowledge of these patterns helps aid agencies avoid them. Understanding how they occur enables aid workers to develop options and alternatives for designing and implementing programs that not only avoid the negative impacts but contribute to peace. Foreknowledge, based on experience, provides a basis for greatly improved work.

The Local Capacities for Peace Project (LCPP) found that for the purposes of delivery assistance, certain knowledge of the context of conflict was essential. Specifically, in order to anticipate and understand the impacts of aid on conflict, aid workers need to understand what precisely in this context divides people, on the one hand, and, on the other, in what ways people—even though they are conflicting—remain connected and interdependent.

Dividers

A careful review of aid programs in conflict showed that it is a mistake to simplify or flatten out one's understanding of conflict. To assume that all conflicts are driven by deep grievance is an error; some are, and others are not. To assume that people fight because they do not understand each other is also sometimes right and sometimes wrong. When conflicts occur, the underlying and proximate divisions are layered. For aid agencies, outlining the things that divide people in the specific context of their work is an important step to anticipating how the aid they provide will either play into and reinforce these divisions or, alternatively, help reduce and overcome them.

Connectors

LCPP found another fascinating reality: in the more than thirty conflicts examined during the project, whether people were engaged in open warfare or in intermittent localized violence, there were a number of things going on in those contexts that connected the groups in conflict. Individuals, of course, had friends, colleagues, associates, and sometimes relatives on the other side. People relied on, and thus maintained, certain systems for survival (such as, in some cases, irrigation or electrical systems) even though they also fought. People from different sides of the conflict continued to trade in markets formally and informally. People shared histories, heroes, holidays, believes, values, culture, language, and so on. Some people in warring societies explicitly refuse to participate. They stake out positions of reconciliation and peacemaking and exert efforts to bring people together. That is, in the midst of conflicts, as people divide along identity lines, they also maintain some common connecting networks.

When aid agency staff come into a war zone to provide humanitarian assistance because of enormous human suffering, they are often so overwhelmed by the violence and division they encounter that they fail to see and acknowledge the existence of any continuing connectors. As a result, they provide their aid in ways that legitimate and reinforce the divisions among groups and that ignore and weaken any connectors.

Recognition of the need to see what precisely divides people in a context and recognition of the need to identify and reinforce, build on, and support connectors turn out to be the two basic clues for aid workers that allow them to avoid worsening the former and ensure they promote and support the latter.

Relevance of the Lessons from Humanitarian Aid for Peacebuilding

What aspects of the learning by aid agencies is relevant to agencies engaged in peace work? Often peace agencies work on such low budgets that they feel sure their "resource transfers" cannot do harm. They do not have warehouses of food that can be stolen, and they do not construct shelter in disputed locations that favor some groups over others.

Although they do not have goods that can be stolen, peace-building programs may have some kinds of negative or counter-productive distributional, market, substitution, and legitimization effects.

Distributional Effects

International groups involved in mediation regularly promote and facilitate intergroup dialogues in areas of conflict. Every time they do this, they make choices and judgments about whom to include and exclude. In one case, a decision to hold all dialogues in English, made so the outside agency could facilitate and in order to avoid reinforcing the intergroup animosities aroused by use of local languages, meant the participants had more in common with each other than each had with its own larger community. The dialogues went well, but their impact on moving the larger societies toward constructive peace was marginal. (Decisions about who to include or exclude can also legitimize certain forces in societies, such as those pursuing warfare and those causing the most suffering.)

A peace agency established a long-term presence in one country in order to become better able to work with local people. Unknowingly, this agency hired all of its staff from one clan. They discovered the hostility they had reinforced when one of their staff members was killed.

Market Effects

Some peacebuilders report that under certain circumstances, they have been "protected" by armed guards as they enter or leave tense locations or even as mediation is occurring. They know, as the aid agencies know, that payments to such guards directly feed the coffers of warring sides in conflict settings.

Substitution Effects

An agency spent many months setting up locations and opportunities for people separated by conflict to meet. One by one, these places became unavailable for a variety of reasons; finally, they found the only remaining places for continued connection. These turned out to be villages on the border between the two groups where, to the surprise of the organizers, people of both groups lived and frequently crossed from one side to the other. This agency had not even known such connections existed and thus felt it necessary to create a range of venues that did not survive.

Legitimization Effects

Decisions about where to carry out dialogue meetings are sometimes criticized for inadvertently legitimizing dividing structures. In one situation, a decision to hold meetings of conflicting groups in a certain location considered to be neutral was interpreted by some as legitimizing the separation of the two groups rather than finding more fully integrated ways of building on existing areas where they were connected.

Implicit Ethical Messages

The assistance agencies involved in the LCPP also discovered that they had inadvertent negative—or positive—impacts on warfare through the ways they worked, interacted with local societies, and engaged with other agencies. They came to term these impacts the effects of implicit ethical messages. One example is the message conveyed by international agencies that compete and even deride each other's work rather than cooperate on shared concerns. The message of such behaviors when carried on in conflict zones is that when one disagrees with the approach of others, one does not have to work with or get along with them. In war zones, this is exactly the mood that prevails.

Peacebuilding agencies may find that they too unintentionally convey messages that reinforce the systems of conflict rather than of peace. For example, when outside agencies initiate programs in conflict areas, there is some evidence that they may appear to local people to be experts who are experienced in many conflict zones and can instruct and guide people in conflicts in the "right" way to make peace. They have worked in many conflict situations and have the experience and techniques necessary to bring peace. People within a conflict, for whom it is their first and only experience, may get the message that they, as locals, cannot make peace without the advice, direction, and support (often financial) of international peacebuilders. To the extent that this disempowers local groups to initiate and direct their own efforts, the dynamic that allows this to occur deserves attention.

Conclusion

Peacebuilders, as aid workers, should be alert to the potential for inadvertent negative impacts of well-intentioned work. As aid workers, peacebuilders may on occasion fail to recognize specific divisions (as in hiring staff from one clan) that, when ignored, mean their work has negative impacts. Peacebuilders would do well to recognize existing connectors and work with these supportively rather than assuming they must create all opportunities for divided communities to meet. More than the explicit work, peacebuilders need also to be aware of the implicit ideas and attitudes they convey by the ways they act. The parallels are not exact. More reflection on experience, across many settings and with many types of peace interventions, can produce greater specific learning about the pitfalls—and as-yet-underused—opportunities of peacework. The Reflecting on Peace Practice Project (RPP),[1] in which over fifty agencies involved in peacework are currently engaged to combine their experience and learn from it collectively, may provide this basis.

Note

1. RPP is a joint project of the Massachusetts-based Collaborative for Development Action and the Swedish organization Life and Peace Institute. RPP commissioned twenty-six case studies of peacework around the world, with the goal of drawing learnings from these cases regarding the characteristics of peacebuilding work as it is actually done.

21

How Can I Evaluate My Work?

Harry Mika

One of the most complicated and daunting questions we get in this field is contained in the simple phrase, "Did you achieve peace?" It is sometimes overwhelming when you are working in settings where the violent conflict has been raging for decades to find a way to explain to friends, colleagues, and most especially donors how your work is contributing in a situation that does not appear on the surface and certainly does not appear in the mainstream media to be improving or making progress. How do we approach evaluation of our peacebuilding endeavors?

We turned to Harry Mika for some ideas. Harry is on the faculty at Central Michigan University. For more than twenty years, he has worked with a variety of evaluation processes, many of these with community-based initiatives in the restorative justice field. Most recently, he lived in Northern Ireland, where he has been working on the design and evaluation of paramilitary roles in transitional justice.

Harry suggests that we reconsider evaluation not so much as something that measures success and failure as we look back at a process, but rather as a tool of learning, transforming relationships, and building peace. In this chapter, he provides some concrete ideas and tools for developing transformative evaluation.

. . . .

The overview of evaluation offered here is decidedly biased toward ideas and processes of evaluation that represent political practice, where evaluation might become a catalyst for transforming relationships. Such an evaluation would stand in stark relief to the more conventional and staid evaluation practices that are technical in nature and actuarial in intent. The more transformative evaluation approach, one that is collaborative and elicitive, will be discussed briefly here as a prelude to a review of the more pragmatic stages of evaluation for the novice peacebuilder. It should be clearly understood, however, that the election of a value orientation is the most decisive and strategic choice one makes in terms of approaching evaluation, for it is only then that the meaning and consequences of fieldwork processes can be understood.

My preference for a transformative approach to evaluation is based on a number of assumptions in the goals, means, and outcomes of evaluation:

- Partnership and participation

- A process (versus outcome) orientation that embraces incremental development and change in study objectives and goals

- Democratic research and evaluation processes

- Commitment to working with disenfranchised groups and working to the well-being of people generally

- A multicultural worldview

- Interdisciplinarity and a holistic approach to knowledge, understanding, and action

- Stewardship of relationships affected by the research and evaluation processes and outcomes

- An intimate relationship of theory and practice, where theory finds its support in practice, and practice is informed by theory

Such a value orientation becomes an evaluation approach through the following imperatives:

- Determining locally what is valued, what is needed, and what is possible through dialogue and consensus building

- Nurturing sensitivity and responsiveness to indigenous values and culture, local definitions of needs, and circumstances on the ground

- Promoting universal articulation of human rights standards as a reflex of local organizational culture, processes, and outcomes

- Minimizing risks and harms to participants in both processes and outcomes

- Building organizational and community capacities by strengthening individuals' skill sets and developing the local reservoir of material and human assets

- Advocating maximum participation, inclusion, and intimate involvement, cooperation, and collaboration of organizational workers in evaluation and research processes

- Emphasizing the means to the end, where the process is at least as important as the outcome, or perhaps where process and outcome are interchangeable or indistinguishable

- Empowering stakeholders by sharing with them control of the evaluation, as well as involving participants in shaping processes and details, determining the use of findings, and acting on outcomes

- Expanding the evaluator role to be both responsive to local needs and receptive to learning with other participants

- Conceptualizing program performance within the larger social structural and community environments

- Employing a mix of methodologies, both conventional and innovative, that are responsive to local needs, resources, and exigencies of the field, such as work in highly politicized settings

- Maintaining overlays of perspectives for the longitudinal, historical, and comparative evaluation that render program outcomes understandable and relevant

- Ensuring transparency of the evaluation and research processes—its goals, rationales, uses, and impact

- Cultivating relationships in the field that presume both long-term reciprocity and accountability

- Promoting coalition building, coordination of work, community development and organization, and mobilization, responsibility, commitment, and resolve to action

Terms and conditions such as these must underwrite evaluative processes if interventions are to suit and serve local needs for improving the performance of programs. It is easiest, of course, if these choices are a reflex of personal values as well.

Only when an architecture of values is carefully laid is one properly oriented to contend with the host of routine issues that shape evaluation activity on the ground. The following ten questions or probes, and a range of possible scenarios, responses, and rationales, describe evaluation work. These constitute a framework for most practitioners; those seeking specific transformative outcomes, however, might be less ambivalent about possible choices here and indeed see fewer ambiguities in these queries to begin with.

Why Evaluate?

There is seldom universal agreement about why an evaluation is set into motion. For some, ideas of evaluation and audit are interchangeable; the clear intent of the latter is to investigate compliance and performance against a contract, for example. Others conceive of the purpose of evaluation to freeze a moment in time and review goals against performance. Is this particular program doing what we think it is, or what we said it would be doing, or what we would like it to do? Evaluation can be targeted to improving program performance over time. Often, with unrelenting pressure to duplicate good programs quickly and replicate good results elsewhere, evaluation may be used to learn—to assemble the best ideas about good practice and pitfalls with which to compose a blueprint for other initiatives. There are other purposes of evaluation as well that suit more strategic purposes, such as program planning, fundraising, crisis management, and responding to political challenges.

Unquestionably, there are a host of darker motives for evaluation. Suffice it to say that the answer to "Why evaluate?" is often quite mixed and multidimensional. The enterprise is assisted enormously with any effort to explore purposes in an open and frank manner, and with some agreement regarding compatible objectives of evaluation. Evaluators themselves have been long and justifiably criticized in the field for pursuing their own personal or professional objectives, at the great expense of doing largely irrelevant (or worse) work and ignoring the needs of other participants.

When Should an Evaluation Be Conducted?

On the surface, there would appear to be relatively straightforward options regarding the sequence of an evaluation. Some are conducted during the initial stages of program development, during or at the conclusion of an implementation phase, to test the chances that the program will survive or thrive, make additional funding available, or make strategic changes in the program. Evaluation can also be oriented to the longer-term processes of a program that are established and in place, usually after some set period of time. Program outcomes or results might also be evaluated at the end of a funding cycle or at program conclusion. Perhaps the decision will be made to terminate the initiative or continue it as is or in some modified way, or even to expand a program based on assessment of its output or impact. Evaluations can also be done longitudinally, with regularity over time to gauge whether certain benchmarks have been achieved.

There are a number of dilemmas regarding sequencing that are very obvious in the field. Many evaluations are not planned but are instead put into motion with a program crisis of one sort or another. Often, the crisis is resolved before the evaluation is completed, as funds are cut, for example, or program personnel are released. Evaluation under crisis circumstances is often a desperate affair. While this might be inevitable, the evaluator must be braced for the facts that there is little consensus regarding the purpose or utility of the evaluation, many disaffected stakeholders will be reluctant or refuse to participate, and significant changes are looming in the not-too-distant future that may change all the rules.

Another difficulty that pertains to the timing of an evaluation concerns duration. In the best circumstance, evaluation is among the earliest discussions of program planning and implementation, and it is anticipated and normalized in organizational culture. This type of evaluation process takes place over the organizational life cycle. Most often, however, evaluations are only impact or outcome oriented, where the evaluator has only momentary contact with a program, not a relationship with a program and its participants. That is as desperate as the crisis circumstance.

Who Extends the Invitation to the Evaluator?

It is most often the case that an evaluator is invited to participate. Sometimes this is the result of a competitive bid process, or a direct solicitation due to a reputation, recommendation, or specific experience. Who is making the invitation can be a function of why the evaluation is to be conducted in the first place. Outside funders or donors increasingly require evaluation of some sort of all their grantees, mandating that a portion of the budget be reserved for this purpose. That funder might select the evaluator, or perhaps it is left to program administrators. Funders appear to be increasingly relying on evaluation as an intervention for purposes of crisis management. Programs themselves, when, for example, they are committed to strategic planning or trying to manage a program crisis, may initiate contact with an evaluator. A program director or manager or a board of directors or management committee may be designated to make the approach.

What is especially critical about who extends the invitation is to appreciate their motives, their particular agenda (there is nothing inherently devious about motives and agenda; everyone has them), their power within the organization, and the representational quality of their views and sentiments. More of this will be said later in the context of possible problems in the field.

Who Are the Participants in the Evaluation?

This should be a complex and vital area of concern to evaluation work. I like some basic premises:

- The more people who become involved, the more ownership there will be for results and outcomes.

- Evaluation as a learning opportunity increases as participation is expanded.

- The coherence of an evaluation (its ability to capture a broad range of input) is directly related to levels of participation.

Often, a challenge to evaluation is to look beyond the obvious stakeholders to individuals and groups who are marginalized. Those who use programs, for example, are often ignored in evaluation. Organizational and program culture might actively diminish the input and impact of women, certain ethnic or religious groups, the young or the old. Participation is an exercise of power in both a service program and an evaluation. Expansive ideas and strategies about participation (for example, enfranchising the disenfranchised in evaluation processes) serve the evaluation very well.

Having said this, what does participation mean? Democratic decision making? High levels of consultation? Broadly based input into how the research questions are formulated, how the data will be used and controlled, and what the final action plan will be? Development of individual skill sets and organizational capacity building? Unquestionably, this is about sharing power in the evaluation process, as the cornerstone of participation.

What Is the Nature of the Relationship of Evaluator and Participants?

There is always a relationship between an evaluator and the stakeholders in a program and organization. The questions are, What is the nature and character of the relationship, and how does it affect evaluation work and outcomes? It is not difficult to enumerate an ideal list of positive attributes. The challenge for evaluators, however, is to weigh these against countervailing forces, involving time and commitment, risk, and personal values and disposition. Accepting the core relational character of evaluation work to begin with, I propose that a relationship between evaluator and participants should be marked by honesty and openness, predictability and accountability, sensitivity and respect, inclusiveness and equality among participants, tolerance, good communication (avoiding the professional babble that disenfranchises), protecting the vulnerable (informed consent), and avoiding unintended consequences. These ingredients are the culture of good relationships under any circumstance.

What Is the Evaluation Design?

Design is the road map of evaluation, designating in bold relief its strategic points of interest but allowing as well any number of side excursions. Evaluation design should not be too rigid, and it must be accommodating to circumstances at hand. At a minimum, design decisions are opportunities for collective input and for enfranchising participants in the more technical aspects of evaluation work.

There is a logical sequence in devising an evaluation design. One begins with a host of preliminary considerations, including perhaps the ten questions posed here and also issues of cost, logistics, and time line. It is critically important to clarify and conceptualize the ideas and foci of the study and creatively manage and operationalize concepts (translating them into data points, such as questions to be asked in interviews). Deciding on methods and techniques of evaluation and identification of individuals or groups who will be consulted as part of the study are reasonable next steps. Attention to the information includes collecting and organizing (processing) data and interpreting or analyzing the results. Finally, strategic decisions must be made about application and the uses of the study (such as publication and plan of action). The entire design sequence should have an overlay of critique, such as various feedback loops that allow ongoing monitoring and, if necessary, revision of design elements.

What Is the Evaluation Methodology?

Many assume that evaluation is itself a methodology or a narrow range of number-crunching techniques. Very often, evaluation uses methods or techniques of evaluation that revolve around analysis of the written record. But evaluation, like research generally, is enhanced through the use of multiple methods and data opportunities. In addition to creating and analyzing data sets from written records, evaluation might incorporate individual interviews, group interviews (focus groups), surveys, participant observation, and organizational and community audits.

Being expansive in one's thinking about methodology has important implications for evaluation work. Many methods involve establishing relationships and having access to key stakeholders. The addition of methods almost certainly involves more time in the field and is likely to be financially more costly as well. However, a very narrow-minded focus on evaluation as methodology, and a very limited set of techniques for producing only a particular type of data or insight, is surely missing the forest for the trees.

What Are the Appropriate Evaluator Roles?

I am disposed to a broad redefinition of appropriate evaluator roles that are characterized by catalytic intervention and facilitation. Above all else, the types of appropriate roles must be driven by the needs and the trust of participants in host organizations. What is the range of appropriate roles? While monitoring, documenting, and analyzing are expected, perhaps training, facilitating, planning, organizing, and advocating are needed as well.

It is clear that evaluators, like the venues where they labor, are highly variable in a number of key assets they might possess. Gaining local trust and having opportunities to display competencies as a precursor to such trust take time. We are then speaking of an evaluation relationship of some duration. Embracing multiple roles implies as well that the skill sets and competencies of evaluators are adequate for local needs and demands. This involves an investment of time to acquire those needed skills.

It is also prudent to make a concession here to variable comfort levels of evaluators to becoming involved in the life of an organization or program in areas of conflict resolution, technical assistance, and the like. It is not for everybody. In addition, there always seems to be someone in close proximity to remind you that you have ventured beyond their narrow view of what is appropriate for an evaluator to be or to do. In my experience, such criticism seems to arrive at the most vulnerable and inopportune moments. Suggesting that one should develop an appetite for such criticism is certainly asking too much; some tolerance, however, is most helpful.

What Problems Might Occur During the Evaluation Process?

Evaluations, with planning and attention to the details raised in this chapter, can be rich and rewarding experiences for seemingly everyone involved. However, one should pay very close attention to problems that have the potential to create misunderstandings and disappointment. There are some clear tendencies. Very often, many of the most comforting assumptions that evaluations begin with—assumptions about the nature of problems or the nature of the evaluation—are in the end discredited. While you might intend to design an evaluation process that is productive and of use in facilitating problem solving, others might wish the evaluation to accentuate conflict, or to promote it, or to raise it in its starkest detail to the light of day. Relationships might become strained during an evaluation, as participants are often unclear initially about their vested interests that will be challenged and are at stake in the evaluation process. Evaluation can involve labor-intensive strategies for finding and giving information, and they can involve substantial and unanticipated (or budgeted) investments of time and energy. Perhaps an evaluator cannot say no to the many proposals that are made to expand the work of the evaluation by improving its processes, though there might be substantial resistance in the end for a collective admission of responsibility for having promoted such proposals or the delays they have caused.

Treating all participants as repositories of valuable data and expertise, entitled to respect for expressing their points of view and their willingness to participate, can certainly gall those who place less value on the input of a selected few. The process of the evaluation has (or should have) more impact than any tangible product or document produced from the evaluation. Some participants will find the end to be anticlimactic, which may be disappointing. Avoiding the political agendas or the simmering conflicts that may exist between individuals and groups may be impossible, and even inappropriate.

Tactfulness is an art, but honesty is a moral imperative. Both belong in the evaluator's tool kit. An obsession with data and a short-summaries approach to what information counts or is needed exerts considerable pressure to concede to unreliable, unverifiable, or self-serving data. The collective evaluation task is unique, and the process may be uncharted; hence, strict time frames and schedules, proposed with the very best of intentions, often become unworkable. While groups and organizations may need to get information quickly, ensuring the integrity of study findings and recommendations may require more time. These issues reflect routine problems in the field.

What Is the Expected Outcome from the Evaluation?

Finally, planning and energy seem to be in very short supply as an evaluation nears its end. A very large issue, however, must be resolved: What is next?

Optimally, the uses of a study outcome are deliberated very early in the evaluation, where issues of responsibility to act and the commitment to act are sorted out by study participants. Is the evaluation to result in a report? If so, who is to receive the report (is it public? confidential and private?)? Does the report go through in-house drafts for deliberation or redrafting? How is the report to be disseminated, and who takes on this responsibility? How is the report to be written or cast? Is its purpose to be accessible to professionals or to the public at large?

Even when the emphasis is not on a report but rather on some plan of action (strategic planning, implementation of changes, another type of intervention), it is critically important to have lines of decision making and responsibility clearly understood, including that of the evaluator role. It is my experience that while a good evaluation and process reduces the fright of the final product, there is an ever-present danger that a report will only join others in a study graveyard, deep in a dusty file. Thinking and planning in terms of an action plan help to facilitate future processes and uses of the collective evaluation product.

Conclusion

Evaluation that is transformative is first and foremost mindful of its value orientation and is then concerned with the articulation of value imperatives in its fieldwork. If indeed exclusion is the bellwether of injustice, a highly inclusive and collaborative evaluation approach appears suited and fit for the rigors of peacebuilding.

Part V

. . . .

The Decision

We started this book with a telephone call that left us facing a decision: Do we accept and begin a journey into a new endeavor? Through the preceding chapters, we have explored some of the ways experienced peacebuilders have created criteria and guidelines for orienting their decision around entry, the development of the work, and the ethical dilemmas inevitably faced in the complexity of working in difficult situations. But we are back at our deciding point.

The chapters in this part explore three interrelated concerns. The first is to address in a straightforward way the question, "Do I go?" The second question adds a reality check about time and how you might evaluate what length of commitment this will represent. And finally, we add the suggestions and advice from people who have worked for multiple decades in the field and their reflections about how they sustain themselves over the long haul.

22

Do I Go?

Ronald S. Kraybill

Inevitably, no matter how much you process it, you will face this decision: Is this the right thing for me to do, or should I say no? Perhaps the hardest thing we must face in the field of peacebuilding is knowing when to say no. How do we make this decision?

We asked seasoned practitioner, trainer, and mediator Ron Kraybill to reflect on his experiences. Ron teaches at the Conflict Transformation Program at Eastern Mennonite University and has worked in the field of conflict transformation for more than twenty-five years. He was the founding director of the Mennonite Conciliation Service and director of training at the Center for Conflict Resolution in South Africa where he lived with his family for five years. He has conducted training initiatives and consulted and mediated conflicts of nearly every shape and variety in dozens of countries. His telephone is constantly ringing with requests for help. Here is how he responds when a request comes in.

• • • • • • •

After almost a decade as director of a national network of mediators and trainers in the United States, I relocated in 1989 to South Africa. I spent six and one half years at the Cape Town–based Centre for Conflict Resolution (CCR), much of that time as director of training. Although I had conducted training in the United States, Europe, Asia, and Canada during previous years with the Mennonite Conciliation Service, the intensity, significance, and difficulty of events in South Africa dwarfed all I had previously done. The progression of political talks between Mandela's African National Congress and the white government made it finally apparent to South Africans and the eagerly watching world that apartheid would meet its demise not under the barrel of a gun but across a bargaining table.

Increasingly, it also became clear that more than one table would be required to bear the weight of the political transition. Virtually every sector of human activity would have to be reconstituted. In addition to national talks, extensive negotiations would be required at regional and local levels to work out details of the new dispensation. When we arrived in 1990, negotiation was opposed by all parties; by late 1992, South Africans of all political and ethnic backgrounds were interested in improving their skills in it.

Overseas conflict resolution organizations were among the first to sense the potential. The week that I moved to Cape Town with my family in 1989, a group of American trainers were conducting a series of workshops at the CCR, where I was based. Over the next several years, what began as a trickle of queries from trainers abroad eager to come to South Africa and train swelled to a steady flow. Often these offers were to train for free and sometimes even to fund meals and housing for participants. For the first time in my life, I was on the receiving end of international largesse apparently dedicated to the peaceful resolution of conflict.

The experience cost me considerably. I lost forever the bliss of packing bags to travel and train abroad with an easy conscience. I still travel and train, but since South Africa, ambivalence hounds me. I still believe that traveling trainers have important contributions to make to the challenge of building a peaceful world, but today I am a reluctant skeptic of myself and my own kind: the conflict resolution trainer with a suitcase.

An early learning was that there is no such thing as a free workshop. A significant slice of precious organizational energy goes into the production of a workshop. Even the trainers who came at no charge cost our Cape Town organization considerably in the form of staff time to publicize, organize, and support the workshop. Although the contribution to our work by some international trainers was significant, it was not always apparent that what we gained justified the cost.

A cost the South African experience forced me to reckon with was the phenomenon of "foreign expertise" delivered to "less knowledgeable" locals. I felt sad and frustrated to see confident foreigners present in smoothly prepared packages skills that I knew existed among members of our own staff and colleagues in the region. It is probably true that no one in Cape Town was able at that time to deliver things quite so nicely stitched together as some of the international trainers did, but it is also true that little was delivered that was not already available from people around us. Besides, South African trainers desperately needed the self-confidence that results from experience and recognition as successful trainers. Gradually, I came to feel that a flood of veteran trainers from abroad could actually stand in the way of the emergence of promising local trainers.

My South African colleagues were keenly interested in improving their skills. They were receptive and polite to the traveling trainers. But their comments after the trainers were gone made it clear they too were ambivalent. Eventually, we decided to stop scheduling workshops for foreigners except in response to gaps we had specifically identified that could not be met by local expertise. Within a year of making this decision, several of our staff were leading excellent workshops. Within two years, I had relinquished my role as director of training and was reporting as trainer to a training director whom I had hired and trained.

The longer I train, the more complicated I discover it to be. When should trainers say no to training opportunities? Below follow some possible instances when it may be inappropriate to start packing a suitcase. Perhaps more important, in each instance, I seek to define the yes behind the no, to identify positive values that can guide in decision making about training.

Transparency About Motives

Say no when the values and motivations of the trainers are unclear or heavily diluted by self-interest.

The underlying value: Trainers, funders, and sponsors should be aware of and transparent about the benefits that accrue to them in doing training and reflective about how these affect the choices they make.

Accountability to local contexts requires a commitment to placing the well-being of the recipients higher than consideration of rewards to the trainer or organizations abroad. Accountability begins with honesty about the multiple ways in which training rewards the givers of such training.

For trainers, doing training abroad provides invaluable experience. It adds to the trainer's professional reputation and marketability, increases the trainer's self-confidence, gives prominence to his or her home institution and thereby increases the trainer's status and influence within it, generates income and establish contacts for more work, and provides grist for books and research. Funders and sponsors of training often benefit significantly as well: they may gain increased visibility and credibility if others perceive them as initiating or supporting significant work in challenging places; this in turn may bring an increased ability to raise funds. Successful training is likely to increase the ability of funders and sponsors to promote their own values and ideologies among the recipients of training, and this may increase their influence abroad and at home. Their own internal sense of morale and confidence in doing good work may receive a boost.

There is nothing inherently wrong with these rewards. The important thing is to acknowledge these often obscured self-interests consciously. Many desires play on trainers in addition to desires to be accountable. It is possible to be accountable to the communities being trained and still reap many of these rewards. However, often these rewards compete with true accountability. Rarely is it possible to maximize these rewards to self and still hold the well-being of recipients as the highest value. For example, the well-being of communities is strengthened when they are able to take steps toward constructive responses to conflict in such a way that people feel that they did good work and that their success comes from themselves and their resources. This important need for community credit for success is blocked when funders and trainers publicly highlight their role in providing training.

It is difficult to assess the mix of motivations of those doing training, perhaps especially when we are ourselves the trainers or funders. The key is constant reflection and dialogue on these issues. Trainers, funders, and sponsors unwilling to engage thoughtfully and openly in the constant self-scrutiny this calls for may contribute more by staying at home.

Roots in Local Commitments

Say no when the request for training comes from people outside the local context and no local groups have demonstrated deep commitment to the training.

The underlying value: Training should be deeply rooted in the local context.

Some years ago the Conflict Transformation Program where I teach and work received a request to do a training workshop from a big American organization seeking to respond to a situation of large-scale violence abroad. Who had requested the workshop, we inquired? It had been proposed by Washington-based staff who felt it important to be doing something in this crisis. Our staff considered this request carefully. The organization had prestige, money, and some high-level connections. But it had no track record of work on the ground in this context and no real current connections there. Neither did we. Politely, we declined.

Our experience has taught us that when the stimulus for training comes from outside the place of training, particularly from organizations that are not deeply rooted in a web of active relationships there, training leaves little impact. Commonly, such requests arise from a desire to be seen to be doing something good, more than from a true commitment to the well-being of the people involved. Even when the motivation is deeply altruistic, the odds of sustaining the long journey of developing persons and institutions in context are low.

Honoring Local Resources

Say no when local trainers are available who could do the training as well as a visitor could.

The underlying value: Make empowerment and recognition of local trainers a very high priority.

The mere presence of a foreign trainer is itself a troubling metaphor: This host society and these people are so poorly equipped to respond to their own problems that outsiders are required to come in and teach them. We have grown so accustomed to the reality of exporting technology and instruction that we rarely reflect on the message implicit in our presence as outside trainers.

The context of this message is a world ravaged by colonialism. Overt political colonialism is gone, to be sure, but the impact lives on in the soul of the world. I will never forget the words of a friend in South Africa, an internationally recognized figure in the black consciousness movement, a leader who wrote and spoke constantly about black empowerment. A conference was being planned, staff had botched the logistics, and major revisions were required as a result.

"Trust a black guy to mess things up," growled my friend to his companion in an unguarded moment. The comment was so untypical and so spontaneous that even years later, it seems unfair to cite. Yet I believe it reveals a painful reality that must be named. At a deep level, a large number of people in the North and the South share an unspoken, barely conscious conviction: the South is inferior; it needs the North as teacher.

To the extent this conviction is present on either side, it is terribly damaging to the work of peacebuilding. Peacebuilding, after all, requires self-reliance and self-confidence. Creating peaceful societies and communities requires people who are strong and confident enough to stand between angry neighbors and redirect that anger toward a joint search for solutions. Thus, developing peacebuilders is about much than teaching skills. It is about nurturing the foundations of individual and cultural strength required to undergird the application of skills. A critical dimension of those foundations is self-respect and self-reliance.

So there is a dilemma here: How do we assist people when our mere presence symbolizes perpetuation of the problem? In the world we live in, no trainer from the North has the ethical luxury to pick up a suitcase and head South—or to any other location where people are deeply demoralized by conflict—without wrestling constantly with this dilemma. We must consider its implication at every phase of our work:

- Do we carry in books and outside training materials or develop what is needed in situ?

- Do we bring in role-plays or use local situations?

- Do we bring a list of skills and concepts to teach, or interact with people about their own insights and responses?

- Do we use local trainers?

- Who is announced as the sponsor?

- How is the trainer described?

I have never given a purely elicitive "local resources" answer to these questions, but in every workshop I wrestle with them. There are also times when I have declined to go, in part because I felt there were others in the local context or close by who could train as well as or better than I could. Other times when I have accepted a role, I have actively encouraged planners to bring in local trainers as well.

Train with a Long-Term Perspective

Say no when there are no signs of commitment to a long-term effort.

  The underlying value: Encourage planners of training to view training events from the very beginning in the context of a larger vision or plan.

As much as anything else, peacebuilding training is about arousing hope. The message implicit in our work is that it is possible to improve the way in which conflicts are dealt with. However, accomplishing this requires time, effort, and organization. We should not arouse false hopes unless there is good reason to believe that at least some of these hopes can be realized.

Accountability to Local Communities

Say no when planners demonstrate no marks of commitment to accountability to the context in which training will take place.

  The underlying value: Encourage planners to view themselves and all peacebuilding efforts as primarily accountable to the needs and structures of the local context, and not to outside organizations

What are the marks of accountability? Planners should be in consultation with local persons and organizations about the planned training and demonstrate responsiveness to local guidance. They should demonstrate specific knowledge about the conflicts and realities of the local context. They should demonstrate respect for local resources and eagerness to use and honor them. Rather than using the event for organizational gain, they should demonstrate a willingness to keep a low organizational profile if called for in order to increase the credibility and effectiveness of the training event.

Conclusion

I wish I could say I have succeeded in consistently applying these values in full, but I have not. The only way I can continue my work is if I recognize that I work in an imperfect world. I seek to be faithful to my values as far as possible. When I can apply them fully, I am delighted. When I cannot, I pray that the damage will be minimal. I am in this work for the long haul. Over time, I believe that even flawed efforts can be gradually brought to serve the values that must undergird authentic peacebuilding.

23

How Long Will It Take?

John Paul Lederach

When you receive an invitation to be involved in a new piece of work, your conversation immediately turns to the details. When would this work take place? Who will I work with? How long will this trip last? More often than not, we think about the time it will take in reference to our own calendar. Can we go for two weeks in April? What we may not factor in as explicitly is the evolution of the work over time. "How long?" is not just a question of whether we have two weeks available in April. It is also about whether we can think through the implications of starting something new and following it through as it develops over time.

So how long will it take?

In this chapter, John Paul discusses his framework for assessing his involvement over a longer period of time. He suggests that if we do not have a tool that helps us see the longer-term picture, we may inadvertently fall prey to not being prepared for what comes our way. He suggests that different types of peacebuilding work require different kinds of time commitments and that we need to understand and be aware of what those activities will require in terms of our calendar and availability from the start.

H ow do I assess the impact of time on the decisions? I have found a few keys from my practice over the years that create a frame of reference for sorting through a decision from the standpoint of what it will mean in terms of my commitment and whether I can actually follow through and deliver what is being sought. I have become increasingly convinced that we do not pay enough attention to the challenges of time. This is true in two ways. First, we pay too little attention to making the connections between short-term emergency responses and long-term strategic change goals. Not having clear time horizons in mind makes these needed connections more difficult to achieve. Second, we have not given enough attention to the ways in which different kinds of roles require different time frames. This is important to recognize in order to make appropriate decisions about our involvement and the integrity needed to fulfill the range of work needed.

Keys for Sorting Through a Decision

Here are the keys that I have found helpful.

Key 1: Assume Things Will Take Longer Than Is Initially Proposed or Expected

On nearly every occasion, when it comes to activities related to peacebuilding, you should start from the assumption that even what appears as a clearly defined, discrete, and time-bounded task usually requires more work and has more spin-offs than initially meet the eye. By far, the hardest aspect of my work over the past decades has been the challenge of not getting overly committed. For many of us, and certainly for me, our eyes and ideas envision a horizon that our feet cannot always reach.

Key 2: Be Explicit About Your Limitations

If there are specific limits to your time, from standards that you have set for yourself or the realities of other work and commitments, try to be as clear and transparent with people about what those are and the impact they may have on your work together. What you want to avoid at all costs is to raise the expectations of others in reference to your availability and then not be able to deliver. There may be nothing more painful than not being able to fulfill the expectations of people relying on you because you have not been uncompromisingly honest about your limitations. Be clear and honest, early and often, when it comes to the realities of what you can and cannot do.

Key 3: Create a Capacity to Think Long Term

I have said on many occasions that I think it takes as long to get out of a conflict as it took to get in. I first said that in Belfast in the early 1990s to a roomful of peace advocates, and I remember a palpable sigh of near despair (and felt as if I was about to be chased from the room). This is not a literal mathematical formula. It is a metaphor. Change processes take a long time, so prepare yourself for a long haul if you are truly interested in supporting large-scale change processes in settings of protracted conflict. The metaphor should help you develop a time horizon. Think out ahead, not just of the moment at hand.

Key 4: Remember That You Are Entering a Relationship

Peacebuilding and the constructive transformation of conflict is not just a piece of work or a contract; it is a process of building and sustaining relationships. This certainly involves concrete activities and work, but it will also involve entering the flow of lives and contexts affected by a significant level of trauma, seemingly overwhelming challenges, and difficulties. You will come up against the complex realities that people you respect and care deeply about face. Although it is important to know your boundaries and responsibilities, it is equally true that this arena of work requires the kind of time that is not punched on a clock.

Key 5: Recognize That Different Requests Require Different Time Horizons

As my work has developed, I have come to recognize that I receive very different kinds of requests that require of me different types of roles in support of broader peacebuilding initiatives. These roles are not equal in the intensity and time horizon of commitment. Knowing how to recognize and distinguish this early on in the process has been very helpful in assessing whether it is something I can do. Listed here are a series of different roles and activities I have typically carried out and how I assess them in terms of time when I begin to think about a response to the invitation. This is not an exhaustive list but is used here as an example of finding ways to be more intentional about the nature of the work and the time implications. What it suggests is that you think early on about the likely ways this initiative would conclude and what level of time commitment in the process it will require of you.

Seed Planting

I refer to seed planting as events, like conferences, speeches, and seminars, where what is being asked of me is to help present ideas to get some new or different thinking going. The time commitment is short, often very discrete in terms of the event. Typically, though not always, other activities may come as a follow-up at a later stage. However, the immediate request can be thought of as short-term investment for longer-term return.

What I weigh in these decisions is whether this seems to be a good use of my time, whether there are others who could do it equally well or better, and how many of these events I have taken on in the overall flow of my calendar. One of my roles is to help plant seeds, but not all the time. I also want to tend to a few plants over a longer lifetime.

Participation to Provide a Training Component

Typically in these circumstances, I am asked to join an existing training program or initiative. My time commitment is around the actual delivery of the component, but not for the full development of the program or initiative infrastructure. For example, I have often worked with the Life and Peace Institute in helping to deliver a training program in the Horn of Africa to different constituencies, like a national church body in Ethiopia, or the national staff of the institute in their Somali grassroots peacebuilder program. My time is limited to serving as a trainer for certain components of an overall training process. I join a team of people who have ongoing responsibilities for the design, implementation, support of educational application and practice, and logistics. I can say yes to these invitations knowing that I have a more limited role to help with a portion of an overall effort rather than fuller responsibility for the whole process.

Training Design and Implementation

Logically, the next step up from what I just described are initiatives where I am part of a team responsible for the design, implementation, and follow-up support for an education process. This requires a horizon of commitment that is much greater in terms of my time and the intensity of involvement. I have helped this happen, for example, in Colombia with Justapaz, a local conflict transformation and peacebuilding center, and its "permanent course" training model.[1] This approach involved the design and implementation of a capacity-building initiative delivered over multiple years with numerous training events each year. Such a commitment meant continuous consultation, regular availability for training in Colombia, and responsibility for fundraising, monitoring, and evaluation.

I have to think carefully about the implication of time and calendar when I take on this kind of commitment, which I refer to as a strategic commitment. *Strategic* means that the commitment creates a backbone to a five-year calendar and that subsequently I must weigh other invitations against the existing responsibilities. This kind of decision is much different from juggling whether I can attend a two-day conference; that decision is placed in the context of the strategic commitment as a lesser priority, not the other way around.

Mediation and Facilitation

Over the years, I have received invitations to work with a mediation process, at community, organizational, and national levels in international settings.

I have had very few direct involvements in national-level mediation processes aimed at negotiating an end to a war. When I was involved, I can say unequivocally that it changed my life, my calendar, and everything I was doing. I literally did little or nothing other than work with the mediated process full time. When and where these kinds of initiatives appear to be emerging, I take very seriously two sets of consultations: with family and friends and with professional colleagues.

In my discernment process, I look for a number of things. First, is it possible to distinguish specific roles that I might play in support of people who are working full time within the process? These activities and roles provide discrete and manageable functions. For example, I have often found that a useful role is to be available for consultation by telephone, e-mail, or on occasion a quick trip. In these instances, it is a support function to the team and the process, but I am not directly involved in the day-to-day rush. If regular and constant availability is needed, the second inquiry begins. Am I willing to call off, cancel, and open my calendar to take on this role exclusively? And am I personally and at a family level prepared for the consequences of the decision? I cannot overemphasize the importance of taking seriously the level of intensity this kind of process will involve.

When I receive a request to help with a mediation process at other levels, for example, with an organization experiencing difficulties, or within a national network of organizations, or with a community conflict, I have a similar process of consultation and thinking related to calendar and consequences. I have generally found that a process of mediation in international settings always takes more time than is originally proposed. I have a theory of mediation creep: once the process begins, more people, more consultation, and more activities are needed. Usually, these need to be done in a timely way, they require availability, and they require a great deal of integrity. I have become increasingly reluctant to accept these invitations for several reasons. First, I generally find that for these processes, a team made up of people who are close to the situation is the best approach. I never accept an invitation for mediation unless it has a local team component. Second, even requests that appear rather straightforward but seem to have a significant component of mediation will translate into an intensive process. I pay careful attention to my sense that this is leading toward mediation and, by virtue of that, toward a much greater time commitment than was originally proposed.

A Case Example

I recently received a letter and e-mail from a colleague known to me by organizational affiliation in Northern Ireland. He wrote on behalf of a coordinating committee asking me to consider coming to Northern Ireland for what I understood to be the facilitation of a meeting and the creation of a process for dealing with conflicts and significant differences of perception between a range of organizations working on conflict and justice issues in that context. The differences and potential of greater conflicts between them was paralyzing the efforts to create a coordinated impact and develop new applications that were much needed in the context in the broader Northern Ireland change processes. The people who had been involved in developing their coordinated efforts came from different bases of operation: some in the communities, some from international nongovernmental organizations, and others more directly linked to the official and state institutions. The suggestion in the early inquiry was that an outsider respected by most of the participants would be seen as useful at this stage for getting things moving and facilitating the initial meeting.

I responded that I was willing to consider the possibility of participation in this role but that I would need more details about the nature of the situation and the request. The initial inquiry was a confidential one. I was asked not to talk about or share the information in reference to the request. On this account, I asked permission for two things. First, I needed to consult with a colleague in my university program who was widely recognized by many of the organizations and people who would be involved in the process. Second, I indicated that for more than eight years, I had worked with colleagues in a mediation organization in Northern Ireland whom I felt would be capable of doing the facilitation (and were well known to most of the participants) and that I would appreciate receiving my Irish colleagues' advice on whether this was an appropriate role for me to play.

At this early stage, I also lifted up several other concerns that I needed to explore more fully before responding. Did he think this would be a single meeting to develop a recommendation or multiple facilitation meetings in a longer process? Was this oriented toward the development of a process design for dealing with the issues accepted by everyone, or would this naturally move toward a fuller mediation role working over time, through multiple meetings, until an agreement was forged?

I shared with the caller my own feeling that from his description, it seemed much more likely this would involve a longer mediated process and that I was not sure a one-time facilitation would be likely. My intuition was telling me that if I started this process and it went well in the first round of contacts, a much greater pressure would build to continue, and I would need to be prepared to follow through. This worried me for two reasons. First, my calendar was too full to do much more than a one-time meeting. It would be very hard to be available to this process with integrity over any amount of time. Second, I was concerned that I was being asked as an outsider to provide some support for the process, but it was not clear at this stage whether a team of facilitators would include skilled people from Northern Ireland. I would much prefer the model of a team, well rooted in the context, of which I would be a member.

In the course of raising these questions, I was granted permission to talk about the request with my colleague at home and on a discrete level with colleagues in Northern Ireland. In the next days, I received divergent responses.

My colleague at home, who had worked with many of these people in the preceding year, indicated that it was clear to him that the process of sorting out conflicts and differences was much needed and that I likely had the profile and respect needed to make a contribution. He suggested that if my calendar permitted, I respond positively to the request. In particular, he felt it would be useful to get a good process going, and an initial support from outside would be important.

The mediation colleagues from Northern Ireland responded with greater caution. They suggested that some initial contacts were being made with the networks in question and that there was a good chance that a team of people from the context could be identified to work as a facilitation team. They advised that I not move too quickly in accepting the invitation but rather wait for further consultation to take place.

Based on this round of information, I concluded two things that I tried to convey back to the friend who had sent the original invitation. First, everything I was hearing indicated that this would be a process requiring ongoing support and availability. While it may be useful to help with the first meeting, my experience suggested that once it got going, it would be hard to extricate myself from the process. This would require a much greater time commitment than I had available. Second, although there were strong indications that I might be useful, there were equal signs that there were resource people available closer to the context. It could well be that a joint team of action would be helpful. But it also seemed to me that further consultation should be done in seeking appropriate facilitation resources with people there. I feared that my acceptance of this role might cut short that process and could potentially get in the way of a more adequately contextualized and available set of resources.

I declined to accept the invitation, but I also indicated that I would be glad to explore this further if at a later point it seemed necessary. One of the keys for me was the recognition of how the role I was being asked to play had potential time consequences that I was not clear I could make.

Conclusion

I find it useful to think through the time implications of invitations not just from the standpoint of what appears on the surface, but from the implications of the kind of work it will involve. I think through my calendar in a strategic way, so that to the degree possible, I create commitments of a longer-term nature as the backbone and then fill in other requests that appear to be possible for me to accept. While it can be difficult in this line of work, where much of our energy is spent on crises, I try to be careful about not overcommitting, and I think through the implications about the evolution that is likely to rise from an invitation.

Note

1. Lederach, J. P. *Building Peace: Sustainable Reconciliation in Divided Societies*. Washington, D.C.: United States Institute of Peace Press, 1999.

How Will I Sustain Myself?

Amy C. Potter, with Ronald S. Kraybill, Louise Diamond, and Joe Campbell

Working in a setting with extensive and long-term cycles of violence, a great deal of trauma, and pain, poverty, and structural injustice takes a toll on peacebuilders. This is especially true when you have worked for a longer period of time and in the course of that experience have lost friends and colleagues to the violence or watched your hopes rise that progress was being made, only to live through the despair of a collapsing peace process or a renewed cycle of fighting. How do peacebuilders keep going? A few of us have suggested that perhaps the field should be renamed hope-building, in the sense that the biggest challenge for significant change is keeping hope alive in the face of the overwhelming odds of history that seem pitted against the building of justice and peace.

We turn in this chapter to a conversation among several old hands who collectively have seen nearly a century of peacebuilding. Amy Potter engaged these colleagues in a discussion of what keeps them going. Amy is a graduate student working on approaches of building positive peace and has been particularly interested in how people who have dedicated their life to this field have kept themselves alive and healthy. Among the three, you have already been introduced to Ron (in Chapter Twenty-Two) and Louise (in Chapter Three), so here are a few words about Joe Campbell. Joe grew up and worked all of his professional life in the troubles of Northern Ireland. Currently director of training and education at Mediation Network Northern Ireland, he is among the forerunners of developing applications of mediation to the community and national sectarian conflicts in his homeland. He and his colleagues have worked on the street during the heat of parading seasons, behind the scenes in the Maize Prison, and in the halls of churches and corridors of political offices. He has watched the rise of great hopes and the dashing of the same in more than one decade.

Listen to the voices woven in the conversation in this chapter. They suggest tapping deep into your resources, knowing yourself, and remembering that this race is to be run with patience.

She stands on the line looking over her shoulder as she awaits the handoff. The sun is beating down, and beads of moisture slide down her face. She has been preparing for this moment for many years and is filled with curiosity, passion, and trepidation. The fascination of different cultures, the love of peace, and the desire to make a difference have been growing and expanding through years of study. When will the other runner get there, and when he gets there, will she be ready to carry the baton?

As she waits, three people approach her. She recognizes them as experienced peacebuilders who have done the sort of work that she is hoping to begin. Despite their years of experience in the midst of conflicts, they have vitality in their steps and calm on their faces. They are there to give her parting advice. The first reminds her that her race is a relay race; she didn't see the start, nor will she see the finish. It will be a race that will go on for generations, and it will be important for her to have a team to cheer her along her stretch. The second reminds her to breathe. Be aware of and intentional about your breath; breathe in and out in a constant rhythm. Finally, the third tells her to stop frequently to drink water from the spring. The spring will never dry up, but it may become blocked from view if she diverges from her path. Equipped with these important insights, she sees her teammate round the bend. Hand stretched behind her she gracefully takes the baton and begins a well-paced journey.

This story introduces the themes in this chapter, which are a combination of the experience and insights from interviews with three individuals who have been doing peace work for at least twenty-five years. The three interviews were with Joe Campbell, assistant director of the Mediation Network for Northern Ireland, father, church leader, sailor, and gardener; Louise Diamond, founding president of the Institute for Multi-Track Diplomacy, author, mother, and nature lover; and Ron Kraybill, father, founding director of Mennonite Conciliation Services, and hammer dulcimer craftsman. Despite their long years in the field, they are energized by their work and identify working in a sustainable way as a key to long-term peacebuilding work. Their combined experience spans frequent travel to conflicted areas, living in a conflicted area for several years, and being a resident of a community involved in long-term conflict with insights on foreigners coming to work on the conflict.

The content of the chapter is a compilation of ideas and advice from the interviewees (and unavoidably my own interpretation), as if their voices have been combined into one. The majority of ideas under each metaphor were shared by the individual who articulated it. However, the other interviewees' ideas are mixed into each section. Imagine you are hearing multiple voices as you read.

Derive Energy from Your Center

> *Sustaining yourself is like a spring. It's that source*
> *of connection . . . centeredness. That energy is there*
> *if we make a space for it. Even if we use it up too*
> *quickly, it won't just dry up, but it can get blocked.*
>
> Ron Kraybill

To begin this journey in a sustainable way requires first looking at yourself. At your center is your source of energy. The closer you are to your center, the energy will continue to flow. However, you need to know if your center is really in line with the work before you. What are your motivations? Why are you doing peacebuilding work? If you feel a deep sense of call to contribute to peace, keep moving forward. If you are energized by the approval of others, there may be times when you'll be satisfied, but you'll never have the satisfaction that will keep you in this work over the long term. "Sustainability is very closely connected to whether or not we are grounded in a sense of call as the motive of the work rather than approval or recognition." Looking outside yourself for approval will block your inner source of energy. Be aware that others may think this kind of work is glamorous, but don't let that influence your purpose for being involved.

Another motive that will cut you off from your source of energy is the desire to "save" or "fix" people. This assumes that somehow a peacebuilder can control other people and "put them right." Of all the different motives, this can be the most dangerous. Fixing people isn't possible, and it doesn't connect you with local people. In fact, it does harm and sets back local efforts. It's outside the energy that comes from your center.

Know What Comprises Your Center

Once you have become clear about your motivation, look at what comprises your center, that is, your wholeness and who you are. It will be important to find more than only peacebuilding skills. "It's the whole person that makes the impact, not just the skills each one brings." You have many qualities, interests, talents, and needs. Make sure you are ready to bring these with you. Being in touch with your whole self will give you the widest channel to your source of energy.

Another important element of doing effective peacebuilding work may seem to conflict with this advice, which is try to fit into the local culture. You may find that the way you give voice to the many aspects of yourself may be different in different contexts. Appreciating the local culture and building the trust with local people that is required for peacebuilding work may require some shifting. For example, if you like to run for exercise and it's not safe in that locale or will make you stick out there, it may be helpful to find another way for you to be athletic and stay fit. Try to fit in as best you can while at the same time being true to yourself.

Another key to maintaining your energy is by doing work that you enjoy. Peacebuilders usually work in the midst of conflict situations, surrounded by hopelessness and discouragement. This is not a reason to take yourself too seriously and limit the range of emotions you feel at work. It's important to find deep joy and satisfaction in your work. In fact, that is what helps you know you are at your center. It is also what you bring to others in a conflict situation. You need to be a hope giver and life giver, and you can't give away what you don't have.

Be Self-Reflective

To stay connected with your motivation and center of energy, it is important to be self-reflective and ask yourself questions frequently:

- Why am I here?

- Am I trying to save the world?

- Am I thinking and acting based on what others are thinking (or what I think they are thinking)?

- What are my mind, heart, and body telling me right now?

- Am I attending to all of the dimensions of what comprises my whole self?

- Am I really helping?

- How am I helping?

Maintain a Sense of Rhythm and Balance

> *Sustaining yourself is like breathing. Breathe out, and*
> *breathe in. If you only breathe in, you can't breathe*
> *out. The natural flow of energy in life is reciprocal.*
> *You breathe out; you breathe in to the same degree.*
> *If you breathe in and you don't breathe out, you're*
> *tightening, you're holding. If you try to breathe out*
> *and don't take much in, it's the same thing.*
>
> Louise Diamond

Rhythm and balance help maintain a focus on living from your center. All three peacebuilders emphasized the importance of having a balanced life. Family, prayer, meditation, music, art, friends, hobbies, exercise, work, and sleep are keys to living in a sustainable way and will allow you to do your best work. Peacebuilding work will have plenty of intensity and seriousness; include lightheartedness and humor in the mix as well. Working too much without spending time with family and being engaged in other life-giving activities will lead to suffocation or implosion. Breathe out, and breathe in.

Know When You Are Off-Balance

There are clear signs to be aware of that will let you know you are off-balance. Sickness, fatigue, despair, and loss of hope may be signs that you have lost a sense of balance that maintains your connection to your center. Another sign might be if you find yourself getting sucked into the behavior of the conflict that surrounds you. You may find yourself treating colleagues the same way those in the conflict are treating each other. You may become indifferent in terms of relationships with protagonists. Secondary trauma is another danger. Secondary trauma is the trauma a caregiver experiences when he or she is exposed to the trauma of others. This can also manifest itself through despair and loss of hope. "What is really important is that you know where your center is. You recognize when you are off-center and bring yourself back."

Get Back in the Rhythm

There are several things to do when you find yourself off-balance. Each person has a unique individual rhythm, so it will vary from person to person, but these are some things that have worked for others:

- Talk with others. Talk about what you are hearing and experiencing with those in your support network. This is especially important in the case of secondary trauma.

- Just say no. Don't agree to be involved in more projects than you can do while being engaged in your other important life activities. Turning down projects now will allow you to do much more work over the long term.

- Ask yourself what you offer in a situation. If you can't bring a sense of hope and energy, back off for awhile, and let someone else take over, or figure out what else you may be able to offer that requires a different kind of energy and involvement.

- Keep your work at work. Don't bring it home.

- Discover what is life giving for the locals, and become engaged in those activities. In spite of the conflict situation, there will be activities that will be positive and life giving.

- Reengage in the activities that give you a sense of balance.

- Go to your sanctuary. This can be a place within the conflict situation where you find rest and renewal, or it could be the place you come home to between trips.

We know that it is not at all possible for anyone to stay at his or her center all the time. However, it's important to know where your center is and how to get back to it.

Think Generationally, and Be a Team Player

> Living sustainably is being a runner in a relay race. We are on part of this race, and we'll not see its completion. Neither have we seen the start, and we will hand it on to the next generation. Building sustainable peace is a multigenerational event.
>
> Joe Campbell

Being part of a relay team is two-dimensional in terms of thinking sustainably. First, being on a relay team can be seen in the dimension of time. Those you are getting the baton from have started before you, and those you will pass it on to will be in the future. This understanding will help you pace yourself and be realistic about what you can accomplish. The other dimension of the team is being with a team of people in your present work that forms a network of support. Two keys to being sustainable, in addition to working from your center and keeping a sense of balance, are thinking about the work generationally and working with a team. Peacebuilding work is not about instant gratification or being a lone ranger.

Be Responsible for a Piece of the Peace

"Being sustainable is the ability to make decisions about how we're going to allocate our time based not on what is right in front of us but on a thoughtful, long-term or life-time perspective." The piece you have to contribute to the peace is significant, but it's still only a piece. Thinking you can do it all will quickly lead to disappointment. When asked how they dealt with disappointment when an initiative falls apart after having put in tremendous effort, all three peacebuilders said they couldn't take responsibility for the whole situation. They did their parts diligently, and that's all they could do. They did not give up because they were committed to the long term. Success can be defined in terms of small steps in the context of the greater vision. "Success would be the small but significant changes in the lives of individuals . . . finding more in the lives of individuals than in big societal shifts." To remain hopeful in times of disappointment, hold on to examples of individual actions that made a difference, personal transformations, new understandings, and relationships that developed in connection with your work.

Create a Local Support Group

Having a local support network as your team is important. The network acts as a reference board and emotional support. Especially in a place of deep division, it's helpful to have people who represent each side of the conflict on the team. These are people who might not be involved in the conflict, "but have the feelings and guts of those who are. They are people you can be honest and vulnerable with and invite their honest feedback." This support network will help you know how to be the best support and team member to the local people. Part of being on a team is not only doing what is best for your own sustainability, but in order to create sustainable peace, the local people must be supported. As you find a pace for yourself in a foreign situation, understand that the local people need to pace themselves for an even longer run. Your support group will help you understand your best role, which is often listening, asking good questions, and sharing stories from other contexts. Be aware that the support network just described is not what people usually do. Those who are working internationally in a conflicted setting have a strong tendency to get sucked into one side of the conflict and maintain a support network at home rather than creating one locally.

Step Back and Observe the Local Culture

Before forming your support group, it's important to learn about the local culture and try to fit in, though without compromising who you are. Driving vehicles, wearing clothes, and living a lifestyle very different from the local people will make it harder for them to accept and trust you. It will also be harder for you to make connections with local people so you know what will be helpful. If you're trying to create sustainable peace and especially if you're going to be in that context for some time and want to create a sustainable life for yourself, observe what is going on around you first.

Go Out in Peace

Lessons of living sustainably will come throughout the journey, and there will certainly be times when you will feel that you've gone off the path. Some of the ideas here from those who have had experience on and off the path and observing others in the field will be helpful in avoiding or dealing with those times. Go out in peace as you work in a way that sustains you and helps you contribute your best over the long run.

> Our runner is well on her way. She has been doing peacebuilding fieldwork for several years now. When she got to her first destination, she stood back, observed, and listened carefully. She created a local support network and learned about the different perspectives. She was able to contribute her talents and insights in partnership with the local people. She celebrated the small triumphs and expressed her disappointment with her team. Frequent reminders about why she was doing the work helped her make sure her actions were in line with her motivations.
>
> During this time, her life was much broader than her work. She painted, joined choirs, worked with her church's youth group, and remembered to laugh. She was able to contribute to peacebuilding because she lived it. She's still going, and she and others like her are and will be ready to pass on the baton.

Part VI

. . . .

Good Advice from
Gray Hair Hard Won

In Chapter Fifteen, our West African colleagues suggested we should take care to recognize the voices of and wisdom of elders. We would be remiss in a handbook on international peacebuilding that wished to provide advice to those entering the field if we did not seek the counsel of our elders. If you ask any seasoned peacebuilders in this field what got them started in this work, we would wager a guess that the vast majority would answer not with what but who. They would talk about somebody who had gone before them, who had set an example, whom they looked up to, and who provided them guidance and mentoring.

We have asked four people from different walks of life, different countries, and different professional applications to answer this question: Looking back across your work and life, what would you recommend to younger colleagues entering the field? Their words are worth reading slowly and carefully, and more than once.

25

Embody Peace

Hizkias Assefa

Based in Nairobi, Hizkias Assefa is active in mediation, training, education, and the support of peace processes across his native African continent. He has been a forerunner in the development of reconciliation applications in some of the most difficult conflict settings, from West Africa to Rwanda and Ethiopia. His book, Mediation of Civil Wars: Approaches and Strategies—The Sudan Conflict *(1987), remains one of the best on the short period of negotiated settlement in the 1970s in that four-decade-long war. In addition to his international work, Hizkias teaches courses at Eastern Mennonite University and George Mason University.*

. . . .

In writing this chapter, I have been told to address a North American practitioner in some aspect of peacebuilding who is interested in working abroad for the first time. Because most overt conflicts are located in the South, I will assume that this person would most likely be trying to work in the South. I am writing from two perspectives: as a peacebuilding professional who has lived in North America and East Africa and from those bases worked in a number of conflicts in the South for almost two decades and as an African who comes from a society that has been on the receiving end of this kind of assistance.

Lesson 1

The issue in these complex conflicts is not only about how outsiders feel they can help correct things that in their view are wrong, but also how the parties to the conflict ultimately are helped to live harmoniously with each other.

Peacebuilding is a broad field that consists of many kinds of activities, including development, human rights monitoring and enforcement, political advocacy, training, mediation, and reconciliation work. Some of these activities are quite sensitive as to who does them and how they are done, and others are less so. For some, the need for an in-depth knowledge of culture, broad experience, discipline, worldview, and cultural sensitivity is critical, and for others it is more peripheral.

For example, peacebuilding work based on international and national legal norms such as human rights advocacy and enforcement is less sensitive than mediation and reconciliation work to the factors already noted. Political advocacy, that is, mobilizing international or national public opinion in support of one position or another in a conflict, is higher on the sensitivity scale. Because advocacy groups claim to take their stance and actions based on some notions of what is right, just, or proper, they may not be very worried about how their actions are perceived by all parties to the conflict. Their aim is to make a case in the court of public opinion for their favored party's position so that it receives wider support and finally prevails over its contender.

In very complex conflict situations, simplistic advocacy that reduces issues to mere right and wrong often does more harm than good for the overall situation. Doing advocacy work in the context of peacebuilding is different from doing it outside that framework. The advocate must consider the impact of the advocacy on the conflict itself. The process might help bring victory to their favored side, but ultimately, if the victory makes the underlying conflict worse or impossible for the conflict parties to live with each other, one might have undermined the very purpose of the peacebuilding exercise. Peacebuilding advocacy requires more discipline, more knowledge of the intricacies of the conflict, and a higher sensitivity to the perceptions of the protagonists involved.

I recently had an encounter with a fellow who had just finished his studies at a prestigious institution in North America and was starting his first mission outside the North. He was going to a war-torn African country to do advocacy work under the auspices of a Northern organization. He came with very strong views about how to end the civil war there and was gathering information to mobilize international public opinion for the option he proposed. From what I knew of the local situation, it seemed clear that his option would most likely increase the deaths and destruction in that society. Notwithstanding the merits of his position, it was disturbing and ethically challenging to meet an outsider so certain about the solutions who was trying to mobilize international public opinion to make such a life-and-death decision for the people of the country in whose interest he and his organization were ostensibly acting.

Lesson 2

Building trust and honest relationships are more important in the long run than skills or methodology.

The level of sensitivity required is even higher when it comes to mediation and reconciliation work if that work is to be effective in the long run. Mediation work can be driven by a power-based approach that relies on leverage garnered by the third party to reward or punish the parties to the conflict for their cooperation with the mediator or for their lack thereof. An alternative approach relies on a high level of trust (trust-based approach) that the mediator builds with the parties.[1] Such trust can be a powerful mechanism for helping the parties overcome their fears and defenses and search for mutually rewarding solutions to their problems.

From my research and experience, it seems that the trust-based approach lies at the core of true mediation and reconciliation work and is an essential ingredient for the genuine transformation of the relationship between the former adversaries. How such trust is gained is a complex matter. In my experience, it emerges from empathy and a strong sense of identification that emanates from deep intellectual and emotional understanding. The parties' perception of whether the third party understands what it means to be on the receiving end of the pain that they are enduring goes a long way in terms of establishing credibility and trust with them.

I remember an encounter with a Sri Lankan bishop who was one of the courageous champions of peace in his country. When we met for the first time, he received me by saying, "Thank you for offering to help. One who has suffered knows what it means to suffer." Since I too was from a place that had undergone an intractable internecine civil war, he felt that I could know what it is to live with conflict and could therefore more readily understand the complexity of his people's situation.

Lesson 3

When we attempt to build peace without being embodiments of peace ourselves, we inflict violence without even knowing that we are doing so.

Mediation and reconciliation work draw deeply on who we are. It took me a long time to understand what the Vietnamese Buddhist monk Thich Nhat Hanh meant by "being peace," as described in his book *Being Peace* (1987). I contrast this with what we call "doing peace," which is implicit in terms such as *peacemaking* and *peacebuilding*. *Being peace* means living out the values of peace and leading the parties in conflict by example. It is having respect, empathy, and humility and coming to terms with one's own self in order to reserve judgment so that one can understand deeply.

I have found that being peace is much more difficult than doing peace. Ultimately, doing peace is not very meaningful or effective unless it emanates from being peace. That might be why we professionals have not been very successful in our peacebuilding efforts, especially when it comes to going beyond stopping war and transforming relationships and society.

Lesson 4

To have credibility as a peacebuilder within other cultures, you must also work at peacebuilding within your own context.

This way of looking at mediation and reconciliation work poses special challenges to peacebuilding work in the context of North-South relationships and for Northerners who want to be engaged in peacebuilding work in the South. Although many conflicts in the South are generated by dismal national leadership, as well as political, economic, and sociocultural systems that are ill adapted to their societies, the roots of many of the problems underlying these conflicts are also connected with the global order dominated by the North. The economic system that is increasingly being globalized continues to generate unprecedented wealth in the North and abject poverty and misery in the South. The political and cultural hegemony of the North has meant the dehumanization of the South, which is more or less two-thirds of humanity.

This economic marginalization and cultural denigration have not only poisoned relations between North and South but also fomented a great deal of social unrest, alienation, and civil wars within the South revolving around either the distribution of the ever-shrinking economic pie or the ill-adapted social systems that have emerged as a result of trying to live up to the dictates of the North. If indeed peacebuilding is about addressing and transforming root causes of conflicts, then there is a great deal of peacebuilding work that has to be done in those societies that are benefiting from this global system at the expense of generating injustice and crises in other societies.

Here is where Northern peacebuilders can make a large contribution to peace in the South since they are in a position to access and positively influence the forces in their own society that in one way or another contribute to conflict and destruction in the South. This is what, in my view, it means to do peace out of being peace. This is also how a Northern peacebuilder can establish credibility and trust in the South as a committed peacebuilder working in the interest of the South, and ultimately the rest of the world, shared by all. In fact, from my observation, peacebuilding work in the North might be even more difficult since conflicts and problems do not manifest themselves in overt wars as in the South. Therefore, the citizens of those societies are often not aware of the injustice and structural violence that their systems are generating to their own detriment as well as to others.

Lesson 5

We have to be very humble about what it is that we are bringing as outsiders into the situation that the people there cannot do on their own.

Another issue of perception that the North American peacebuilder has to deal with is the notion that the South has been seen as being perpetually on the receiving end of things. Ideas and practices about how the South should go about economic and social development, how it should govern itself, how it should educate itself, and how it should build its society, even how it should worship, have been largely imposed from the North at the great cost of undermining the cultures, values, and to a very large extent the humanity of people in the South. It would be important to avoid making peacebuilding another avenue where the South is once again on the receiving end. It would be very important to be sensitive to understanding that these societies have their culture, people, and history that if understood and supported could help build meaningful peace and social relationship in their communities.

I am reminded of an encounter I had with an international nongovernmental organization (NGO) from the Far East operating in a Southern country where I was working. The NGO was keen on facilitating peacebuilding work in that country. I was once invited to visit the organization and give a lecture on peacebuilding to its staff. When I went, I found that the organization had a lot of young graduates from its home country who had come to work for the NGO. I was told that they were to be attached to various local organizations so that they could learn about peacebuilding and then equip themselves to work in that country.

I found it a bit ironic that the nationals of that country were to teach the outsiders about how the foreigners could do peacebuilding work in their country. I wondered if it did not make more sense to give this opportunity to the nationals so that they could be trained by their own compatriots or, alternatively, for the organization to use its resources to work in more depth with those originally doing it. It reminded me of an analogy of a seriously ill patient lying on an operating table being expected to give detailed directions to an inexperienced surgeon on how to proceed through the surgery.

Conclusion

There is no question that the field of peacebuilding will benefit greatly if more people are engaged in it in the genuine sense of the term. The fact that a North American professional is interested in peacebuilding in the interest of societies in the South, even if that person is not very experienced, is commendable and to be encouraged. However, the best contribution that can be made is not necessarily by operating in the South. There is a lot of peacebuilding work that needs to be done in the North that can have a positive impact on peace in the South, and often it is Northerners who would be placed to do such work.

As a practitioner, I have often felt that the peacebuilding work currently going on in the South cannot produce meaningful results if the larger global system continues to foster conflict and crises. In other words, working at the subsystem level without addressing the forces at the larger systemic level that undermine the work at the subsystem level will not lead to any durable outcome. This means that in order for peacebuilding in the South to generate sustainable peace, there also has to be similar and complementary work at the global systemic level. What is needed is a coherent and coordinated peacebuilding vision and strategy that allows peacebuilders to work not only on the South but also on the North and their interrelationships so that ultimately the cause of peacebuilding is enhanced everywhere.

What I would offer to peacebuilders from the North may not be advice on how they could work in the South, but a partnership on how we can work together to transform the global system into a more just and humane order for the benefit of not only the South but the North and all who inhabit the world.

Note

1. For a more detailed discussion on these two kinds of approaches to mediation, see Hizkias, A. "The Challenge of Mediation in Internal Wars: Reflections on the INN Experience in the Ethiopia/Eritrea Conflict." *Security Dialogue*, 1992, 23(3), 101ff.

26

Commit to People,
and Commit to Time

Harold H. Saunders

Harold Saunders, former under secretary of state across five administrations, earned his early credentials in the Middle East peace processes having formed a part of shuttle diplomacy at an official level. Hal subsequently left his official role in Washington to take up his deepest passion: creating and sustaining dialogue and building relationships in war-torn societies. His recent book, A Public Peace Process *(2001), brings together many of the lessons he learned in both official diplomacy and informal efforts. He is currently director of international affairs for the Kettering Foundation and remains actively involved in the Inter-Tajik Dialogue, an effort to create and sustain dialogue in the public sector in Tajikistan over the past eight years.*

W orking with people in deeply rooted human conflict is a calling, not just another job. Moreover, no one can ever be completely prepared for the task. It is more important than in many other situations to look inside yourself and think deeply about your personal and practical support systems before you commit yourself. A "fact-finding" trip may be essential provided you make it clear that such exploration is essential to your ultimate decision. While you are considering whether to go even that far, you will want to ponder a number of questions.

Does It Feel Right for You?

Does the project proposed to you connect with what you are all about: your experience, your knowledge, your capacities, your intellectual curiosities, and your commitment?

Be imaginative as you probe deeply in answering these questions. The connections between a possible project and your own interests may not be obvious on the surface. A problem may capture your interest because it resonates with some earlier, though seemingly quite different, experience. You may not initially even recognize the connection, but somehow you sense it. Or it may intrigue you because you believe that an approach you have developed in other situations may be useful here. It may seem to offer an opportunity for you to pursue more deeply questions and analysis that interest you. It may seem to offer an opportunity for enhanced learning that would both extend your horizons and permit you to bring to bear a larger but relevant perspective from other experiences. Or it may just not feel right for you. Pay serious attention to your visceral reaction, and try to understand it.

Can You Give This Project the Time It Deserves?

There are two aspects to your answer. First, it is essential to recognize that most intractable problems require extended commitments. Short, one-time interventions may on occasion have their place, but normally they risk doing more harm than good or having no impact at all. Sustained involvement is normally required, and *sustained* may mean a commitment of years.

Recognize that in dealing with most deeply rooted conflicts, the purpose is to produce not palliatives but peace, or at least a fundamental change in destructive relationships. Don't count on parachuting in and flying right out. You need to see a coherent process through to a point of identifiable change or a moment when you can judge that such is not possible now. That will require time to give the process a fair trial.

The second aspect of answering this question is a personal one. Don't say yes if you know that you will not be able to carve out the time that the project will ultimately require. Many projects are tempting because they are so compelling or so interesting, but viscerally we know that other commitments already made will make it virtually impossible for us to give this one the time it deserves.

Exceptions to this heavy warning may be fact-finding missions for the purpose of learning enough to answer these questions. But even a fact-finding mission is often the first step in a larger process. Be honest with yourself about your own limits of time.

Are There People on the Ground Willing and Able to Work with You?

A colleague often quotes a friend who is an African American educator: "Find what is growing, and help it grow."

An outsider has very little capacity to change a political culture or conflictual relationships in ways that are often essential with deeply rooted human conflicts unless some collection of individuals within a conflict wants to change.

In 1992, a Russian-U.S. task force I had worked with for a decade was deciding how to use the process of sustained dialogue that we had developed in our own interactions in one of the conflicts that had broken out on the territory of the former Soviet Union. Tajikistan slipped into a vicious civil war immediately after independence, and we decided to investigate what might be possible there. Many people in the field of conflict resolution would have thought in terms of sitting down with representatives of the factions in the civil war to mediate a peace agreement. Ultimately, a mediator representing the secretary-general of the United Nations brought the parties together in a mediated negotiation.

Our proposal for help in funding our project stated that we wanted to see whether a group could be created from within the conflict to analyze its dynamics and to design a peace process for their country. The ongoing Inter-Tajik Dialogue, more than eight years old as of this writing, has become what we call "a mind at work in the middle of a country making itself." The group has formed its own nongovernmental organization, the Public Committee for Democratic Processes, to develop spaces in their country where citizens can resolve their differences peacefully and deal with challenges such as economic development together.

In short, it is essential to determine whether one's involvement can serve as a catalyst for on-the-ground efforts to achieve the kinds of fundamental changes in relationship and political culture that are essential to conflict transformation.

Can You Develop an Open-Ended Process for Transforming Relationships?

Often, changes in relationships and political culture occur through carefully conducted sustained interactions, the outcomes of which we cannot know at the beginning of a process. In some ways, an open-ended political process itself contains the elements of solution, and our task is to create space in which approaches to challenges can be generated.

Unfortunately, *process* has become a pejorative word. I have been told, "You are all process and no substance." I do not understand why *process* has become a negative word; we all admire effective manufacturing processes or medical processes for healing. For me, an effective political process of continuous interaction that produces changes in relationships and even in political culture is a powerful idea. The concept of a multilevel peace process, learned in the intensity of the Kissinger shuttles of the Arab-Israeli war in 1973, is a powerful framework that permits us to understand the potential for political, social, and economic initiative from all levels of a body politic. It is the only conceptual framework that I have found that is large enough to encompass the kinds of fundamental changes that are essential in building peace.

I do not care whether anyone accepts my framework; I deeply care that each person in this field has a framework that works for her or him. It is only with such a framework that one can enter a new situation about which he or she knows little initially and begin to analyze the dynamics that must be dealt with if relationships are to be changed.

Do You Have a Set of Principles to Guide Your Work as an Outsider?

The question is not so much whether a third-party intervenor is appropriate as it is how that person will conduct herself or himself with respect to the sensitivities and needs of the people he or she is working with.

The most important precept for me is captured in John Paul Lederach's word *elicitive*. The point is to find the mind-sets and habits of the people you are working with and help those people bring their traditional ways of doing things to bear on their problems while helping them to find additional approaches to enlarge their capacities.

Another way I have found it useful to put this point is to recognize that there is a citizens' political process in every community—a way in which citizens traditionally go about dealing with problems. It may be that they need to find ways of altering those traditional approaches, but they must be the ones to generate the change because they may learn more effective ways of working. The outsider can introduce ideas, model different ways of approaching problems, provide training and education, inject powerful new ideas, and maybe even provide financial support, all at appropriate moments in the participants' own process so as to help them change their own process rather than trying to impose changes from outside.

Timing is extremely important. Groundwork needs to be laid for the introduction of new approaches and new ideas. All must be done in a way that enables participants to change themselves. All must be done with utmost respect for who they are.

Who Will Provide Sustained Support?

Although any peace process is far less costly than the continuation of the violent conflict, it does cost money to bring together the people who need to come together, especially if a process is going to reach over considerable periods of time.

Unfortunately, the attention span of some funders extends over only relatively short periods of time. I have been incredibly fortunate to work with three foundations that have stood by our Inter-Tajik Dialogue and its civil society follow-on through these more than eight years. I believe I am almost alone in the good fortune of these deeply supportive relationships. Anyone committing oneself to this work over time will need to be prepared to argue the case that it is only with an extended commitment that progress in the field is possible.

A New Paradigm

I believe a new paradigm is necessary for this work. Instead of the old focus on governments and institutions, I believe we must think in the following context. Relationships between groups and countries are a multilevel process of continuous interaction among significant elements of whole bodies politic across permeable borders. Citizens outside government are political actors. Only governments can negotiate formal agreements, but only human beings can change conflictual relationships.

That means we are dealing with whole human beings in whole bodies politic. We must be prepared to work toward changing human relationships so that citizens outside government can resolve problems among them. The job of the outsider is not to "make peace" but to create space and help generate processes for people to form peaceful relationships.

Peacemaking is a way of life. Peace is never made; it is always in the making. Only citizens outside government can make peace for themselves and among themselves.

27

Practice Love and Sustain Hope

Elise Boulding

Elise Boulding is often considered the matron saint of the peace studies movement in the United States. A sociologist by training who taught for decades at Colorado University and Dartmouth College, she is now retired but remains active in writing and networking, and she is a voice of encouragement to all she meets and knows. From a Quaker background, she and her husband, Kenneth Boulding, marked the beginnings of the study, teaching, and practice of peace and conflict resolution and helped found the International Peace Research Association. Elise is especially well known for her work on women and peacebuilding, the development of global networks for civil society, and the Imaging the Future workshops she conducted all over the world for people from every walk of life. Her latest book is Cultures of Peace: The Hidden Side of History *(2000).*

· · · · · · ·

In the summer of 1941, when I joined the Friends Civilian Training Unit for Women in Highacres, Pennsylvania, we were preparing to clean up battlefields and do mass feedings overseas, but no one said anything to us about conflict transformation. In fact, at the end of the summer, I married Kenneth Boulding, and the nearest I came to mass feedings for the next fifty years was never knowing how many people would be sitting around the supper table each evening. Of course, those fifty years were well spent in gaining understanding of the processes and skills involved in mediation, negotiation, and peacebuilding, but today new problems have arisen with the professionalization of those skills.

As a peacebuilder, you do not want to come across as the know-it-all outsider. So how are you going to think of yourself in the situation you are about to enter? I suggest you try out the apprentice role. Even with all your skills, you are nevertheless apprenticing yourself to your new situation as a learner, looking everywhere for clues. Most particularly, you are looking for and listening to the locals who are already working in peacebuilding networks but are badly in need of support and resources. They will be your teachers and your partners in networking for creative problem solving.

Develop Networks with Good Communication

We could all write the stories of our lives in terms of the networks we have developed as we move from place to place in the highly mobile world we inhabit. I instinctively place everyone I meet in terms of overlapping networks of interests, concerns, and contacts and have started more newsletters than I can count (long before the days of e-mail) to help mobilize people for action in different arenas of peace work. It's fun, and each network collects its own stories of how to get things done. Networking will be an important part of your responsibilities wherever you go because you are linked to others.

Make Sure That You Include Women

I have found, as both an activist and a researcher, that women's networks are basic in any conflict situation. They vary widely in visibility from place to place, but they always know what's going on locally, and they always have their own peacebuilding strategies.

· These women's groups may need help in networking in their country, so it will be good for you to know about groups like ISIS, which helps women on every continent gain access to radio and television. Check with ISIS in the Philippines, International Alert in London, and the International Fellowship of Reconciliation's Women Peacemakers Program in the Netherlands, as well as with your own nongovernmental organization (NGO) and faith group contacts about women's networks in the place you are going to.

The United Nations Security Council finally adopted Resolution 1325 in October 2000, which states that the United Nations itself and its member states must see to it that women are included in decision making at all levels in national, regional, and international institutions and mechanisms for prevention, management, and resolution of conflict. That public recognition of the importance of women's roles in peacebuilding is something you will want to build on. International Alert will provide you with a packet on the Women Building Peace Campaign, which includes details on the Security Council resolution and names of the supporting NGOs. For men, access to women's groups may be harder, but not necessarily. Keep networking until you find out how to do it.

Make Sure You Include Children and Youth

Be sure to find the children and young people. In the years that our five children were growing up in Ann Arbor, Michigan, in the 1960s and 1970s, I always found, in listening to them and the groups they were part of in our neighborhood and at school, that they were developing their own ways to witness against the Vietnam War and for the new civil rights movement in the South. They called for days of fasting and wore tags that said, "I'm hungry for peace in Selma and Vietnam"–fasts that even first graders participated in.

Today, there are many international young people's networks. Street Children, composed of exploited child laborers and former child soldiers around the world, are organizing to deal with the violence in their lives through creative self-help initiatives that need adult cooperation and support. They create wonderful newsletters too. The recent International Red Cross project to teach the humanitarian laws of war to fifth and sixth graders in the Balkans, so that when these children are drafted by local armies they will know they are supposed to protect civilians, has now generated another project: Making Peace Where I Live. This project encourages fifth and sixth graders around the world and their teachers to interview local peacemakers, so they can know about and participate in local conflict resolution activities.

Develop Clear, Positive Images of What You Are Hoping to Build

Things may be looking pretty bleak in the setting where you will be working, and you may feel discouraged. Will anything you do make a difference?

In the 1970s, when I was participating in many international working groups focused on disarmament, I began asking the question of my colleagues, "How will the world function when we don't have armies anymore? How will conflicts be managed?" I discovered that activists and professionals alike were all in the same boat: we did not have any mental images of how such a world would function. How could we ever get disarmament if we could not imagine what a disarmed world would be like?

I had just finished translating *The Image of the Future* (1973) by Dutch futurist Fred Polak on how throughout history, societies with strong, positive images of the future were empowered by their own imagery to bring to fruition the possible future they were envisioning. Why not hold imaging workshops focused on imagining a world without weapons?

We began to hold such workshops, and over the decades, they have helped empower activists in a variety of peace and justice campaigns. Try the process, and consider whether such an adventure in envisioning might be useful for you and for the locals with whom you will be working. To give you an idea of what would be involved, the focus would be on a mental journey three decades into the future, when enough time will have elapsed to allow for the envisioned changes to come about.

The group begins by making a list of specific features that participants would like to see in their world three decades from now. Then everyone spends a few minutes daydreaming that they are in that future space in which hoped-for changes have come about. What are people doing? How are differences resolved? Participants write or draw what they see, share it with the group, and then imagine the history of the three intervening decades that brought about that future. After recording this imagined history on newsprint, the discussion logically moves toward what to do to start that process. There are no panaceas, and certainly the envisioning process is not a panacea, but it usually gives people new insights into what is possible in the present.

Build In Fun and Recreation

The tasks at hand are so solemn and so heavy that lightening up becomes very important. I have always been happy to discover the talents of my coworkers. Who can sing, play an instrument, lead dancing, do clowning? There must be time for cavorting. Laughter works its own kind of miracles and brings the spirit to a new place. It may even open a new door into the future.

Practice Love

Frustrations do pile up. By nature, I am a bit on the impatient side and like to get things moving. But what do you do when people are not ready? The most important lesson I have learned is that when I am in danger of getting pushy and cross, it is time to practice loving: loving the people around me just as they are and letting my spirit reach out to their spirit, my heart to their heart. The world is short on loving. But it is we humans who keep it out. Love is there. Whenever we can open ourselves to loving, a little bit of despair melts away, and a new space opens up.

Sustain Hope

Despair must be constantly dealt with. Kenneth Boulding years ago taught me four words that I have used over and over again when I get discouraged, words that are even more important to me at age eighty-one than they were in my youth: *What exists is possible*. Every time a reconciliation takes place among people who have been doing their best to hurt each other, we receive a blessed reminder that it is possible for humans, different as each of us is from every other, to deal with their differences peaceably. Those blessed reminders are everywhere in daily life but rarely make it to the public consciousness, to the media, to our history books. It is up to us to keep noticing peacemaking whenever it happens, no matter how trivial the incident. One smile will do it. One hug. What exists is possible.

. . . .

28

The Simplicity of Peacebuilding
An Interview with Adam Curle

John Paul Lederach, Muzna Al-Masri,
and Rita Ann Litwiller

Adam Curle is eighty-five years old. British by birth but a world citizen, Adam has worked at peace- and conflict-related matters for over five decades. He supported numerous conciliation and mediation initiatives with Quaker Peace and Service in London. He has worked in places like Nigeria during the Biafran war, Rwanda following the genocide, and the former Yugoslavia during the hardest war years. Many of us have sought his advice, wisdom, and practical experience. He has written many books from his experiences and several volumes of poetry. Muzna Al-Masri, a rising peacebuilder in her own right, with significant grassroots conflict transformation experience in her native Lebanon, and John Paul interviewed Adam by telephone, seeking his wisdom for younger peacebuilders. The interview was transcribed and edited by Rita Ann Litwiller, a graduate student who has recently completed research on peace in Nepal, and John Paul.

. . . .

So what does a man who in his eighties traveled frequently from London to Sarajevo propose as the guidepost of his work? To preserve strength, sustain hope, and provide little havens of moral strength, courage, and sanity.

JOHN PAUL LEDERACH (JPL): As you look back across the many decades you have worked in conflict zones on peacebuilding initiatives, what is the key lesson that you would pass on to a person who is just beginning a piece of work in a new place?

ADAM CURLE (AC): First, I would advise the person to be open, proceed very gradually, and wait for the development of relationships. You will need mutual understanding, trust, and confidence with the people who are involved in the situation into which you are moving. Building relationships with people who are already active in the field is the key.

JPL: When people start this work, they often wonder what their role in peacebuilding might be and whether it ever changes. How do you assess the changes that have happened in your roles as a peacebuilder? How have you determined that a particular role was the right thing to do or to change to a different kind of a role at a given point in a process?

AC: When I started, the Quaker tradition began by building up relationships with people who were in positions of power and authority, the decision makers. The problems I considered to be the important ones were those that required a very high level of judgment by the leaders involved directly in the situation. I needed to be in contact with these leaders and gain their trust. In fact, that was my approach until relatively recently. The people I worked with were high officials, up to the highest like presidents, and this covered my work in Nigeria, India, Pakistan, Sri Lanka, Zimbabwe, and in Northern Ireland.

In the last years when I was working in Rwanda and in Croatia and Bosnia, I wasn't in touch with leaders at the high level. The problems we worked with were very local, involving local warlords, local leaders, and the people who were prominent in a particular church or community. The majority of these conflicts, particularly ones in Africa and the Balkans, had great local confusion and disorganization, influenced by warlords rather than official generals and commanders in chief. This was quite different from the sort of thing that I had done in Nigeria during the Biafran war, where everything was focused on the decisions of people who are at the very top of the decision makers in the regime.

This change meant that it was important to have an understanding with a wide range of people, going right down to the scale of taxi drivers and workers in hotels and waiters, through the professional classes and the academics. To get an understanding of the total situation, it was necessary to develop contacts with the people who are ultimately responsible for war or peace.

Two things I learned. First, my view of situations changed. Most conflicts now are not the big international ones involving high-level international meetings, the United Nations, and regional organizations. Second, the key was to focus on preserving people's strength in society to sustain their hope, helping to provide them little havens of peace and constructiveness that would send out rays of moral strength, courage, and sanity, which would affect the communities in which they were living.

Sometimes these distinctions blurred. For example in Sri Lanka, there were the government people, the president, the minister responsible for conducting war. Then there were what I will call the terrorists—the gangs of the people I first encountered not in Sri Lanka itself but in the slums of Madras, where they tend to hide and develop fighting skills. So there was a mixture between dealing with the big shots and dealing with the underground movements. It wasn't a question of great decisions as to what the political structure of the country would be after one gang or another gained power. Peace, it seemed to me, was something that depended on an understanding and the social and spiritual development of a mass of people. So in my work in Bosnia, and particularly Croatia, I never spoke to an official minister. I spoke, if necessary, to local warlords, trying to get them to change their attitudes about one thing or another, getting them to change their attitudes about, for example, attempted assassinations.

MUZNA AL-MASRI (MAM): I want to voice a concern that many of the people have who are just starting in peacebuilding: Does peacebuilding really work? Sometimes we have a lack of trust in whether these efforts are contributing to a more peaceful world.

AC: I think new people coming into a new situation, into a particular conflict field, are less exhausted than people who've been in it for years. I find that many of those people basically want some kind of support and strength, not necessarily to be overwhelmed with new peacemaking techniques. They seek someone who will sympathize and do things that help them, that make life easier for them.

Looking back on my work in Croatia, most of what I did was to try to make life a little bit more tolerable for people, to create a little bit of space in which they were not constantly in danger or some desperate sort of situation. They were obsessed with the terrible problems facing them and needed some degree of peaceful ambience in which they could simply relax and talk and ask questions and where they would not need to feel frightened or guilty.

JPL: Do you have any thoughts on the part of Muzna's question that asked about success? Do you think about or how you have understood and measured the success of your work over these years?

AC: Not really [laughs].

JPL: Well, that is the answer we all love to hear, but it is not the one the students look for or funders seek.

AC: I think if success is anything, it is that loving friendships have developed. That's really the best thing one can hope for. And sharing: to share problems and the difficulties of those you work with and try to find ways out of them.

I have this idea that we are dealing with very simple things. In the early days in the former Yugoslavia, the most important thing I did was come with a computer. I would be asked to bring paper clips.

Paper clips. I would bring the latest book or manual. It happened almost every time I went there. I was taking something that somebody had needed in order for them to do their part of the work better. In the midst of fear and chaos and shelling and bombs, they were trying to create peaceful havens in which they could help people who had economic problems, who were bereaved by the fighting, whose families had been broken up. It is simple: how to help with all these things that people need in order to have the strength to tackle perhaps larger or more serious problems.

Then you would have the times when your partners were faced with moral choices. The local warlord was hostile because they were dealing not only with the general problems but also with the problems of some particular group who were a minority, an unpopular group. Our question was how to help them defend the vulnerable group without alienating the warlord to an extent that he would kill them. These become very practical problems. You get crowds of refugees moving from one place to another, with half their family lost or disappeared. They have lost their money; their farm has been occupied. You've got all that to deal with that, and at the same time you've got to try make the social scene less violent, less dangerous.

Local peace groups are working at all levels. And they need all sorts of help from other people. They would ask me, for example, to find somebody who knew about how to mend bridges—social and physical ones. Or they would ask about someone who knew about peace education because they thought that children were growing up knowing nothing except war and violence.

MAM: What specifically should I be careful with if I am an outsider coming to somebody else's conflict?

AC: Most important is a combination of confidence and humility. People want someone whom they feel is wise, well informed, and helpful—somebody who doesn't show off, somebody who will understand the sort of society, the sort of situation they are in and accept it. But they also want someone who can suggest new things but not in an aggressive or know-it-all fashion.

MAM: Where do you get your own strength and guidance both professionally and personally in the situations of conflict?

AC: Where do I get my strength and guidance professionally and personally? [laughs] Oh, I don't know. From everybody I meet! When I started doing this, I knew absolutely nothing. In my very first situation, I was a member of an opposition group in South Africa. That is not quite what we are talking about here, but I learned some interesting things.

Some of the people I worked with, particularly in Yugoslavia, have become some of my very closest friends, and from the very start, I got all sorts of advice and strength from them. You get into a situation like this and you stop feeling separate from the people you are working with or for. You just become one, part of a team. And you share wisdom, instructive friendship, and love. This is what I received from my counterparts in the Balkans, and it has been a great treasure for me. You don't feel separate from them. You are somebody who is caught up in the same situation, but you have some advantages because you aren't worn down by too long a period of tension and fear, strain, or physical weakness because of the shortage of food. I think that's where you get your guidance.

Then you have your wise mentors whom you meet when you go home again, like Elise [Boulding]. I think formal debriefing is a helpful, good thing. But one needs the time to let the experience sink in and develop its meaning.

JPL: From your five decades of work and eighty-five years of wisdom accumulated, what final words of advice or encouragement might you give us, particularly those who are coming into the field for the first time?

AC: The main thing is one I give myself: try to understand it. These conflicts are extraordinary situations. Take our current situation [a month after September 11, 2001]. We have to try to know what these events are all about. We have to try to understand Islam. I have always been receptive to Islam. When people say it's a cruel religion, I remind them that when any Muslim is going off to anything like shopping, the person starts off by saying, "Bi ism allah ar rah man ar rahim"—in the name of God, be compassionate and merciful. And they mean it. This was my experience with my Muslim friends.

I think that we have to immerse ourselves in the effort to understand what's going on and why. The more we understand, the more we may see things that are helpful to do.

Part VII

· ·

Conclusions and Summary

29

So What Have We Learned?

John Paul Lederach and Janice Moomaw Jenner

L ooking back across the previous chapters, words shared from
some of the most experienced peacebuilders in our field, we
may well feel overwhelmed. On the one hand, many of the authors
provided cautions and even provocative questions about whether
peacebuilding intervention can be accomplished with integrity by
those arriving from outside the setting of conflict. On the other
hand, you can feel the excitement from the words of people who
are learning by doing. Wisdom emerges from experience, not sitting
back and being paralyzed by detail.

If we are to summarize these pages of advice and wisdom, we
might do so by asking ourselves this question: What thoughts and
ideas appeared most often as central across the breadth of these
chapters? We then put together the following lists of good advice
from the voices of experience.

Know Yourself

- Get a clear sense of the roles you can and cannot play.

- Be honest with yourself about the levels of risk you can
accept and feel comfortable in settings that are volatile
and violent.

- Be honest with how much time you have.

- Understand and provide what you need to sustain yourself.

- Be clear and honest about your own cultural biases and perspectives.

- Develop ahead of time a framework for making ethical decisions in your work.

Be Clear About Your Relationships

- Get a good sense of who you are working with and how they fit into the conflict.

- Be clear about expectations people have for you and the expectations you have for them.

- Remember that this is about relationships, people, and lives, not just work.

- Remember that you are coming from outside. Listen carefully to those who are from the setting.

- Develop a clear framework for accountability with people you work with in the setting and those who provide you resources.

Learn About the Context

- Commit yourself to learning about the context, history, and setting of the conflict generally and from different viewpoints of the people in conflict.

- Remember that learning is complex and continuous. Prepare with diligence, but always be open to greater and deeper understanding.

- Pay attention to the cultural understandings and nuances of the different people in the setting.

- Respect and seek to understand meaning systems and religious perspectives of the people in the setting.

Consult, Consult, Consult

- Listen early, and listen often. There is no replacement for the long road of seeking the perspectives and advice of those in the conflict.

- Seek the views of people who are not like-minded and not located in similar positions in or out of the conflict setting.

- Give preferential weight to the concerns and cautions of those who must live with the consequences and decisions you make in the setting.

- Take time to drink tea with people.

Be Realistic About What You Can Bring

- Be clear about your role, and do not engage in activities that you do not understand or are not prepared to do, especially in settings of violence where the consequences affect peoples' lives.

- Understand the time frame of different types of peace-building activities and roles in the context of relationships and commitments. Be clear and realistic about your time frame and calendar.

- Develop a capacity for providing feedback and evaluation, with attention to both learning about your work and for assessing the unintended consequences your activities.

- Remember that saying no requires courage and clarity.

Be Humble

- Remember you cannot do it all, and you cannot do it alone.

- Seek out and recognize others who are doing similar and important work. Foster an attitude of cooperation and transparency.

- Be willing to accept feedback and criticism, particularly from people in the setting. Create a learning rather than a defensive demeanor in reference to assessment.

- Remember that small things count, from bringing paper clips, to a word of encouragement, to carrying a message.

Be Bold

- Practice love and compassion.

- Ask questions when you do not understand.

- Commit yourself to stand with your colleagues even when the times are tough.

- Be an ambassador for justice, compassion, and change in your home country and setting, particularly where the policies of your country affect other people.

For rising practitioners, the preceding chapters and these lists of suggestions may feel as if there are so many things to reflect on that if they took the time to attend carefully to each piece of this good advice, they may never venture into the actual work. This is true. Peacebuilding requires preparation and careful attention to detail. However, it is equally true that peacebuilding requires us to learn by doing. There is no shortcut around the rich school of direct experience.

All of these seasoned practitioners who have spoken to you in this book learned their greatest lessons from venturing into the eye of the storm. Good advice is a guide, not a rulebook. Accumulated wisdom does not answer questions. It helps you ask better questions.

We send you off with the sage words of a prophet shared by a number of religious traditions that stand us all well on the pathways of building peace: Do justice, love mercy, and walk humbly. But by all means, keep walking.

Bibliography

Anderson, M. B. *Do No Harm: How Aid Can Support Peace—or War*. Boulder,
   Colo.: Lynne Rienner, 1999.
Anderson, M., and Woodrow, P. *Rising from the Ashes: Development Strategies
   in Times of Disasters*. Boulder, Colo.: Lynne Rienner Publishers, 1998.
Assefa, H. *Mediation of Civil Wars: Approaches and Strategies—The Sudan
   Conflict*. Boulder, Colo.: Westview Press, 1987.
Augsburger, D. *Conflict Mediation Across Cultures*. Louisville, Ky.: John Knox
   Press, 1992.
Avruch, K. *Culture and Conflict Resolution*. Washington, D.C.: United States
   Institute of Peace Press, 1998.
Boulding, E. *Building a Global Civic Culture*. Syracuse, N.Y.: Syracuse University
   Press, 1988.
Boulding, E. *Cultures of Peace, The Hidden Side of History*. Syracuse, N.Y.:
   Syracuse University Press, 2000.
Brett, J. M. *Negotiating Globally: How to Negotiate Deal, Resolve Disputes and
   Make Decisions Across Cultural Boundaries*. San Francisco: Jossey-Bass,
   2001.
Burgess, G., and Burgess, H. *Encyclopedia of Conflict Resolution*. Santa Barbara,
   Calif.: ABC-CLIO, 1997.
Carstarphen, N., and Nan, S. A. *Windows to Conflict Analysis and Resolution:
   Framing Our Field*. Fairfax, Va.: Institute for Conflict Analysis and
   Resolution, George Mason University, 1997.
Chew, P. K. (Ed.). *The Conflict and Culture Reader*. New York: New York
   University Press, 2001.
Cohen, R. *Negotiating Across Cultures*. (Rev. ed.) Washington, D.C.: United
   States Institute of Peace Press, 1997.

Curle, A. *Making Peace*. New York: Tavistock, 1971.

Curle, A. *True Justice*. London: Quaker Home Service, 1981.

Curle, A. *Tools for Transformation: A Personal Study*. Stroud, U.K.: Hawthorn, 1990.

Curle, A. *Another Way: Positive Response to Contemporary Violence*. Charlbury, U.K.: Jon Carpenter Publishers, 1995.

Curle, A. *To Tame the Hydra: Undermining the Culture of Violence*. Charlbury, U.K.: Jon Carpenter Publishers, 1999.

Daloz, L. A., Parks, Keen, C. H., Keen, J. P., and Parks, S. D. *Common Fire: Lives of Commitment in a Complex World*. Boston: Beacon Press, 1996.

Dass, R., and Gorman, P. *How Can I Help?: Stories and Reflections on Service*. New York: Knopf, 1999.

Denzin, N. K., and Lincoln, Y. S. *Handbook of Qualitative Research*. Thousand Oaks, Calif.: Sage, 2000.

Diamond, L. *The Courage for Peace: Daring to Create Harmony in Ourselves and the World*. Berkeley, Calif.: Conari Press, 2000.

Diamond, L. *The Peace Book: 108 Simple Ways to Create a More Peaceful World*. Berkley, Calif.: Conari Press, 2001.

Diamond, L., and McDonald, J. *Multi-Track Diplomacy: A Systems Approach to Peace*. Hartford, Conn.: Kumarian Press, 1996.

Eller, J. D. *From Culture to Ethnicity to Conflict*. Ann Arbor: University of Michigan Press, 1999.

Evans-Pritchard, E. E. *Witchcraft, Oracles, and Magic Among the Azande*. (Abridged ed.). Oxford: Clarendon Press, 1976. (Originally published 1937)

Fitzduff, M. *Beyond Violence: Conflict Resolution Processes in Northern Ireland*. Tokyo: United Nations University, 1996.

Gopin, M. *Between Eden and Armageddon: The Future of World Religions, Violence, and Peacemaking*. New York: Oxford University Press, 2000.

Gopin, M. *Holy War, Holy Peace: How Religion Can Bring Peace to the Middle East*. New York: Oxford University Press, 2002.

Hall, E. T. *Beyond Culture*. New York: Doubleday, 1976.

Hanh, T. N. *Being Peace*. Berkeley, Calif.: Parallax Press, 1987.

Hizkias, A. "The Challenge of Mediation in Internal Wars: Reflections on the INN Experience in the Ethiopia/Eritrea Conflict." *Security Dialogue*, 1992, 23(3), 101ff.

Huntington, S. *The Clash of Civilizations and the Remaking of World Order*. New York: Simon & Schuster, 1996.

International Committee of the Red Cross. *ICRC Guidelines on Humanitarian Action in Conflict Zones: Coping with Stress*. Geneva: International Committee of the Red Cross, 1996.

InterAction. *The Security of National Staff: Towards Good Practices*. Washington, D.C.: InterAction, 2001.

International Committee of the Red Cross. *Respect for and Protection of the Personnel of Humanitarian Organizations*. Geneva, Switzerland: International Committee of the Red Cross, 1998. [www.icrc.org.]

Jenner, J., Ayindo, B., and Doe, S. G. *When You Are the Peacebuilder: Reflections on Peacebuilding from Africa*. Harrisonburg, Va.: Conflict Transformation Program, Eastern Mennonite University, 2001.

Jongman, A. J. *World Conflict and Human Rights Map*. Leiden, The Netherlands: PIOOM-Interdisciplinary Research Programme on Causes of Human Rights Violations, 2001–2002.

Kvale, S. *Interviews: An Introduction to Qualitative Research Interviewing*. Thousand Oaks, Calif.: Sage, 1996.

Langer, E. *Mindfulness*. Reading, Mass.: Addison-Wesley, 1989.

Lederach, J. P. *Preparing for Peace: Conflict Transformation Across Cultures*. Syracuse, N.Y.: Syracuse University Press, 1995.

Lederach, J. P. *Building Peace: Sustainable Reconciliation in Divided Societies*. Washington, D.C.: United States Institute of Peace Press, 1997.

Mahoney, L., and Eguren, L. E. *Unarmed Bodyguards: International Accompaniment for the Protection of Human Rights*. West Hartford, Conn.: Kumarian Press, 1997.

Making Peace Where I Live. A Learning Guide Designed to Support Young People in Researching Their Peacemaking Traditions in Their Own Communities. West Hartford, Conn.: Making Peace Where I Live.

Marks, S. C. *Watching the Wind: Conflict Resolution During South Africa's Transition to Democracy*. Washington, D.C.: United States Institute of Peace Press, 2000.

Martin, R. "NGO Field Security." *Forced Migration Review*, Apr. 1999, pp. 4–7.

Mayer, B. *The Dynamics of Conflict Resolution: A Practitioner's Guide*. San Francisco: Jossey-Bass, 2000.

McDonald, J. *Newcomer's Guide to Track II Diplomacy*. Washington, D.C.: Institute for Multi-Track Diplomacy, 1993. [www.imtd.org.]

Mitchell, C., and Banks, M. *Handbook of Conflict Resolution*. New York: Pinter, 1996.

Moore, C. *The Mediation Process: Practical Strategies for Resolving Conflict.* San Francisco: Jossey-Bass, 1996.

Muggah, R. *Perceptions of Small Arms Availability and Use Among Oxfam-GB Field Personnel.* London and Geneva: Small Arms Survey and Oxfam-GB, 2001. [www.smallarmssurvey.org.]

Nan, S. A. *Complementarity and Coordination of Conflict Resolution Efforts in the Conflicts over Abkhazia, South Ossetia, and Transdniestra.* Fairfax, Va.: George Mason University, 1999.

Nordstrom, C. *A Different Kind of War Story.* Philadelphia: University of Pennsylvania Press, 1997.

Quintyn, L. "Managing Stress." In L. Reychler and T. Paffenholz (Eds.), *Peacebuilding: A Field Guide.* Boulder, Colo.: Lynne Rienner, 2001.

Polak, F. *The Image of the Future.* New York: Elsevier, 1973.

Reason, P., and Bradbury, H. (Eds.) *Handbook of Action Research: Participative Inquiry and Practice.* Thousand Oaks, Calif.: Sage, 2001.

Rogers, C., and Sytsma, B. *A Shield About Me: Safety Awareness for World Vision Staff.* Monrovia, Calif.: World Vision, 1998.

Samovar, L. A., and Porter, R. E. *Intercultural Communication: A Reader.* (9th ed.) Belmont, Calif.: Wadsworth, 1999.

Saunders, H. *A Public Peace Process.* New York: St. Martin's Press, 2001.

Schoeny, M., and Wallace, W. "Reconnecting Systems Maintenance with Social Justice: A Critical Role for Conflict Resolution." *Negotiation Journal,* 2000, *16,* 253–268.

Sheik, M., and others. "Deaths Among Humanitarian Workers." *British Medical Journal,* 2000, *321,* 166–168. [www.bmj.com.]

Stringer, E. *Action Research.* (2nd ed.) Thousand Oaks, Calif.: Sage, 1999.

Thomas, J. *Doing Critical Ethnography.* Thousand Oaks, Calif.: Sage, 1993.

Tirman, J. *Making the Money Sing: Private Wealth and Public Power in the Search for Peace.* Lanham, Md.: Rowman & Littlefield, 2000.

Trompenaars, F. *Riding the Waves of Culture.* Burr Ridge, Ill.: Irwin, 1994.

Uehara, E., and others. "Toward a Values-Based Approach to Multicultural Social Work Research." *Social Work,* 1996, *41,* 613–622.

Van Brabant, K. *Operational Security Management in Violent Environments.* London: Humanitarian Practice Network, 2000.

Van der Merwe, H. W. *South Africa: Morality and Action: Quaker Efforts in a Difficult Environment.* Chicago: Progressive Publisher, 1981.

Van der Merwe, H. W. *Pursuing Justice and Peace in South Africa.* New York: Routledge, 1989.

Van der Merwe, H. W. *Peacemaking in South Africa: A Life in Conflict Resolution.* Cape Town: Tafelberg, 2000.

Wallace, W. "The Potential for Local Zones of Peace in Moving from Civil War to Civil Society." *Peace Review,* 1997, 9:2, 249–255.

Warfield, W., and Schoeny, M. "Reconnecting Systems Maintenance with Social Justice: A Critical Role for Conflict Resolution." *Negotiation Journal,* July 2000, pp. 253–268.

Williams, S., and Williams, S. *Being in the Middle by Being at the Edge: Quaker Experience of Non-Official Political Mediation.* London: Quaker Peace and Service, in association with Sessions Book Trust, 1994.

Working Group on NGO Security. *NGO Security Training.* Washington, D.C.: InterAction, 1997.

Zehr, H. *Changing Lenses: A New Focus for Crime and Justice.* Scottdale, Pa.: Herald Press, 1995.

Web Sites

American Evaluation Association, www.eval.org/publications/publications.html.

Applied Conflict Resolution Organizations Network, www.acron.iwa.org.

European Centre for Conflict Prevention, www.euconflict.org.

Field Security.com, www.fieldsecurity.com.

Humanitarian Practice Network, Publishes papers and reports, including on security training. www.odi.org.uk.

Humanitarian Safety and Protection Network, www.hspn.org.

International Alert, www.international-alert.org.

People in Aid Project, www.peopleinaid.org.

Real World Rescue, www.realworldrescue.com/rwrmain.htm.

RedR Security Training, www.redr.org.

Networking Initiatives

The following are the international headquarters addresses for three major women's peace-related networking initiatives. Each can lead you to others.

International Alert, Women Building Peace Program, 1 Glyn St., London SE11 5HT, U.K.

International Fellowship of Reconciliation, Women Peacemakers Program, Spoorstraat 38, 1815 BK Alkmaar, Netherlands

ISIS International, P.O. Box 1837, Quezon City Main, Quezon City 11200, Philippines

About the Editors

. . . .

John Paul Lederach is professor of international peacebuilding at the Joan B. Kroc Institute for International Peace Studies at the University of Notre Dame and a Distinguished Scholar at Eastern Mennonite University's Conflict Transformation Program. He works extensively as a practitioner in conciliation processes, active in Latin America, Africa, and Central Asia. He is widely known for the development of elicitive approaches to conflict transformation and the design and implementation of integrative and strategic approaches to peacebuilding. He is the author of twelve books, including *Building Peace: Sustainable Reconciliation in Divided Societies* (1997) and *The Journey Toward Reconciliation* (1997).

Janice Moomaw Jenner is the director of the Institute for Justice and Peacebuilding, the practice arm of the Conflict Transformation Program at Eastern Mennonite University. Jenner has worked extensively with community peacebuilding groups in Africa, focusing on work with women and religious organizations. She is the coauthor, with Sam Doe and Babu Ayindo, of *When You Are the Peacebuilder: Reflections on Peacebuilding from Africa* (2001), and several articles on community-level peacebuilding in Africa. She holds a master's degree in conflict transformation from Eastern Mennonite University.

. . . . .

Index

CPSIA information can be obtained at www.ICGtesting.com
Printed in the USA
LVOW102009080513

332766LV00001B/78/P